THE BRITISH ISLES
0
100 Miles
0
200 km
Orkney Islands
Shetland Islands
W0392954
Outer Hebrides
ATLANTIC
OCEAN
Skye
High-lands
Loch Ness
Aberdeen
Ben Nevis
Mull
Scotland
North
Sea
Islay
Glasgow
Edinburgh
Southern Uplands
Hadrian's Wall
Newcastle
Northern Ireland
Belfast
GREAT BRITAIN
Lake District
Pennines
Scarborough
York
Isle of Man
Blackpool
Hull
Irish Sea
Leeds
Manchester
REPUBLIC OF IRELAND
Dublin
Holyhead
Liverpool
Sheffield
Conway
Wicklow Mts.
Caernarvon
Snowdon
Chester
Nottingham
Shannon
Derby
Midlands
England
Cambrian Mountains
Aberystwyth
Birmingham
Coventry
Cork
Wales
Cambridge
Stratford-upon-Avon
George's Channel
Fishguard
Severn
Oxford
Luton
Milford Haven
Tenby
Caerleon
Watford
London
Swansea
Thames
Cardiff
Bristol
Kent
Dover
North Downs
Folkestone
Southampton
South Downs
Tunnel
Bournemouth
Brighton
Hastings
Isle of Wight
Cornwall
Plymouth
Scilly Islands
Land's End
English Channel
Cherbourg
Le Havre
Channel Islands
FRANCE
Brest

Learning English

Green Line new 3

Unterrichtswerk für Gymnasien

von
Stephanie Ashford, Rosemary Hellyer-Jones,
Marion Horner, Peter Lampater, Harriette Lanzer,
Peter Pasch, Rolf W. Roth, Helmut Slogsnat,
Klaus Stenzel, Gunther Volk,
Margaret Winck, Harold S. Wonham
sowie
Claudia Finkbeiner

Ernst Klett Verlag
Stuttgart Düsseldorf Leipzig

Learning English

Green Line New 3

für Klasse 7 an Gymnasien

von
Stephanie Ashford B.A., Villingen-Schwenningen; Rosemary Hellyer-Jones M.A., Ehingen (Donau); Marion Horner M.A., Cambridge; Peter Lampater, Ehingen (Donau); Harriette Lanzer B.A., London; Prof. Dr. Peter Pasch, Tübingen; Rolf W. Roth M.A., Idar-Oberstein; Dr. Helmut Slogsnat, Neckargemünd; Klaus Stenzel, Bopfingen; Gunther Volk, Villingen-Schwenningen; Margaret Winck B.A., Tübingen; Harold S. Wonham M.Litt., Stone
sowie
Dr. Claudia Finkbeiner, Heilbronn

Beratende Mitarbeit
Dr. Rainer Berthelmann, Halle; Gisela Bullan, Cottbus; Adelheid Kierepka, Apolda; Jürgen Meyer, Itzehoe; Ilsabé Seils, Neubrandenburg; Günter Schubert, Kiel; Dorit Stribel, Nürtingen; Dr. Uwe Vogel, Leipzig
sowie
Jörg W. Mollenkopf, Giengen

Visuelle Gestaltung
Elsie Lennox/Duncan Smith, London (Zeichnungen); Bernd Bürkle, Fellbach (Grundlayout)
Christian Dekelver, Weinstadt (Graphiken, Layout)

Kassetten und CDs zu diesem Band

SB *Begleitkassette zum Schülerbuch* für zu Hause und für den Unterricht mit Unittexten, Liedern, Ausspracheübungen (Klettnummer 546238).
Die *Begleit-CD zum Schülerbuch* mit demselben Inhalt hat die Klettnummer 546285.
Lieferung durch jede Buchhandlung oder, wo dies auf Schwierigkeiten stößt, zuzüglich Portokosten per Nachnahme vom Verlag.

HV *Kassette zum Hörverstehen* für den Unterricht mit den Hörverstehenstexten aller Werkteile (Klettnummer 546239).
Die *CD zum Hörverstehen* für den Unterricht hat die Klettnummer 546286.
Lieferung direkt an Lehrerinnen und Lehrer, Schulstempel erforderlich.

Lernsoftware:

Passend zu diesem Band wird es ein Vokabel- und ein Grammatiktrainingsprogramm geben.
Die Programme bieten abwechslungsreiche Übungsformen, zahlreiche Abfragevarianten, Leistungs- und Lernzielkontrolle und ein Lexikon mit dem Wortschatz der gesamten Lehrbuchreihe.

1. Auflage 1 16 15 | 2010 2009 2008 2007

Alle Drucke dieser Auflage können im Unterricht nebeneinander benutzt werden, sie sind untereinander unverändert.

Die letzte Zahl bezeichnet das Jahr des Druckes.

Internetadresse: http://www.klett-verlag.de

Redaktion: Peter Cole M.A., Ingrid Mathews, Michael Mattison

Herstellung: Eveline Wiest, Stuttgart
Umschlaggestaltung: Christian Dekelver, Weinstadt
Satz: DTP-Verlag und Lihs, Satz und Repro, Ludwigsburg
Reproduktion: Repro Maurer GmbH + Co, Tübingen
Druck: Firmengruppe APPL, aprinta druck, Wemding
ISBN: 3-12-546230-4

9 783125 462304

Inhaltsverzeichnis

Hallo, hier ist wieder Monny!
Ich begleite dich auch durch dieses Buch und gebe dir ab und zu ein paar Tipps.
Damit du dich leicht zurechtfindest, erkläre ich noch einmal kurz, wie dieses Buch aufgebaut ist.

In diesem Band gibt es fünf **Units** und vier **Workshops** mit jeweils unterschiedlichen Themen.
Die *Units* sind wie in den ersten Bänden aufgebaut und enden mit einer *Let's check*-Seite.
Die *Workshops* helfen dir, bestimmte Arbeitstechniken anzuwenden, z. B. für das Sprechen, Lesen oder Schreiben.

Auf Seite 88 beginnt die **Extra line** mit weiteren interessanten Geschichten, einem Theaterstück und ab Seite 97 mit Übersetzungsübungen.

Auf Seite 100 beginnt der **Grammatikanhang** mit einer zweiseitigen Wiederholung.

Das **Vokabular** beginnt auf Seite 118. Hier findest du alle neuen Wörter aus den *Units* und *Workshops.* Wenn du einmal ein Wort aus einer früheren *Unit* nicht mehr weißt, kannst du in der **alphabetischen Wortliste** am Ende des Buches nachschlagen.

Und alle **unregelmäßigen Verben** stehen in einer Liste auf den Seiten 182 und 183.

Du solltest aber auch noch wissen, was die **Zeichen** vor den einzelnen Texten und den Übungen bedeuten:

- SB: Begleitkassette bzw. CD zum Schülerbuch
- HV: Kassette bzw. CD zum Hörverstehen
- Wiederholungsübungen
- Partnerarbeit
- Gruppenarbeit
- Word power: Wortschatzübungen
- Your turn: Hier kannst du über dich, deine Familie oder Freunde sprechen.
- ⟨ ⟩ wahlfreie Aufgaben
- schwierigere Aufgaben, die wahlfrei sind
- für fächerübergreifenden Unterricht

Alles klar?
Na, dann – viel Spaß!

LET'S TALK

1 New friends

The Dixons have been on holiday in the Netherlands. Now they are making the fourteen-hour crossing back from Rotterdam to Hull.

Florian: Mensch, pass doch auf!
Sarah: Oh sorry, I –
Ellen: No, I'm sorry. It was my bag. I – er – I left it in a silly place. Are you OK?
Sarah: Phew! Yes – still alive!
Ellen: And you? Do you speak English, too?
Florian: Er – a bit. – Yes, I'm OK. It was just a big shock!
Sarah: You speak very good English. Where are you from?
Florian: Thanks. I'm Florian. I come from Jena in Germany.
Ellen: And I'm Dutch. My name is Ellen. And you?
Sarah: I'm Sarah. And I'm going back home to Nottingham. Hey, what a way to meet – in an international accident!

1 Collect ideas for your own dialogue

a) *Look at the dialogue again. Find examples of typical questions and answers when people meet for the first time. Start like this:* "Do you speak …?" *Go on.*

You can revise present tenses in exercise 1 on page 13.

b) *Think of more ideas. What else can you ask or tell new friends?*

How old …?
… on holiday?
I'm travelling to/staying … .
Do you like/know …?
…?
… is my favourite … .
…

c) *Imagine you meet an English girl or boy. Make a dialogue with a partner.*

2 Talk about countries and languages

I D NL E GB
F TR PL DK

tip It can be interesting to talk to people from other countries. Don't worry too much about mistakes. Remember – nobody is perfect!

Country	Language	
Denmark	Danish	['deɪnɪʃ]
Poland	Polish	['pəʊlɪʃ]
Italy	Italian	[ɪ'tæljən]
Turkey	Turkish	['tɜ:kɪʃ]
Greece	Greek	[gri:k]
Switzerland		

a) *There are cars from lots of countries on the ferry. What countries do these letters stand for?* 'NL' stands for the Netherlands. 'D' stands for … .

b) *What languages do people from these countries speak? Example:* People from the Netherlands speak Dutch.

c) *Do you know any more countries and languages?*

2 The right words

The next morning Sarah and her father see Florian on deck.

Florian: Hi, Sarah. Good morning, Mr Dixon.
Sarah: Hm. I don't know if you can call it a **good** morning – it's the end of our holiday! You're lucky, Florian. You and your family are just starting your holiday.
Mr Dixon: What are your plans in Britain?
Florian: We want to travel round England. We're going north first. To Edinburgh.
Mr Dixon: Er – I hope you don't mind if I correct you. But Edinburgh isn't in England. It's in Scotland.
Florian: Oh, of course.
Mr Dixon: Britain is more than just England.
Sarah: One of my teachers at school is Welsh. He goes crazy when people call him English!
Florian: Well, thanks for the tip. My parents and I don't want to upset anyone !

You can't call **it** **a good morning**.

§ 1

You can practise sentences like this (where the object has two parts) in exercise 2 on page 13.

1 Use different words for different people

a) *How does Florian say 'Hello' to Sarah and her father? What words does he use? Why do you think he uses different words to each of them?*

b) 1. Goodbye. Have a nice evening. / Bye. See you tomorrow.

2. Excuse me. Can you bring me a glass of lemonade, please? / What have you got to drink? Lemonade?

3. I'm sorry, but I think that's my bag. / Hey, that's my bag!

These words say the same thing, but in different ways. Which words are for friends, and which are for more formal situations?

Example: "Goodbye. Have a nice evening." is for a more formal situation. You can say it to a teacher, for example.
"Bye. See you tomorrow." is what you say to a friend.
Go on.

tip Always try to look and sound friendly. Then it isn't so bad if you make mistakes.

2 Be polite

It's important to choose the right words in English so that you sound polite.

a) *These sentences are not very polite. How can you make them sound more polite?*

Example: 1. "No sugar in my tea." → "No sugar in my tea, thank you."
2. "I'll open the window, OK?" → "Do you mind if I open ...?" *Go on.*

3. "I want a map of this town."
4. "I need that pen over there."
5. "Where's the station?"
6. "Give me a ticket to London."

thank you | Do you mind if ...? | please | Excuse me | Can you tell/pass me ...? | Could I have ...? | I'd like ...

b) *Make little dialogues with the ideas in a). Find good answers, and practise with a partner.*

England	–	English
Ireland	–	Irish
Scotland	–	Scottish
Wales	–	Welsh

3 Check your Geography

Compare these three maps, then answer the questions.

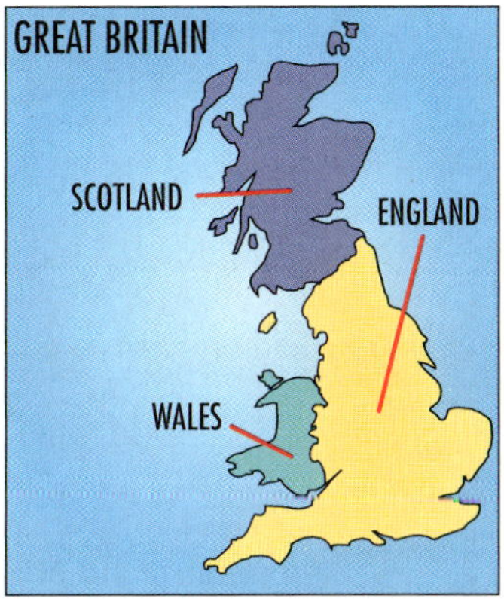

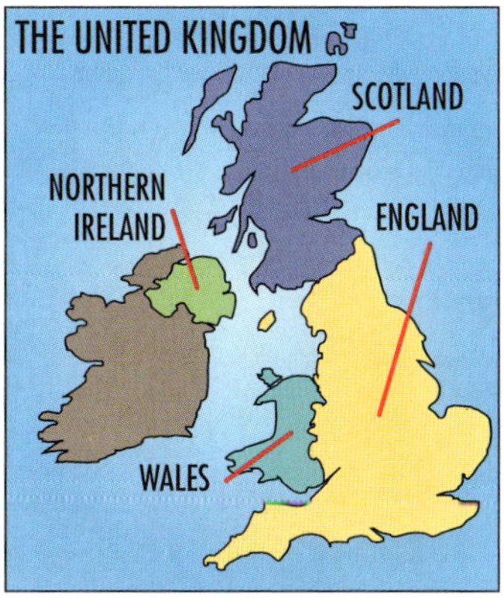

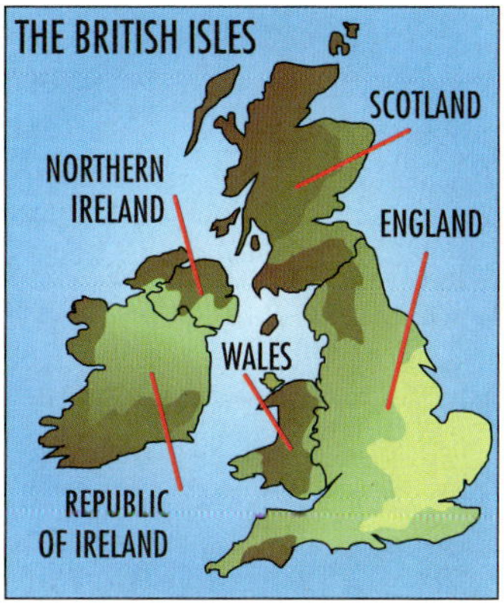

1. How many countries are there in Great Britain? What are their names?
2. What is the difference between Great Britain and the UK?
3. Which part of the British Isles is **not** in the UK?

4 Listening practice: Find out about different parts of the UK

People from different parts of the UK speak with different accents.
Listen to the recording. You will hear English, Scottish, Welsh and Irish voices.

a) *Say which part of the UK the girls and boys come from. Which is the right photo? You can start like this:*
Megan comes from … . That's photo … .

Megan

Asim

Ryan

Kate

A

B

C

D

b) *Work with a partner. Listen to the recording again.*
What can you find out about: Edinburgh, Luton, Glenarm and Belfast, North Wales ?

Example: North Wales
"There are sheep farms in North Wales." – "Yes, and it often rains … ." *Go on.*

c) *Try to find out more about different parts of the UK. Look in books and magazines. Or get brochures from a travel agent's. Bring a photo to school and talk about it. Maybe you can make a poster for your classroom.*

3 On the telephone

1 Practise telephone language

a) *Who is calling who? Read everything first, then find three pairs.*
Start: "A" goes with … . Someone is calling the Crofts, but … .

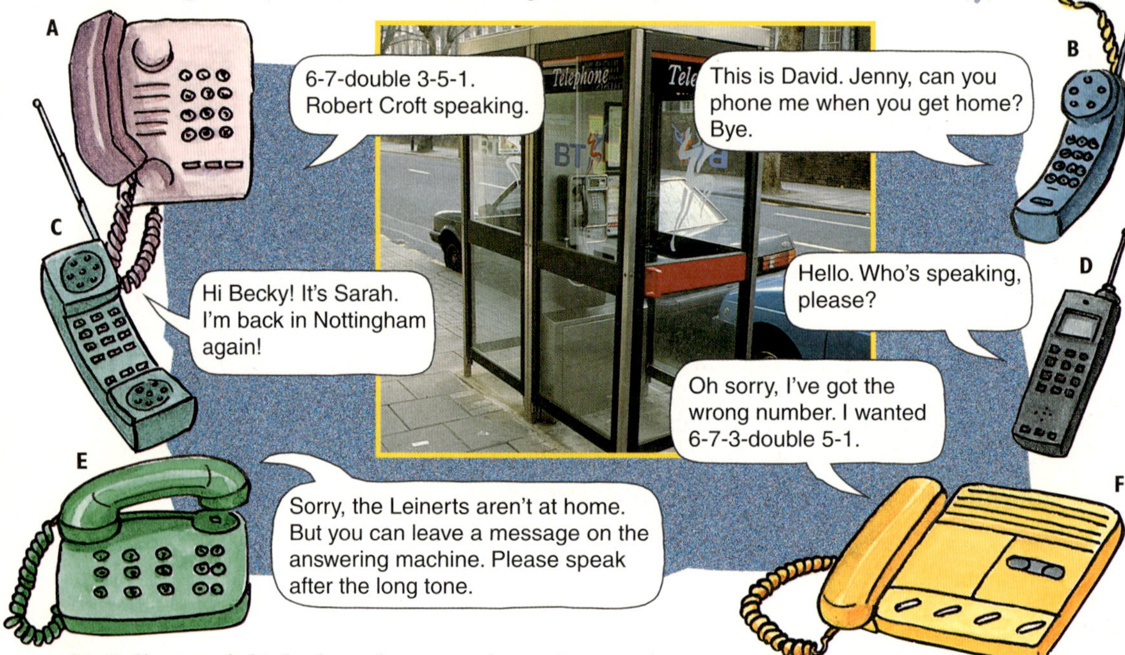

b) *Collect useful telephone language from a).*
Make two lists about – what you can say when you answer the telephone.
– what you can say when you make a call.

2 Listening practice: Take messages

HV

a) *Listen to the recording. You will hear some telephone calls. Write down the message. (Say who phoned, who it is for and what the message is.) You can start like this:*

b) *Listen again. Collect more telephone language for your lists from exercise 1.*

3 Sound practice

SB

You have to be careful: If you say the wrong sound, you often say a different word!

a) *Listen and say:*

1. a big farm – a pig farm
2. a small class – a small glass
3. right away – ride away
4. a TV fan – a TV van

Which sounds make the difference in each pair?

b) *Now practise these sounds:*

1. [b/p]
bark – **p**ark
bath – **p**ath

2. [k/g]
ba**ck** – ba**g**
pi**ck** – pi**g**

3. [t/d]
town – **d**own
ha**t** – ha**d**

4. [f/v]
ferry – **v**ery
o**ff** – o**f**

4 Some useful telephone tips

Ellen and her sister want to stay in the Lake District next weekend. Ellen is phoning the Ambleside Youth Hostel.

1. *Look at the picture on the right. What does Ellen do before she phones? Is this a good idea? Why?*
2. *Listen to the call on the recording. Look at Ellen's notes. How does she use them?*
3. *Now listen and read. Find out:*
   - what you can say if you don't understand what the other person says.
   - how you can help the other person if he or she wants to write down your name. (Don't forget – if you're from another country, your name will be a bit strange!)

Warden: Ambleside Youth Hostel. The warden speaking.
Ellen: Hello. My name is Ellen Jonker. I'd like to – er – to book two beds, please. They're for my sister and me – for next Friday and Saturday.
Warden: Hm. I think we're full. Let me see. – Oh, you're lucky. Somebody has just cancelled.
Ellen: I'm sorry. I didn't understand the last word. Can you say it again, please?
Warden: Somebody has just cancelled. Two other people booked the beds, but now they don't want them.
Ellen: Oh, I see. Well, that's great for us!
Warden: If you can just give me your name again – and spell it, please.
Ellen: Yes, of course. It's Jonker. That's J-O-N-K-E-R. And what time can we ... er ... check in?
Warden: After 5 o'clock on Friday afternoon. We'll see you then. Goodbye.
Ellen: Thank you. Goodbye.

5 Your turn Call a youth hostel

a) *Choose a youth hostel and book beds for you and a friend. (A lot of hostels have family rooms, too. So if you like, you can book a room for your family.) Work with a partner: one of you is the warden, the other makes the call. Write down some notes first to help you.*

Scarborough Youth Hostel
Lots of things to do in this seaside town.
Tel: 01723 3611

York International Youth Hostel
Near the centre of this famous city.
Tel: 01904 6

Ambleside Youth Hostel
Next to beautiful Lake Windermere.
Tel: 015394 323

Malham Youth Hostel
Great for long walks and mountain bikes.
Tel: 01729 83

b) In the dialogue in exercise 4 the warden talked about two other people. *Imagine you are one of them and you want to cancel the room. Write a dialogue for the phone call to the youth hostel. Act it with a partner.*

4 A short talk

Sarah and her friends are back at school now. In the English lesson yesterday they had to give a short talk about a 'travel experience'.

"I want to tell you about a funny 'travel experience'. It happened a few weeks ago while we were on the ferry from Hull to Rotterdam. When we went back to our car, Dad couldn't find the car keys. 'I've lost them – they aren't in my pocket!' he said and ran off to the information desk. Well, all the other cars started to drive off the ferry. Mum was going crazy because we were just standing there. Suddenly my sister Kim said, 'Hey, the car isn't locked. And look – the keys are inside. Dad forgot to lock the car before we left it yesterday!' When Mum heard that, she really went crazy!"

1 How you can use notes

a) Sarah used notes for her talk. *Look at the first part of them. Compare them with the full text. What is the difference?*

- funny 'travel experience'
- a few weeks ago
- on ferry from Hull to Rotterdam
- everything OK

b) *Now go on and finish Sarah's notes.*

c) *When you speak from notes you can sometimes put ideas together with conjunctions.*

For example you can say: It happened a few weeks ago. We were on the ferry from … .
But it sounds better if you say: It happened a few weeks ago **while** we were on the ferry … .

Check how Sarah put other ideas together. What conjunctions did she use?

2 Make a talk from notes

a) *Read the notes for Robert's talk. These words are new:* to cycle, picnic, rainstorm, shelter.

'travel experience' – last month – with David – cycling to Newstead Abbey – wanted to have a picnic – terrible rainstorm – never seen rain like it! – had to stop under a bus shelter – were waiting there – someone else on a bike arrived – from Leipzig in Germany – spending his holidays in England – rain stopped – said goodbye – gave him my address – postcard – yesterday

b) *Use the notes in a). Write down what you think Robert says in his talk.*
Start like this: My travel experience happened last month. I was with my friend David … *Go on.*

SB c) *Now listen to Robert's talk on the recording.*
Compare it with your text.
Check what is the same, and what is different.
Did you use the same conjunctions?

3 Make your own talk

Write notes for a short talk about a 'travel experience'.
Divide into groups of 4 or 5.
Give your talk to your group.

tip

- Don't talk too fast. Stop between sentences.
- Try to look up sometimes.
- Make some words more important than others.

5 ⟨Practice Page⟩

1 Ferry dialogues

Find one verb for each dialogue, and use the right forms: simple present or present progressive

open carry show travel talk

1. *Kim:* What time **does** the restaurant **open**?
   Sarah: Soon, I hope. – Oh good, it's **opening** now.
2. *Mrs Dixon:* Look. Who … Sarah … to?
   Kim: Don't ask me. Our Sarah always … to everyone!
3. *Sarah:* … ferry cinemas … good films?
   Kim: No idea. Let's go and ask what they … on this ferry today.
4. *Sarah:* … you … to England alone?
   Ellen: No, with my sister. We always … together.
5. *Mr Dixon:* Excuse me. How many cars … this ferry usually …?
   Officer: Well, at the moment we … 360.

2 All about Scotland

Sarah is telling Florian about Scotland. Finish her sentences. Add a second part to the object. You can sometimes use your own ideas.

1. "People in Scotland are very friendly. I'm sure they'll make you **very** **welcome**."
2. "There are a lot of lakes in Scotland. You call them … ."
3. "Have you heard of the monster in Loch Ness? I find the idea … ."
4. "Don't be surprised to see men in skirts. They call their skirts … ."
5. "Oh, and I must warn you about bagpipes! Some people like the sound, but I find it … ."
6. "Anyway, I hope you have good weather. Good weather always makes a holiday … ."

3 On holiday in Wales

a) *The Penroses went to Wales. What did they tell their friends about their holiday photos?*

1. *David:* On the first day of our holiday I **caught a fish**.
2. *Mark:* When we were on the beach, Mum and I … .
3. *Mr Penrose:* I felt so silly when I … .
4. *Mrs Penrose:* One day we all … .
5. *David:* Before we left Wales I … . Here it is – a little Welsh dragon.

b) Your turn *What have you done on holiday? Talk about when or where. Ask and answer questions like this:*

Have you ever fallen off a horse?

No, I haven't. But I've ridden a horse. I rode one in Austria last year.

A trip to London

Step A

Famous sights

I've (never) been to … .

I visited … last March /… .

I've seen a picture of / a film about … .

1 Your turn **What do you know about London?**

Talk about the famous sights on the map.

I've heard of … .

My friend sent me a postcard of … .

I know a bit about … . It's … .

…

The exchange visit

Christoph Steffen Katrin Hoffmann Darren Taylor

Samira Sheikh

2 Listening practice: Arriving in London

It is September and some pupils from a school in Kiel are coming to London on an exchange visit. They have never met their exchange partners before and they are all very excited.
Their flight will arrive at Heathrow Airport soon.

Listen to the recording.
Some words are new to you.
Look at the map on pages 14 and 15.
What can the group see before they land?

3 Samira's family

Katrin's exchange partner is Samira Sheikh.
The Sheikhs live in a flat in Bethnal Green.

Katrin: All those different people on the underground – they seem to come from all over the world. Africans, Indians, Chinese, ...

Samira: Well, most of them came to London a long time ago. Look, this is a photo of the Notting Hill Carnival. It takes place in August every year. The West Indians started it ... .

Katrin: People from India?

Samira: No, from the West Indies. You know, islands in the Caribbean.

Katrin: Oh, I see. And what about you? Where's your family from?

Samira: Well, my grandfather came from Pakistan when my dad was four years old. My mum was born in Coventry, but her family is from India. We're Muslims but we often go to the Hindu temple in North London. Look, here. They have lovely Indian festivals. We often take part in them, although we're not Hindus.

Katrin: So you're Indian?

Samira: No, I'm British. I'm a Londoner.

4 Your turn People from other countries

How many people from other countries do you know?
Where did they, or their families, come from?
Find out about the festivals and food of one nationality and write a short report. Example:

My friend Nalan is from Turkey. Her parents came to Germany before she was born. They have different festivals: they don't have Christmas, for example. But at the end of Ramadan

What you can see in London

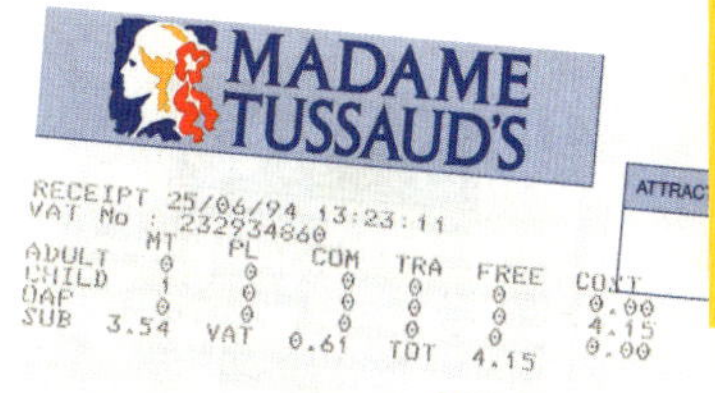

The Taylors were having tea with Christoph. Darren felt disappointed. In the photo his exchange partner looked fun, but Christoph seemed very quiet and boring.
"Oh, dear," Darren thought, "a whole week with him!"
"So, what are your hobbies then, Christoph?" asked Mrs Taylor.
"Er, I like books," came the answer.
"Oh, what about?" Darren's mother asked. "Animals, sports, cars?"
"Well, I really like books about history," Christoph said.
"I think they're very interesting."
"That's nice. You'll love London," said Mrs Taylor and smiled.
"Look, I've got some leaflets about the sights. Here, Darren, pass these to Christoph."
"Here you are," Darren said. "Ugh, history!" he thought.

5 What is it?

Look at the pictures and read the texts.

Which text goes with which picture?
Can you find these places on the map on pages 14 and 15?

In its long history, the Tower has been a castle, a royal palace, a prison and even a royal zoo.

The Queen lives at Buckingham Palace when she is in London.

You can see lots of famous people at Madame Tussaud's waxworks – but not 'live'.

Westminster Abbey is a big church opposite the Houses of Parliament. The kings and queens of England are crowned here.

6 Eastbound or westbound?

Samira and Katrin are looking at a map of the London underground.

Can you find the stops for these sights: the Tower of London, Madame Tussaud's, Hyde Park, Westminster Abbey and the Houses of Parliament, Harrod's, … .

Look at the map on pages 14 and 15, too.

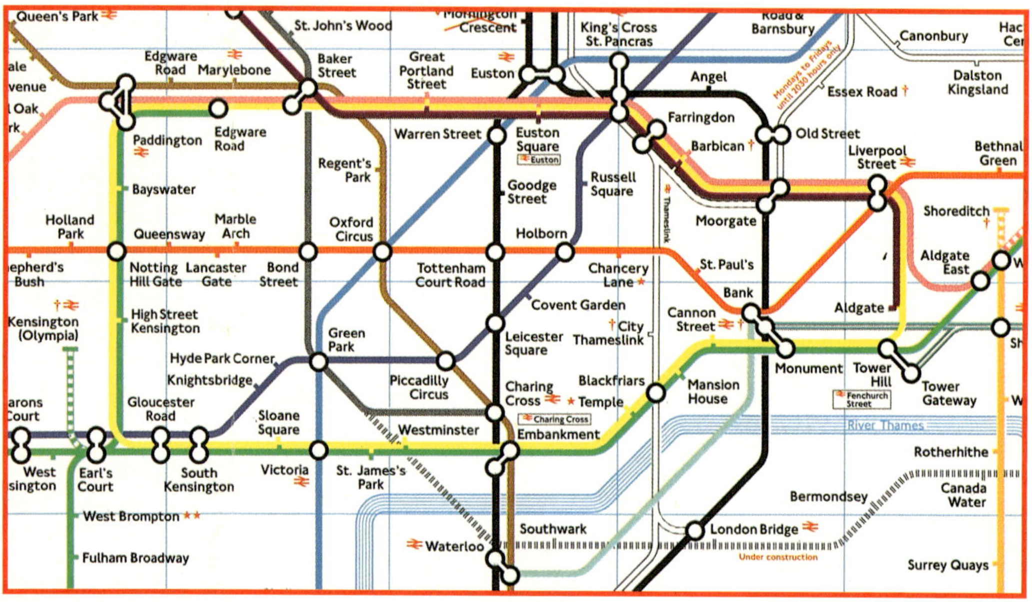

7 Find the station!

Samira and Katrin are on an underground train. They're playing "Find the station". Do you know the answers?

1. You're at Bond Street. Take the Central Line eastbound and go four stops. – I'm at … .
2. You're at Paddington. Take the District Line to Notting Hill Gate and change to the Central Line. Then go one stop westbound.
3. You're at Victoria. Take the Circle or District Line eastbound. Go three stops. Then change to the Northern Line. Go two stops northbound.

Play "Find the station" with a partner.
Example: You're at Green Park. Take the Jubilee Line to … .

8 Your turn Your trip to London

What would you like to see in London? How do you get there by underground from Leicester Square?

Example: I would like to visit Westminster Abbey because … . I'd take the Northern Line to Embankment. Then I'd change to the … .

Step A

At the Tower

Darren and Christoph went sightseeing on their first day. They started at the Tower of London. Darren wanted to know about the history of the Tower, so they looked at some leaflets and talked to one of the beefeaters. They are guards at the Tower and help the tourists.

9 1066

Can you put the information in the right order? Start with A.

Edward the Confessor, King of England, built Westminster Abbey. One week after it was finished, Edward died. They took his body to the new Abbey. **A**

However, William of Normandy (in France) also wanted to become King of England. **B**

King Edward had no children, so the most important men in England met and chose a new king. They chose Harold. **C**

William and the Norman army landed near Hastings on the south coast of England. **D**

Even after William, the kings of England were Normans for the next 200 years. Of course, they all spoke French, not English. **E**

Harold and the English army fought William and the Normans at the Battle of Hastings. **G**

Harold died in the battle and William of Normandy became King William I of England. He was crowned on Christmas Day 1066 in Westminster Abbey. **F**

10 Looking at English

a) *These English words are all from French. Try to make groups for them.*

b) *Now look at the word groups. Who do you think spoke French in those days?*

royal sausage coat charity
parliament abbey lace blue cream
biscuit guard spy officer fruits
religion sugar plate battle dinner
prisoner salad army roast beef

Step B

What do you like doing?

The exchange classes are at school today.
At break they find out more about the others.

Swimming is terrible.
Skiing is my favourite sport.

§ 2.1

I love **reading**.
I enjoy **taking** photos.

§ 2.2

1 Looking at English

a) **Playing** football is great.
I love **reading**.

These -ing forms are called gerunds.
How many can you find above?
Make two lists.

Gerunds as subject	Gerunds as object
Playing football is great.	I love reading.

b) *What verbs come before the gerund as an object?*
love, can't stand, … *Go on.*

2 What do you know about them?

Read the text and talk about the four young people.
Example: Samira likes … .

Make up a dialogue with a partner. You never agree!
You: Playing football is fantastic.
Partner: No, it isn't. Playing football is terrible.

terrible great fun easy fantastic silly stupid difficult

3 Your turn I like …

Say what you like or don't like doing.

go to museums · visit friends · read history books · go to the cinema · cook · play football · listen to music · do homework · dance · work in the garden · read adventure stories · watch sports on TV · work on the computer · go shopping with the family · swim · visit grandma and grandpa · play the guitar · sing

Getting around

In a London restaurant:
– Waiter, there's a fly in my soup!
– Oh dear, it's not very good at swimming!

At the Tower of London:
Small boy: Mum, I'm tired of standing in this queue.
Mother: It's OK, we can go and stand in another queue in a minute, if we want to see the Crown Jewels.

4 Doing things

Use **good at**, **interested in**, **tired of** *and fill in the gerund forms.*

1. If you're … … (read) maps, you won't get lost in London.
2. If you get … … (see) the sights, go for a walk in the park.
3. If you're not … … (remember) sights, take lots of photos.
4. If you're … … (watch) football, go to Wembley Stadium.
5. If you're … … (walk), you could take the underground.
6. If you're … … (see) famous people, go and see the waxworks at Madame Tussaud's.

5 Your turn What are you good at?

Make three lists.

I'm good at…	I'm not very good at…	I'm interested in…
painting	singing	rowing

What is your partner good at? Ask her/him.
Example:

Are you good at painting?

No, I'm not. Are you good at …?

Going out for a meal

One day Mrs Taylor took Christoph and Darren to an Indian restaurant for lunch.
Darren: What's 'Murgh' … er, number 56? It sounds funny.
Mrs Taylor: It's chicken. It tastes nice but it's hot. If you like hot food … .
Christoph: Well, something smells good.
Darren: Yes, look over there – what those people are having.
Mrs Taylor: Would you like that?

It **sounds funny** but it **smells good**.

§ 4

6 What does it taste like?

I think	Italian / Greek / Chinese / Turkish / German	food	tastes / looks / sounds / smells	good. / interesting. / OK. / fantastic. / hot. / funny.

A trip to the British Museum

"Today's trip is to the British Museum," said Mrs Grant to the exchange group. "Are we all here? Samira and Katrin – OK; Darren and Christoph ... where's Darren?" asked Mrs Grant, as she read out the list of names.

"He's ill," said Christoph in a quiet voice.

"Darren just can't stand going round museums," Samira whispered to Katrin.

"Pardon?" Mrs Grant said. "Did you say anything, Samira?"

"No, Mrs Grant," Samira said.

They got on the train. Christoph was upset. Everyone else was talking and laughing with their exchange partners, but he was all alone. Being in London wasn't much fun.

"Cheer up," said a voice next to him. He looked round. Samira was smiling at him. "Come and have some fun with us," she said.

On the way to the museum, Christoph felt much happier. Samira and Katrin talked to him all the way.

"OK," said Mrs Grant when they arrived. "We'll meet here again on the steps at one o'clock. You can go round the museum and fill in your worksheets. Afterwards we'll walk down to Covent Garden, OK?"

Christoph looked at his worksheet. It looked quite interesting. Samira came over to him.

"Hey, Christoph," she said. "Do you really want to go inside?"

"Yes," answered Christoph. "I want to see the Egyptian mummies."

"Ugh," Katrin said. "We're going to play video games. There's a place near the station."

"Come on," Samira said. "Let's have some fun."

Christoph wasn't sure. He was really interested in the Egyptian rooms and some of the other things in the British Museum, but he wanted to go with Katrin and Samira, too.

"What about Mrs Grant and the other teachers?" he asked.

"Them? Look, they're already in the museum. Come on," Samira called to him.

Samira, Katrin and Christoph walked towards the station. It seemed a long way.

"Look, there's the station," Katrin said.

"Hurry up," Samira called. She and Katrin ran across the road.

"Wait for me," Christoph shouted. Samira looked back.

"Christoph! Watch out!" she shouted. "Cyclist!"

But it was too late. Christoph was looking left, not right, as he started to cross the road. The cyclist tried to stop but he was going too fast. He hit the side of Christoph's bag. Christoph fell over and the cyclist fell off his bike.

"You stupid idiot!" the man shouted.

Christoph looked at him. The front wheel of his bike was bent and there was a hole in his jacket. He looked really angry. Christoph was scared. He turned and ran towards the museum.

Samira and Katrin ran after him along the road and round the next corner.

"Hey, Christoph," Katrin called.

He stopped and they caught up with him.

"Is he coming?" Christoph asked.

"No, it's OK," Katrin answered and looked back at the corner.

"Are you all right?" Samira asked him. "Why did you run away?"

Christoph looked very white. "I don't know," he said. "I was scared and … ouch, my hand hurts."

"Let me look," Samira said. "Here, put my scarf round it."

"Thank you," Christoph said. "Can we go back to the museum now?"

"Yes," Katrin said. "I'm not interested in playing video games any more."

"What are we going to say to Mrs Grant?" Christoph asked.

"Oh nothing," Samira said. "She won't notice anything. Just act normal."

They walked slowly back to the British Museum.

When they got there they went straight to the first Egyptian room.

"I can't see Mrs Grant," Katrin said.

"Good!" Samira said. "Then we're OK. Have you got your worksheet? Look, two of the others are over there. We can copy the answers from them."

Christoph was already in the next room. He was looking at the mummies.

At one o'clock Christoph, Katrin and Samira went out to the front steps. A man was sitting there. "Oh no," thought Christoph. The man had a hole in his jacket and next to him was a bike. Its front wheel was bent. Christoph turned round. Mrs Grant was just coming out of the museum.

"Oh good, you three. You're here already," Mrs Grant said. "And so is my husband. Hello, dear."

The man turned round.

1 What do you think?

What do you think happened next?

1. What did the man say?
2. What did Mrs Grant say?
3. What did Christoph and the girls say?

2 How do they feel?

1. How does Christoph feel when the exchange partners meet?
2. How does Christoph feel when they arrive at the British Museum?
3. What do Samira and Katrin think of museums?
4. Does Christoph want to go into the museum?
5. How does Christoph feel after the accident?
6. How do Samira, Katrin and Christoph feel when they see Mr Grant?
7. How does Mr Grant feel when he sees them?

3 Christoph's story

When Christoph gets back to Darren's flat, Darren asks: "Did you enjoy going to the museum?"
What does Christoph say? Write the dialogue.

HV 4 Listening practice: A visit to the British Museum

You want to go to the British Museum but you don't know when.
You can get information on the phone about when the museum is open and how you could get there.
Read the questions first, then make a checklist and listen to the telephone information. Now answer the questions.

1. Can you visit the British Museum on a Sunday morning?
2. What about 4 o'clock on Sunday afternoon?
3. Can you get there by underground?
4. Where can you buy postcards?
5. Can you take photos?
6. Where can you get something to eat or drink?

SB 5 Sound practice

Some words sound the same, but you spell them differently.

Listen to these sentences. How do you spell the missing words?

1. **Where** is my London T-shirt? I want to **wear** it to school tomorrow.
2. My [ɑ:nt] and uncle [ɑ:nt] here at the moment. They've gone to London.
3. There's something wrong with my [nəʊz]. Maybe the doctor [nəʊz] what it is.
4. [ðeə] partners are waiting for the plane over [ðeə].
5. I can [si:] the [si:] from my bedroom at home.
6. What are you saying? I can't [hɪə] you from [hɪə].
7. [nəʊ] , sorry, I don't [nəʊ] the way to Baker Street.
8. I'll [raɪt] your name on the list. Is that all [raɪt]?
9. Who [θru:] this ball [θru:] the window?
10. Have you [red] this poem about the [red] London buses?

6 London thoughts

The pupils from Kiel have written about London.
Can you complete their sentences?

1. I like all the sandwich bars – the sandwiches always … super.
2. London is a big city and the people … busy.
3. I love travelling by underground. It always … so exciting.
4. There are too many cars and buses in London. They often … terrible.
5. If you're standing in front of Big Ben at 12 o'clock it … very loud.
6. People in London speak in a different way – their voices … strange.

sound feel smell taste seem look

Step D

Let's check

1 London questions

When the pupils got back to Kiel, they made a questionnaire about their visit to London.

Example: Most of the pupils enjoyed travelling by underground. One person couldn't stand … .

	love	enjoy	don't like	hate / can't stand
travel on the underground	3	20	2	1
walk around for hours	2	4	12	8
go to museums	4	10	10	2
buy souvenirs	25	1	0	0
stand in queues	0	0	12	14
take photos	7	13	4	2

What about you? Talk about what you like.
Example: I love going by underground … .

2 What are they good at?

Example: Darren is good at playing football, but he isn't … .

– = not good at
+ = good at

3 Word power Travelling in London

Find the rhymes for these sentences? They're all about travelling.

1. Don't go too far
In that old … .

2. Come with us Maxi
Get in the … !

3. Could you show me round?
We'll go by … .

4. Get up on your feet
Then let's walk down this … .

5. Was the plane all right?
Did you have a good … ?

6. Bond Street has good shops.
And it's only two more … .

7. Your idea was really fine.
But we're on the wrong … .

8. This queue is for us.
It's the number 12 … .

WORKING WITH WORDS

1 Understanding new words

1 Find the picture

Selby School in London is going to have a Sports Day. *Read the texts. (You won't know all the new words, but don't worry.) Which person goes with which picture?*

Jackie Mc Carthy: "I'm a member of the tennis team. We're lucky – our school has got its own tennis courts. I want to compete in two cycling races, but I've got to mend my bike first – one of the wheels is bent."

Samira Sheikh: "I've hurt my foot, so I'll just stay in the gym and watch my friend Jane. She's going to do jazz dance."

Lee Jones: "I play rugby for the school, and I'm good at running, too. I'm training for the 200 metres race, so I go jogging every day."

Darren Taylor: "I'm goalkeeper in the football team, but there won't be any football matches on Sports Day. The school needs the sportsfield for athletics, like the high jump and running."

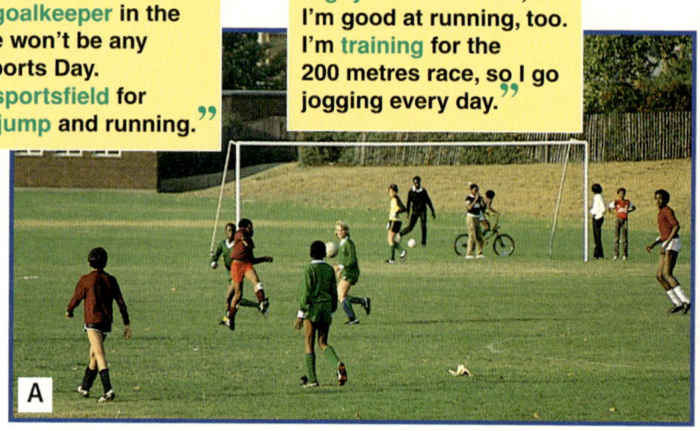

2 Can you guess?

Read the texts again. Look at the coloured words and guess what they mean. The tips will help you.

tip

- You can often guess the meaning of a word from its context.
- If a word is like one in German, it probably means the same.
- Is the word a noun, an adjective or a verb? Maybe you already know the word in a different form.
- If you still aren't sure, ask someone or look it up in the word list.

I know the words 'bike' and 'bent', so I can guess the word 'mend' from the context.

'Training' looks like the German word 'trainieren'.

I know the noun 'competition', so I can guess the verb 'compete'.

I looked up 'goalkeeper'. It means 'Torwart'.

3 Listening practice: What's the situation?

a) *Listen to the dialogues. You won't understand everything but don't worry. Just try to imagine the situation.*

b) *Read the questions and then listen again. Take notes this time.*

1. Where are the people?
2. What have they just done, or what are they going to do?

2 Organizing words

Lee cut out a report about his favourite rugby player from a sports magazine.

The New Zealand Express

Jonah Lomu was born in Tonga in 1975. He plays for New Zealand's national team, the All Blacks, and became famous when he played in the Rugby World Cup in South Africa in July 1995. On the pitch, Lomu looks like a bear. He weighs 120 kilos and is 1.98 metres tall. His size helps him to tackle, but he moves fast, too. He can run 100 metres in just 10.6 seconds! He is like an express train when he fights his way with the ball past his opponents.

Workshop B

1 Collecting and organizing words

Collect the new words in the text and look them up in the word list on page 156.

Read the tips on the right before you write the words in your vocabulary book.

tip
- You can write the word in German: **queue** – (Warte-)schlange
- You can explain the word in English: **to mend** = to repair
- You can write a sentence: **to whisper** – I can't hear you when you whisper.
- You can show the meaning with an opposite: **to lose** ⟷ to find
- You can draw a picture: **cup** –

2 Your turn Writing about a person

Choose your favourite star. Find out as much as you can about this person and write a report. Collect photos or draw pictures. Then tell the class about your star.

- Where and when was your star born?
- What does he/she do now? Why is he/she famous?
- What does he/she look like?
- What other interesting facts do you know about him/her?

3 Word banks

a) *Start a word bank for 'sports'. How many more words can you add?*

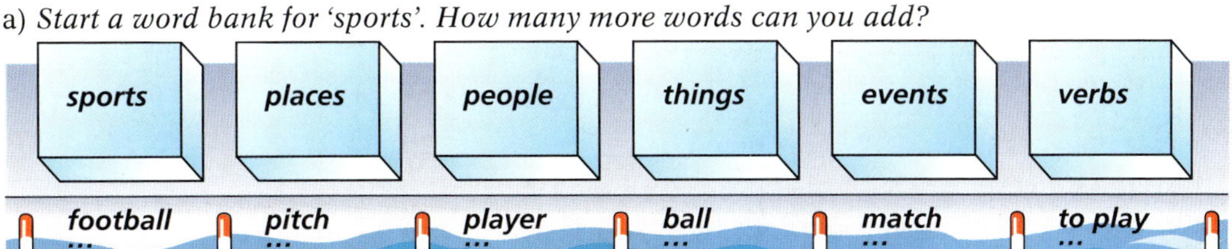

b) *Start a word bank with one of these words here. Make two teams. Someone from team A says a word for the word bank, and someone else writes it on the board. Then the other team says a word. Go on until you can't think of any more words. The winner is the team with the most words at the end of the game.*

food
animals
clothes
shopping
school
at home
jobs

4 Word partners

You should learn some words with their partners.
Can you remember these?
Do they go with 'make' *or* 'do'*?*
Write two lists.

make	do
a cake	homework

a mistake · nothing · a request · athletics · the washing-up · a plan · a test · a cup of tea · an exercise · sandwiches · housework · money · a poster

5 Verbs with prepositions

There are some crazy races on Sports Day.
Describe what these children are doing.
Use the verbs with the prepositions.

put · go · get · come · pick · take · …

on · off · to · up · down · away · in · …

6 ⟨Just for fun⟩

3 Saying things in different ways

Samira and Katrin are going to play table tennis at the youth club.

Katrin: Have you got a racket for me, Samira, or can I get one at the youth club?
Samira: Racket? We're going to play **table** tennis! We'll use the youth club's bats.
Katrin: Bats? Oh, so you've got two words for 'Schläger'. Racket and bat.
Samira: Yes. A racket is a kind of bat, but a racket has got strings on it. Like a badminton racket.
Katrin: Aha! If it hasn't got strings, it's a bat, right? So do you say 'hockey bat'?
Samira: No, we don't! We say hockey **stick**!
Katrin: Oh, what a terrible language!

1 In other words

a) *How can you explain these words? Example:* A kilt is **a kind of** skirt.

fast, helmet, to practise, to catch, to jog, racket, kilt, gym, big, to cycle, match, pitch, to win	is the opposite of is a kind of means the same as	sportsfield, to ride a bike, hat, to lose, small, to throw, bat, slow, skirt, to train, to run, sports room, competition

b) *Think of a different way to explain these words.*
Example: You can play tennis with a **racket**.

2 Listening practice: What does it mean?

Katrin is talking to her English friends. She doesn't understand all the words. So they explain them to her. These are the words: ***changing room*** ***referee*** ***to dive***

Listen to the dialogues. What do the words mean in German?

3 ⟨A song⟩

We are the champions

I've paid my dues,
Time after time.
I've done my sentence,
But committed no crime.
And bad mistakes,
I've made a few.
I've had my share of sand,
Kicked in my face,
But I've come through.

Refrain:
We are the champions –
My friends
And we'll keep on fighting –
Till the end.
We are the champions,
We are the champions,
No time for losers,
'Cause we are the champions –
Of the world.

I've taken my bows,
And my curtain calls.
You brought me fame and
Fortune and everything that
Goes with it –
I thank you all.
But it's been no bed of roses,
No pleasure cruise.
I consider it a challenge before
The whole human race,
And I ain't gonna lose.

Refrain

4 Words in grammar

ⓐ

They're looking at themselves.

myself	ourselves
yourself	yourselves
himself	themselves
herself	
itself	

§ 5

They're looking at each other.

1 Reflexive verbs

Selby School is having a sports quiz. There are prizes for the best answers on Sports Day. These are the rules. Put in -self/-selves *or* each other.

1. Pupils must fill in the answers … .
2. If pupils help … they won't get a prize.
3. Pupils mustn't talk to … .

This is what Mrs Grant said to herself while she was correcting the quizzes.

4. Some people didn't do all the work … .
5. Yes, I'm sure they helped … .
6. Darren said he was talking to … . But I think he and Wayne were talking to … .
7. This is good! Did Samira really do it …?
8. Oh, this is easy. I could even do it … .

ⓑ

Dear Diary,

Jazz dance isn't so difficult after all – I even enjoyed myself! Today we met in the gym and practised our Michael Jackson dance for Sports Day. Dad and Julie are coming to watch us –
I feel nervous already. I know I won't be able to concentrate on the steps if they're both there.
Samira isn't speaking to me. She asked me to cut her hair this afternoon. I thought I cut it really well, but when she saw herself, she screamed and dropped the mirror! Then, while we were picking up the pieces, I cut myself – what a mess!

tip Some words are reflexive in German but not in English:
concentrate, feel, meet, remember, sit, …

2 *Watch out:* -self/-selves or nothing

1. Don't make so much noise. I can't concentrate … .
2. I've dropped the bottle. Be careful! Don't cut …!
3. These photos are fantastic. – Thanks. I took them … .
4. Well done! You've just won the race. How do you feel …?
5. Your pullover looks very nice. – Thank you. My mum made it … .
6. We mustn't worry about Sports Day. We should try to enjoy … .
7. What did we do at Sports Day last year? Can you remember …?

5 Word building

When Sports Day came, Lee wasn't there.
When he arrived at school, the races were already over.
This newspaper article explains why.

LONDON SCHOOLBOY TACKLES THIEF

Lee Jones, 13, of Elf Row, Shadwell, caught a thief in King's Park on Wednesday morning. The man took a woman's bag from a bench while she was feeding the ducks. Lee ran after him, caught him and threw him to the ground. "He was really surprised," said Lee. "He gave me the bag right away, and then I threw it back to the woman." The woman, Ms Nora Duncan of East Cheam, went to call the police while Lee sat on the thief. "My rugby training was useful," said Lee. "It helped me to tackle the thief. I sat on him for 10 minutes until the police came!" Ms Duncan agreed that it was careless to leave the bag on a bench. "I'll be more careful next time. Not many people are as helpful as Lee," she said.

1 Looking at English

Find the words with -ful *and* -less *in the text. What do you think these endings mean?*

2 Word endings

Make adjectives from these verbs and the endings -less *and* -ful.

help — care — use — sleep

1. Look at this 'do-it-yourself' book. It's very … .
2. Little babies can't do anything for themselves. They're … .
3. He loses things all the time. He's so … .
4. My pen is broken again. It's … .
5. Be … or you'll fall.
6. I'm so tired. I had a … night.
7. Robert often does the shopping. What a … boy.

3 Making nouns

Sometimes you can make a noun from a verb + *er*.

Example: sing + er → singer
win + er → winner

Can you make nouns from these verbs? Check what they mean in the word list.

read — work — ride
learn — write — run
drive — swim — dance

4 Adjectives from verbs

You can also make adjectives from verbs. The ending -able *means 'you can do this'.*

Example: wash + *able* → washable

Is this shirt washable?
– Yes, you can put it in the washing machine.

understand — wash — read — change — break

Find the right adjectives for these sentences:

1. Be careful with those glasses. They're … .
2. We'll need anoraks. The weather will be … .
3. Lee was proud of himself when he caught the thief. That's … .
4. This is a good story. It's very … .

Trouble at school

Step A

> **tip**
> - What kind of question is it?
> - Is it a yes/no question?
> - Or is there a question word (who, where, what ...)?

The video conference

1 Questions and answers

Haywood School has organized a video conference between pupils in the German course and pupils at Haywood's partner school in Karlsruhe. They are talking about school life in Britain.

a) *Read all the questions. Look at the tip box. Then look at the answers to find the right ones.*

b) *Collect facts about British schools. Make a list.*

2 Karlsruhe questions

There wasn't enough time to answer all the questions at the video conference. So the Karlsruhe class sent some more questions to Year 9 by e-mail. These are the answers.

Work with a partner.
Look at the e-mail messages.
What do you think the German pupils asked?

How much time …?
When do …?
Are there …?
Do you …?
What happens if …?

Example: A: **Do you** do all your subjects together?

What can you tell British pupils if they ask you the same questions about German schools?

Creating Mail

Out Basket | Send Now | File a Copy… | Delete

Reformattable
Send as Shown

To: Name: Kepler Gymnasium Address:
Subject: Video conference
Recipients:
Options
Auto-File

A Up to Year 9 we do all our subjects together. Then, in year 9, the teachers put us in different groups for English, Maths, Languages and Science.

B We don't have many tests during the term, but there are exams at the end of every school year. They test us on what we've learned during the year.

C Children start primary school when they're 5. When they're 11 they go to secondary school. They can leave when they're 16 or 18. Most secondary schools are comprehensives, like Haywood.

D We can take GCSE exams (that's General Certificate of Secondary Education) when we're 16, and 'A' Levels when we're 18.

E We spend about half an hour on each subject, so that's an hour every evening, and an hour and a half at weekends. The teachers usually collect and check all our homework.

F If pupils get bad marks in the exams, teachers give them special help. They don't have to repeat a year.

G Yes, there are other secondary schools. In some places there are grammar schools and some children go to boarding schools. That's "Internat" in German.

Wrap To Window | 77

3 Right or wrong?

Four of these facts are wrong.
Can you find them?
Write the correct sentences in your exercise books.

1. Children in Britain go to primary school for 4 years.
2. Pupils can leave school before they are 18.
3. If pupils get bad marks, they have to repeat the year until their marks get better.
4. Children are not allowed to take sandwiches for lunch.
5. Pupils in Year 9 are in different groups for some subjects.
6. All secondary schools are comprehensives.
7. Many British schools have libraries. They lend books to pupils.

4 ⟨Just for fun⟩

May I be excused?
My brain is full.

Unit 2

5 Sound practice

Say the words. Are the sounds long [iː] *or short* [ɪ]*? Then listen to the words and repeat them.*

sit	we'll	chip	this	it	he's	leave
seat	will	cheap	these	eat	his	live

St. John´s School for Boys
School Report, Summer Term

Name: **Edward Clark**
Tutor: N. Grant
Tutor group: **8NG**
Number of pupils: 24

Subject	Mark	Teachers' comments
Maths:	A	Edward is a quick thinker and he learns easily. He did very well in all his tests.
English:	B	Edward writes very well and he has interesting ideas. I always enjoy reading his stories.
German:	C	He could do better than this. He is good at languages, but he doesn't work hard enough.
French:	B	He has done well this term. I am very pleased with his progress.
Science:	D	Edward should try to concentrate more. He was very careless with some of his experiments.
R.E.:	D	Edward is too lazy. He should show more interest in the subject.
History:	C	He has a good memory for details, but did badly in tests. He should read the questions more carefully.
P.E.	E	Edward does not like any kind of sport. He really must try harder!
Art:	C	He is working more carefully now. He has made some progress this term.
Geography:	B	Edward's project on rivers was the best in the class. He put a lot of work into it.
Music:	B	He is getting better at reading music. And what a lovely singing voice!

Tutor's comments: Edward is a quiet but helpful pupil. If he works hard he will do well at his new school.

Tutor *Nigel Grant* Headteacher *W Smith*

6 Edward's report

Edward Clark, a new boy at Haywood, went to a boarding school near London while his parents were working in Asia.
Now they are back in Nottingham and he's living at home again. When he started at Haywood, Mrs Benson wanted to see his old school report.

a) *In which subjects were Edward's teachers pleased?*
In which subjects were they disappointed?

b) Your turn *Write comments about your own progress in three subjects.*
(You can make them funny, too.)

A = very good
E = very weak

Unit 2

The new boy

Robert: Have you seen the photos Edward Clark brought to school?
David: Yes, he's shown them to everyone!
Robert: What a show-off! So now we all know about the horse he got for his birthday, the big house he lives in, the swimming pool, … .
David: And all the countries his mum and dad have lived in – without him. And all the famous people they know!
Robert: The photos they took in China were great.
David: Yes, really interesting. Did he show you the photos of that boarding school he went to? It must be thousands of years old – like Dracula's Castle.
Robert: And the silly uniform! It's even worse than ours.
David: There weren't even any girls there. I'm not surprised he was miserable. You know, I don't think Edward is a show-off. He's just trying to make friends.
Robert: Well, he's trying too hard!

Edward brought some photos. Have you seen them?
→ Have you seen the photos **Edward brought**?
Edward went to a boarding school. It was very old.
→ The boarding school **Edward went to** was very old.

§ 7

1 The photos everyone saw

a) *Make sentences.*

1. The people	Mr and Mrs Clark took in China	was a horse.
2. The present	the Clarks live in now	are famous.
3. The photos	Edward went to	is very big.
4. The boarding school	Edward's parents know	is very old.
5. The house	Edward got for his birthday	are interesting.

b) *Why does Robert think Edward is a show-off? What does David think?*

2 Talking at break

Often a contact clause sounds better than two sentences.

Example: 1. I've found the book. You know, I lost it last week.
→ I've found the book I lost last week.

2. Have you seen these photos? I took them in Scotland.
3. Did you like the postcard? I sent it from Fort William.
4. The report looks quite good. Edward got it from his old school.
5. I can't stand that new teacher. You know, we've got her for Maths.
6. I enjoyed the new experiments. Remember? We did them in Science on Monday.
7. That joke book is good. You know, Robert brought it to school yesterday.

Wayne gets into trouble

It is assembly. Wayne and Emma from 9MD are standing in the back row.

Mrs Benson: When I arrived at school this morning I saw something that made me very angry. Someone has sprayed graffiti all over the wall behind the gym. It was the same wall on which we found graffiti last month. But then the person who did it used a spray that was washable. This time we won't be able to get rid of it so easily. The pupil who did it is probably listening to me now. Usually this is a case for the police. But we want to give the boy or girl that did it a chance. If you come to me after assembly, we'll find a way to settle it.

Emma (whispering): You did it, Wayne. I saw you behind the gym after school.

Wayne: What? You're crazy, Emma! Shut up.

3 Word power School words

Can you answer the questions?

1. What is a school meeting which takes place at the beginning of the day?
2. What do you call the person who usually speaks at assembly?
3. What do you call a boy or girl that has lessons at school?
4. What do you call the writing that was all over the wall of the gym?
5. What do you call the people who come if someone has done something wrong?

4 Looking at English

Look at the text and the questions in exercise 3 again. Collect the nouns that go in front of the relative pronouns 'who', 'which' and 'that'. Make a list

Then complete the rules.

We use … with things.
We use … with people.
We use … with … .

who	which	that
person		

5 'who' or 'which'?

Pupils from 9MD have sent more information to their partner class in Germany.
Put in 'who' or 'which'.

1. Pupils … go to a boarding school don't go home in the evening.
2. We have to pay for library books … get lost.
3. Exchange pupils … stay just for a short time don't have to wear school uniform.
4. We've sent you a class photo … is really funny.
5. Children … don't like school meals usually bring sandwiches from home.

A meeting on the stairs

6 Matching the parts

Make sentences with the relative clauses on the right.

1. Bullies are people		knows everything.
2. A frog is an animal	which	comes from Asia.
3. A curry is a meal	who	skin is green and slippery.
4. A teacher is a person	whose	enjoy bothering other people.
5. German is a language	that	has a very long nose.
6. An elephant is a big animal		English people often find difficult.

7 Looking at English

Please compare these two sentences.

What is the subject in the first relative clause? 1. That's the boy who took the sweets.

What is the subject in the second relative clause? 2. That's the boy who we saw in the canteen.

For number 2 you can also say: That's the boy we saw in the canteen.

We call this a contact clause. Can you think of a rule?
When can you leave out the relative pronoun?

8 ⟨A limerick⟩

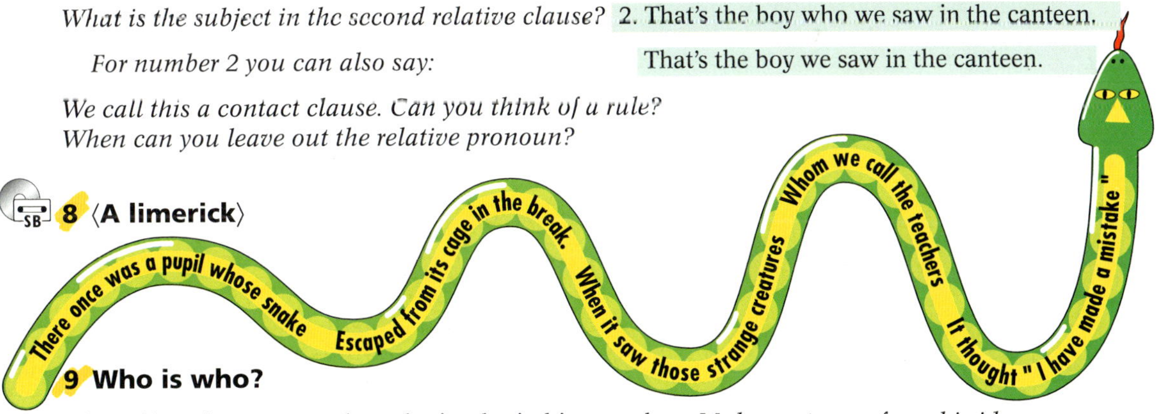

9 Who is who?

Edward is trying to remember who is who in his new class. *Make sentences from his ideas.*

1. Becky – nice – her poster won a prize
   Example: Becky is that nice girl whose poster won a prize.
2. Mario – Italian – his jokes are so funny.
3. Robert – friendly – his mother works for Radio Nottingham.
4. Daniel – clever – his father is our Science teacher.
5. Maggie – Irish – her sister is a pop star.
6. Thomas – crazy – his dad takes him to school in a tractor.
7. Jenny – really pretty – her parents come from Germany.

A busy week

Edward: Hi, Jenny! Can I carry something for you?
Jenny: Oh, thanks. Here, you can take my folders.
Edward: Let me carry your hockey stick, too. W-what are you doing tonight, Jenny? I'm going to the youth club and I don't really want to go alone. So maybe you'd like to … .
Jenny: Sorry, Edward! I'm playing in a hockey match after school.
Edward: We can go after the match.
Jenny: Well, I'm meeting Robert at 6 o'clock. We're acting in Romeo and Juliet at the end of the term. We're practising a difficult part tonight. Robert is a fantastic Romeo!
Edward: Oh, I see.

10 No time for Edward

1. When is Jenny playing in a hockey match?
2. What is she doing at 6 o'clock?
3. When are Jenny and Robert acting in Romeo and Juliet?
4. What are they doing tonight?

What tense did you use for your answers? You can sometimes use this tense to talk about the future!

Monday	4.30pm - hockey 6 pm - meet Robert (his house)	Friday	Emma - Victoria Centre at 5pm - Fiona's birthday present (CD?)
Tuesday	4pm - Aunty Pat, hospital (flowers!!)	Saturday	theatre trip (Romeo and Juliet)
Wednesday	5.45 pm - haircut at Victoria Centre	Sunday	3.30 pm - Fiona's party
Thursday	Becky - Sports Centre 5pm (take swimming things)		

11 Jenny's diary

Talk about Jenny's diary with a partner. Ask and answer questions about her arrangements.

What is Jenny doing after school on Monday?

She's playing hockey.

12 A fantasy diary

a) *You are a V.I.P. – a very important person. Write a fantasy diary for a week, but leave one day free.*

b) *Invite other V.I.P.s in your class to do things with you on your free day. Write the arrangements you make in your diary. If you can't make an arrangement with someone because you are busy, explain why.*

Would you like to fly to Africa with me on Saturday evening?

I'm sorry, I can't. I'm singing in a pop concert on Saturday evening. Thousands of fans are coming to watch me.

Emma

Emma: Hi, Becky. You look nice today!
Becky: So do you! Your hair is great. How did you do it?
Emma: It's easy! Shall I show you?
Becky: Thanks, but not just now, Emma.
Emma: OK. Hey, listen, Becky. I know who did the graffiti.
It was Wayne! Do you think I should tell Mrs Benson?
Becky: Well, only if you're sure.
Emma: Of course I'm sure! Will you come with me to Mrs Benson's office?
Becky: No, I'm waiting for Jenny.
Emma: Is she late again? She's probably with Robert. I can't stand the way those two go round together.

13 Shall I help?

Try to help these people. What do you say?

close lend call mend get carry ✓ show

Example:
1. You see an old woman with some big shopping bags.
– Shall I carry your bags?
2. It's very cold outside. The window is open.
3. Your friend's bike is broken.
4. An accident has just happened. You think someone needs an ambulance.
5. A small child is trying to get a book from the top shelf.
6. Your friend wants to buy a magazine but he hasn't got any money.
7. A new pupil at your school can't find the way to the toilets.

14 A teacher

You are the teacher. What can you say to the pupils? Start each sentence with 'Will you ...?'.

Example:
The pupils are running around the classroom.
You: Will you sit down, please?

1. The class is very noisy.
2. The board is dirty.
3. The door is open.
4. The pupils haven't given you their homework yet.
5. You have more books than you can carry.
6. A pupil has dropped a sweet paper on the floor.

15 ⟨Just for fun⟩

Step C

A thief in the school

1 Listening practice: In assembly

Mrs Benson is talking to the pupils in assembly.

Listen to the recording. Why is Mrs Benson worried? What advice does she give to the pupils?

2 Find the clues

Now read the text. Try to find clues. Who is the thief?

"This queue is terrible!" said Jenny. She was waiting in the lunch queue with Robert. Just before it was their turn, Wayne appeared.
"Hey, can I go in front of you two?" he asked. "I'm in a hurry."
"Don't let him in!" said a girl who was behind Jenny.
It was Emma – a girl Jenny couldn't stand because she was only friendly to her when Becky was around. "Of course you can go in front of us, Wayne," she said quickly.
Robert didn't mind because he wanted to ask Wayne something. "Do you remember the money I lent you, Wayne? When are you going to pay me back?"
"Oh, sorry, I've forgotten it again," said Wayne. "I'll bring it tomorrow, Robert, I promise!"
Robert was annoyed, but he didn't say anything else about it. Wayne was one of the boys who got free lunches, so Robert knew that Wayne's parents didn't have much money.

The dinner lady gave Jenny her tomato soup and salad. "That's one pound, please!"
Jenny looked in her bag for her purse. It wasn't there!
"I'm sorry," she said. Her face was now as red as the soup. "I haven't got any money with me!"
"You've probably lost it," said Emma nastily. "You should be more careful with your things."
"Oh, shut up, Emma!" said Jenny.
Then a voice next to her said: "Shall I pay for you, Jenny?" It was Edward.
"Oh, thanks! I'll pay you back tomorrow," said Jenny. Maybe Edward wasn't so bad after all.

Jenny ate her lunch with Becky and told her about the missing purse.
"That's strange!" said Becky. "The same thing happened to me this morning! I wanted to buy some crisps, but I couldn't find my purse. Maybe the school thief took it! But I was lucky, like you. Edward didn't just pay for my crisps. He bought me a drink, too!"
Then Jenny remembered something. "Becky, was Emma standing near you?"
"Yes, she was. Why do you want to know?"
Jenny couldn't answer. Emma was coming to their table.

After lunch, Jenny met Robert behind the gym.
"Everyone thinks Wayne is the thief," said Robert.
Suddenly Wayne came out from behind the corner.
"Who are you calling a thief? I heard every word you said!"
He pushed Robert against the wall. "I'm not a thief!"
"Don't push me!" Robert shouted and kicked Wayne.
"Watch out!" cried Jenny. "Mr Stuart's coming!"
Wayne left as quickly as he could.
"Come on, let's go and tell Mr Stuart about him," said Robert.

"No, wait!" said Jenny. "We're making a mistake. I think Emma could be the thief."
Robert laughed. "What, Emma? Are you crazy?"
Jenny explained. "Emma's jealous of me! And she tells lies, too!"
"We must be sure who the thief is before we tell Mr Stuart," said Robert. "Listen, I've got an idea." Together they made a plan.

The next morning, Robert and Jenny were too excited to concentrate on their Maths lesson. Just before break Mr Stuart said, "I hope you've all brought your money for the theatre trip. You can give it to Mrs Taylor after break, but don't forget to put it in a safe place."
Robert put his money under his pencil case. It wasn't a safe place, but that was part of the plan.

When the bell rang, most of the pupils left the classroom quickly. Only Robert and Jenny stayed. They climbed into an empty cupboard which was big enough for both of them.
For a while nothing happened. But then they heard a noise. Someone was coming into the classroom! Robert opened the cupboard door a little and looked out. He saw two legs which were walking up to his desk, but whose legs were they?
"That's the thief," whispered Robert. "Come on!"
They jumped out of the cupboard and saw the thief – with Robert's money!
"So it's you!" they shouted.

3 Who did it?

Who do you think is the school thief? Explain why.

4 Listening practice: Who is the thief?

Were you right about the thief? Find out why the thief stole the money.

5 What should they do next?

Talk about a possible ending for the story. What should Robert and Jenny do now? Should they tell Mr Stuart, or should the thief tell Mr Stuart? Is there anything else that Robert should do now?

6 ⟨A song: Can't buy me love⟩

**Can't buy me love, love.
Can't buy me love.
I'll buy you a diamond ring, my friend,
If it makes you feel all right.
I'll get you anything, my friend,
If it makes you feel all right.
I don't care too much for money,
Money can't buy me love.**

**I'll give you all I've got to give,
If you say you love me too.
I may not have a lot to give,
But what I've got I'll give to you,
I don't care too much for money,
Money can't buy me love.
Can't buy me love, ev'rybody tells me so,
Can't buy me love,
no, no, no, no.**

**Say you don't need no diamond rings,
And I'll be satisfied,
Tell me that you want the kind of things
That money just can't buy,
I don't care too much for money,
Money can't buy me love.
Can't buy me love, ev'rybody tells me so,
Can't buy me love, no, no, no, no.**

7 The most interesting film I've ever seen

a) *Work with a partner. Find out more about each other.*

Example: What's the most exciting film you've ever seen?

What's Who's	the funniest/craziest the most beautiful the best/worst the most frightening the most expensive the most interesting/exciting/boring …	book place person film thing	you've ever	done? met? read? bought? seen?

b) *Now tell the class about your partner.*
Example: The most exciting film Michael has ever seen is … .

8 A word game

Choose five nouns you know. (The alphabetical word list will help you.)
Write a definition for each word. (Only use a relative pronoun if you need one.)
Then give the class your definition, but don't say the word. The others must guess the word.
The group that guesses the most words wins.

Example: A kind of a car people use on a farm. – Is it a van?
– Is it a tractor?

A book that gives you ideas for meals. – Is it a recipe book?

9 Word power Nice or nasty?

a) *Put the words in order from the nicest word to the nastiest word. Then find a partner and compare lists.*

school uniform ***breaks*** ***P.E.*** ***exams***

nicest ← nice ↔ nasty → nastiest

homework ***holidays*** ***Maths*** ***detention*** ***computers***

Example:

My favourite word is … .

Then comes … .

… is a nice word, too.

… is a nicer word than …

But … is a nasty word.

And … is even nastier.

The nastiest word is … .

b) *Make your own 'nice–nasty' list with ten other words. Can you explain your list?*

Step D

Let's check

1 Word power At school

Do you know the words? They are all in this unit.

1. A place which lends books.
2. Haywood is this kind of school.
3. You often do this in Science.
4. Some schools have this before the lessons start.
5. If you get into trouble, your teacher might give you … .
6. It rings at the end of the lesson.

PENTEMERIX LELB
EVERSHOPMINCE
BRAILRY BLESSMAY
NEDTONITE

2 At Haywood

a) *Put in the relative pronouns: which/that; who/that; whose.*

b) *You can make three of these sentences into contact clauses. What relative pronouns are missing?*

1. Mrs Benson hasn't found the person … wrote graffiti on the wall.
2. GCSEs are exams … pupils take when they are about 16.
3. The coach … is taking pupils to the theatre is late.
4. Pupils … marks are very good can win prizes.
5. Jenny is the girl … father is German.
6. Teachers don't like pupils … play tricks on them.
7. Somebody took the money … was on Robert's desk.
8. Mrs Dane always asks me questions … I can't answer.
9. Emma is the girl … Jenny can't stand.

3 About me

What are you doing in the next few days? Write seven sentences, one for each day.

Example: I'm doing sports tomorrow afternoon.
I'm going swimming on Friday.

4 Helping each other

What are the people saying? Write four sentences with 'shall' or 'will'.

1

try

2

be quiet

3

feed

4

drive

Unit 3

Welcome to Wales

Step A

Country and people

7

8

9

1 All about Wales

Look at the map and photos of Wales. Read the texts and say which photos go with them. Talk about the photos, too.

Example: Text **a)** goes with picture **1**. It shows Caernarvon Castle in North Wales. The castle looks very big and strong.

a) The English King Edward I conquered Wales in the 13th century. This is one of the castles he built. Edward I made his little son the first Prince of Wales.

b) Cardiff, the capital of Wales, is in the south. In the past, there was a lot of heavy industry in South Wales. Now new industries are growing. Millions of TVs, video recorders and telephones, for example, come from Welsh factories.

c) Snowdon, the highest mountain in Wales, isn't very difficult to climb. There are six different paths to the top – and a railway, too.

d) Rugby is very popular in Wales. The Welsh fans are good at singing, too. Sometimes there are 60,000 people in a "rugby choir" at a big match!

e) The valleys of South Wales are famous for their coal. Now nearly all the mines are closed but some of them have opened again as museums.

f) A lot of Welsh people work in the tourist industry – now the biggest industry in Wales. Most of the visitors come from England. You can see 'B & B' signs in all the pretty villages and seaside towns.

g) Only about one in five Welsh people speak Welsh at home. But all road signs are in both languages, and there are TV and radio programmes in Welsh, too. "Never forget your Welsh!" the Welsh say.

h) At Caerleon, in South Wales, you can see an old Roman camp. Some people think Caerleon was also the place where King Arthur had his castle: Camelot!

i) There is a lot of wild countryside in Wales – with only a few sheep farms on the hills.

SB 2 A ticket to Llanfairpwllgwyngyllgogerychwyrndrobwllllantysiliogogogoch

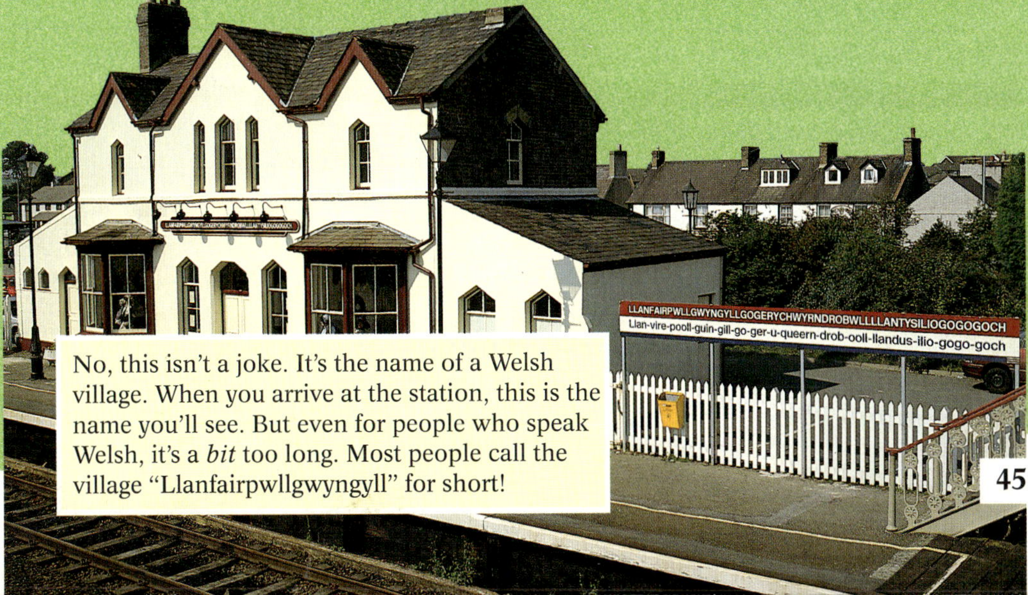

No, this isn't a joke. It's the name of a Welsh village. When you arrive at the station, this is the name you'll see. But even for people who speak Welsh, it's a *bit* too long. Most people call the village "Llanfairpwllgwyngyll" for short!

3 Describing Wales

Collect facts from the map and photos of Wales – and from the information in exercise 1.

Make a mind map.

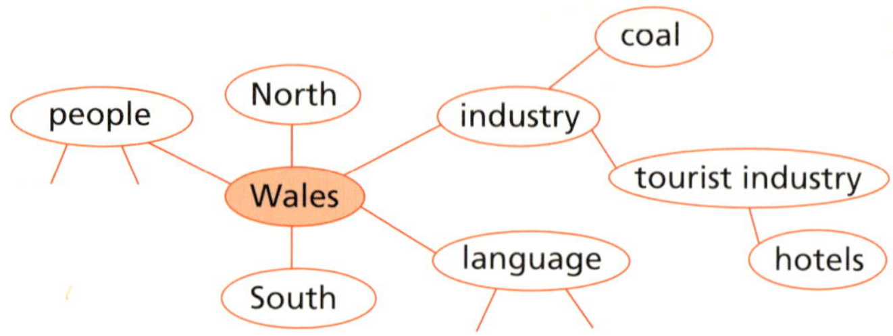

4 Your area

Work with a partner, and make a page for a British magazine about Germany – or about the area where you live.

Try to get interesting pictures of the countryside, of towns, villages, castles or museums. You can add information about the countryside, about industries, or about popular sports or other activities.

5 Listening practice: Arriving at the Snowdon Hotel

The Walkers, a family from England, have just arrived at the Snowdon Hotel in North Wales. While Mr Walker and the two children are getting the bags out of the car, Mrs Walker goes inside. Now she is talking to Mrs Pritchard – she works at the hotel.

First listen to the dialogue.

Now Mr Walker and the two children, Steve and Kate, have come into the hotel with the bags.

Read their questions and listen to the dialogue again. What are Mrs Walker's answers?

1. *Steve:* Oh, you've got our keys already, Mum. Are the rooms next to each other?
2. *Kate:* What's that brochure you've got, Mum?
3. *Mr Walker:* What a huge castle it is! Maybe we could go there tomorrow. Or is it too far away from here?
4. *Mr Walker:* I'd like to go up Snowdon while we're here, perhaps on Sunday. But what about the weather?

6 Sound practice

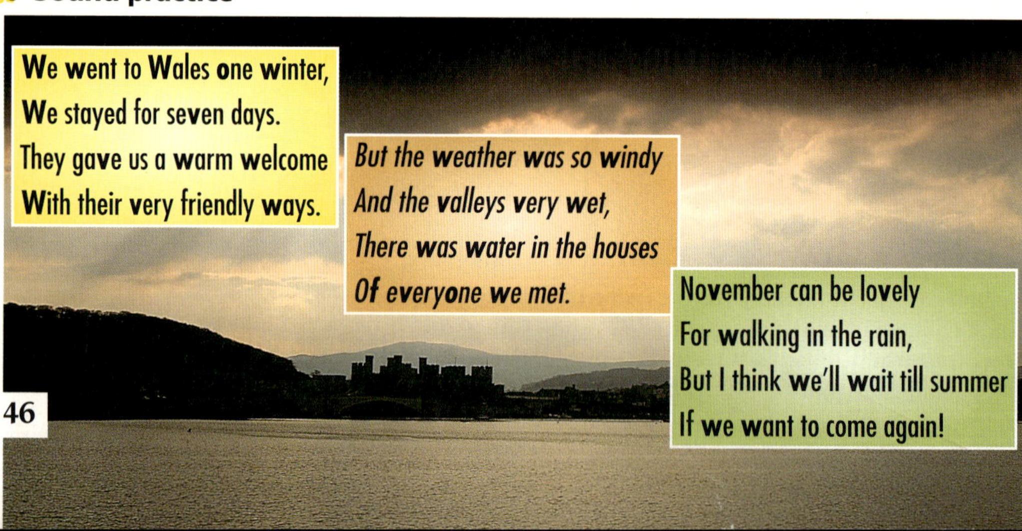

The Pritchards

Gwen Pritchard lives in North Wales. This is the first page of a letter she has written to her new French penfriend.

Dear Michelle,

It was so nice to get your letter - with all the news of you and your family. Now I'll tell you something about myself and my family.

We live in North Wales. But really we come from the South. We've only been living here since last August. You see, my dad lost his job last year. Then the same thing happened to my mum. So they were both out of work! Anyway, then we moved to North Wales, and my parents started work at the Snowdon Hotel. Mum and Dad have been working there for six months now.

My brother Hugh (15) and I are at a new school. We've been going there since September. A lot of people here speak Welsh. Some of my new friends even speak Welsh at home!! I've been learning Welsh for three years but I still find it very difficult!

Your English is good! How long have you been learning it? I

She **has been learning** Welsh …
We **have been living** here …

§ 12

1 Gwen and her family

Fill in the verb forms.

1. *Mr Pritchard:* I … *(work)* at the Snowdon Hotel since September. Some of my old friends … *(look)* for a job for years, and they still haven't found one. So I'm lucky.
2. *Mrs Pritchard:* Now that we live up here, I can visit my sister more often. She … *(live)* in Caernarvon for six years now.
3. *Gwen:* Welsh is a much older language than English. People … *(speak)* Welsh here since the time of King Arthur. Or even before that, I think! We … *(do)* Welsh history for the last few weeks at school.
4. *Hugh:* I … *(learn)* Welsh for four years. Now I'm beginning to find it useful! My new friend Owen speaks Welsh at home. He … *(speak)* it since he was little! So he can teach me a lot, of course. And for the last month or so I … *(listen)* to more Welsh on TV and radio. Owen's uncle … *(work)* for Welsh radio since 1993.

2 Looking at English

The Pritchards have been living in North Wales	**since August.**
Mr and Mrs Pritchard have been working there	**for six months.**

Look at all the examples of the present perfect progressive in Gwen's letter and exercise 1. When do we use 'since'? When do we use 'for'? Can you find the rule?

3 How long?

Here is some information about the Pritchards. First read the sentences. Then work with a partner. One of you asks questions, and the other gives the answers. Always start your questions with "How long ...?" Use 'for' or 'since' in the answers.

Example: 1. The Pritchards live in North Wales now. They moved there six months ago.
– How long have the Pritchards been living in North Wales?
– They've been living there for six months.

2. Mr Pritchard is a waiter now. He works at the Snowdon Hotel. He started his job last September.
3. Mrs Pritchard works there, too. She works in the hotel office. She started five months ago.
4. Gwen and Hugh go to a new school now. They started there at the beginning of the autumn term.
5. They both learn Welsh. Gwen started three years ago, and Hugh started four years ago.

4 Your turn Facts about you

First write down some facts about yourself.

1. Where do you live – and when did you move there?
2. What sports or games (or instruments) do you play – and when did you start?
3. What subjects (choose 2 or 3) do you learn at school – and when did you start them?
4. What activities do you do – and when did you start them?

Now work with a partner again – and "interview" each other. Use 'for' and 'since' in the answers.

Example:
– Where do you live, Florian?
– I live in Gartenweg.
– How long have you been living there?
– I've been living there for six years/since last May/all my life.

5 People at the hotel

It is Saturday. Some of the guests at the Snowdon Hotel aren't very happy.
Why not? What do they say? Make up little dialogues, too.

Example: 1. – Waiter! I've been sitting here since half past twelve/for an hour!
– Sorry, sir! Your meal is nearly ready now.

Tips for visitors

SNOWDONIA NATIONAL PARK

How to travel around

Half a million walkers and climbers go up Snowdon every year – so if you're wondering whether to come by car, DON'T! The only car park is always full, and there's no roadside parking. Use the Park & Ride Service or the bus service from Caernarvon.
(For more details, see page 2.)

Where to stay

Youth hostels, hotels, B & B, farmhouses, holiday cottages ... The choice is yours!
(See page 4 for details.)

What to do

Walking, riding, fishing, water sports, golf ... And for climbers, there are 1,500 climbing routes. *(See page 7.)*

6 Very useful!

a) 1. If you've got a good map, you'll always know ... .
2. Look at the railway timetable, then you'll know ... .
3. Ask the bus driver if you're not sure ... .
4. Your doctor or chemist will tell you ... .
5. Ask the youth hostel warden if you want to know ... .
6. Listen to the weather forecast, then you'll know ... .
7. Ask a farmer if you want to know ... .

b) *Can you find endings for these sentences?*
8. Travel brochures can be useful if you're not sure ... .
9. Get a recipe book if you've got no idea ... .
10. Write a shopping list if you can never remember ... .

how often to take your medicine
how to milk a cow
where to get off
which train to take
when to be back in the evening
which way to go
whether to go climbing or not

7 They don't know

Example: 1. She doesn't know where to have lunch.

The Celts and their language

About half a million people in Wales speak Welsh as their first language. Welsh is a Celtic language, much older than English.
From about 500 BC Celtic people came to the British Isles. They were the people who lived in Britain when the Romans came.
In AD 410 the Romans left Britain. But soon the Angles and Saxons from North Germany began to invade the country. The Britons were not strong enough to keep them out. So when the Angles and Saxons came into the country, a lot of Britons moved west. Many of them settled in the hills of Wales and south-west England. There they felt safer. And their Celtic language lived on. Different forms of it still exist today in parts of Scotland, Ireland and Cornwall. But Welsh is the only Celtic language that has 'official status' in Britain.
Where the Angles and Saxons settled, the Celtic language died. They called the country England (land of the Angles) and they called themselves – and their language – English.

SB 8 ⟨A song: Bachgen bach o dincer / The little tinker lad⟩

© Traditional

Bachgen bach o dincer
Yn myned hyd y wlad,
Cario'i becyn ar ei gefn
A gweithio'i waith yn rhad;
Yn ei law 'roedd haearn
Ac ar ei gefn 'roedd bocs,
Pwt o getyn yn ei geg
A than ei drwyn 'roedd locs.

Cydio yn y badell,
Y piser neu'r ystên;
Taro'r haearn yn y tân,
A dal i sgwrsio'n glên;
Eistedd yn y gongol,
Un goes ar draws y llall,
Taenu'r sodor gloyw glân
I gywrain guddio'r gwall.

Holi hwn ac arall
Ple'r aeth y tincer mwyn,
Gyda'i becyn ar ei gefn
A'i getyn dan ei drwyn.
Bachgen bach o dincer
Ni welir yn y wlad;
Ow, mae'n golled ar ei ôl
I weithio gwaith yn rhad.

Dafydd Gwynn, the tinker,
Was walking through the land,
On his back his boxes slung,
His hammer in his hand;
Working for a trifle
And singing as he goes,
In his mouth a bit of pipe,
And whiskers 'neath his nose.

Taking up a pitcher,
A pot or frying pan,
Talking as he heats his iron
As only Dafydd can;
Sitting in the corner,
One leg across his knee,
Covering with the solder all
The flaws that none may see.

We are seeking round us
The way the tinker goes,
On his back his boxes slung,
A pipe beneath his nose,
Dafydd Gwynn, the tinker,
Has vanished from the land;
So his working for a song
Is missed on every hand.

Plans for the weekend

Owen: Bye, Hugh! See you on Monday.
Hugh: Hey, wait a minute, Owen. Today's Friday. We're going to the cinema tonight, aren't we?
Owen: Gosh, I forgot! Yes, of course we are. I'll come back again at seven. That'll be early enough, won't it?
Hugh: Fine. See you later then. … Mum, can you give me my pocket money now?
Mrs Pritchard: Isn't tomorrow early enough? You don't want to go anywhere tonight, do you?
Hugh: Well, yes, I do. Owen and I want to go to the cinema. That's OK, isn't it?
Mrs Pritchard: *I* don't mind. – Well, here you are then. Enjoy yourselves.

\+ –

You can come tonight, **can't you**?
The film starts at eight, **doesn't it**?

§ 14

– +

You won't be late, **will you**?
They don't sell chocolate, **do they**?

§ 14

9 These are easy, aren't they?

a) *Put the different parts together. Then write the sentences in two lists.*

haven't you? is he? can't I? isn't he? will it? do you? are they? doesn't she?

+	–

–	+

1. Gwen comes from South Wales, …
2. Hugh is interested in King Arthur, …
3. It won't rain, …
4. You don't like reading, …
5. I can sit here, …
6. Mr Pritchard isn't English, …
7. You've finished the book, …
8. The visitors aren't here yet, …

b) *Now make two more sentences yourself – one for each list.*

10 Knights of Camelot

Can you finish the dialogue with the right question tags?

Gwen: Hi, Hugh. You were at the cinema yesterday, …? Did you enjoy the film?
Hugh: Yes, it was great!
Gwen: It was about King Arthur, …?
Hugh: Yes, that's right. It was really good.
Gwen: You went with Owen, …?
Hugh: Yes, I did. His older sister came, too. You don't know her, …?
Gwen: I don't think so.
Hugh: Look, Owen's lent me this old video – "Knights of Camelot". You haven't seen it, …?
Gwen: No, not yet. Mm, it looks exciting, …?
Hugh: Yes, it does. Let's watch it tonight then. There's nothing good on TV, …?
Gwen: Not really. OK then.

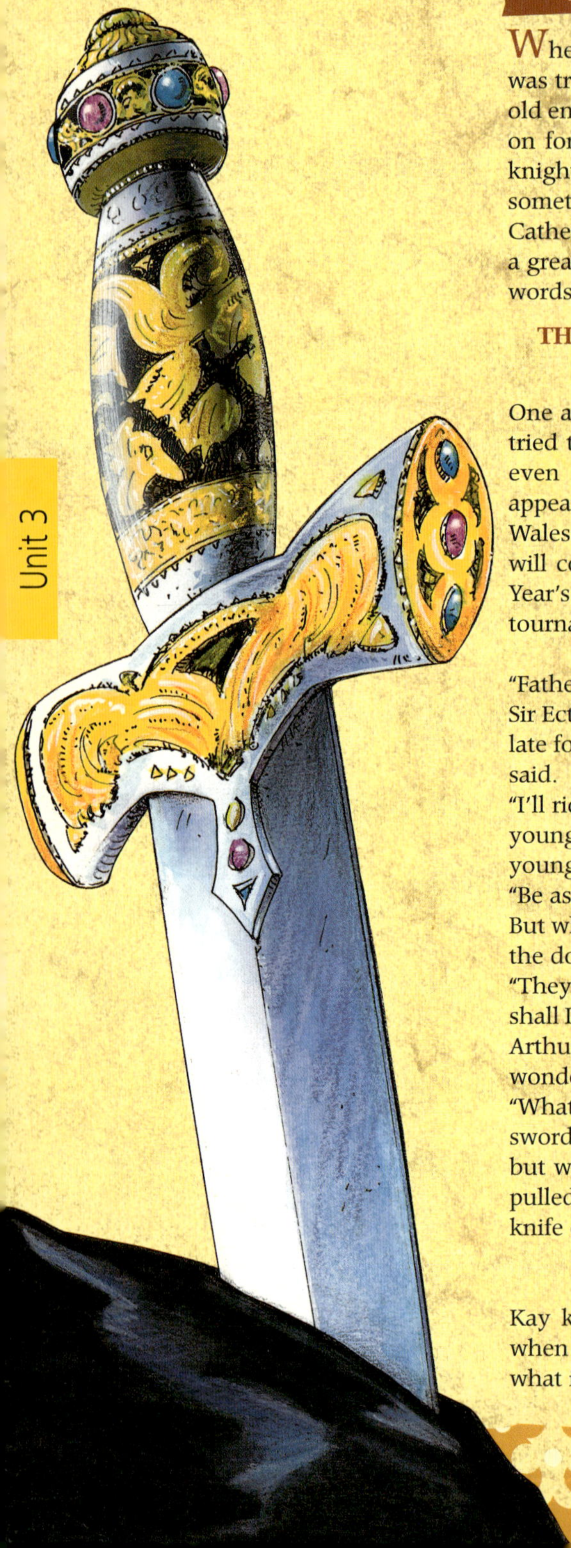

The sword in the stone

When Uther, King of the south-west of England, died, there was trouble. There was nobody to follow him as King and his old enemies tried to take over the kingdom. The fighting went on for years and years. Then, one Christmas Day, when the knights of the land came to the Cathedral, they saw something very strange. A huge stone lay outside the Cathedral – and in the middle of the stone was the handle of a great sword. When the knights came nearer, they saw these words on the great stone:

THE ONE WHO PULLS THIS SWORD OUT OF THIS STONE IS YOUR TRUE KING.

One after the other, all the knights went up to the stone and tried to pull the sword out. But nobody could move it – not even the strongest knight. Suddenly a strange old man appeared from the crowd. It was Merlin, the old wizard from Wales. "Our true King is not here yet!" called Merlin. "But he will come! And then there will be a miracle. Wait until New Year's Day when more knights will be here for the big tournament."

♦ ♦ ♦

"Father! Wait a moment!" called Kay. "I've forgotten my sword!" Sir Ector stopped his horse and looked at his son. "But we'll be late for the tournament if we go back into town for it now," he said.

"I'll ride back to the inn and get it for you," said Arthur, Kay's younger brother. Arthur was only fifteen, so he was still too young to fight in tournaments.

"Be as quick as you can then, Arthur!" said Kay. "Off you go!"

But when Arthur got back to the inn where they were staying, the door was locked. Nobody was there.

"They've all gone to the tournament!" thought Arthur. "What shall I do? Kay will be angry if I come back without his sword."

Arthur rode slowly through the quiet streets. While he was wondering what to do, he came to the Cathedral Square.

"What a piece of luck!" Arthur thought when he saw the great sword in the stone. He didn't notice the words on the stone, but went straight up to it, took the handle of the sword and pulled. The sword came out at once. It moved as easily as a knife cuts through butter.

♦ ♦ ♦

Kay knew from Sir Ector about the sword in the stone. So when Arthur brought him the great sword, he saw at once what it was.

"Here's a sword for you!" Arthur began. "Sorry I couldn't get yours, but –"

"Give it to me!" said Kay, took it and ran off to find Sir Ector. "Look, Father! The sword from the stone! I pulled it out last night – and I kept it till now, as a surprise!"

Sir Ector gave Kay a long look. "Well," he said slowly, "then you must show me how you did it. We'll go back to the Cathedral right away. We'll miss the tournament – but never mind!"

Sir Ector fetched Arthur, and they all rode back to the town. Soon they were outside the Cathedral.

"First put the sword back in the stone, Kay," said Sir Ector. But when Kay tried to push it in, he couldn't do it.

"That's very strange!" said Sir Ector. "Now, Kay, don't tell any more lies. Explain how you really got the sword!"

"Arthur gave it to me," said Kay quietly.

"I can't understand what all this trouble is about!" said Arthur. He took the sword from Kay. "Look! It goes in and out of the stone quite easily!"

Arthur pushed the sword into the stone – and then pulled it out again. When he looked at his father and brother, he couldn't believe his eyes. Sir Ector and Kay were down on their knees in front of him.

"Arthur! The miracle has happened. You are our true King," said Sir Ector. "I've been wondering how to tell you this for a long time. I've always known you will be King!"

"King?" said Arthur. "But how can I be King?"

♦ ♦ ♦

That evening, the wizard Merlin stood with Arthur and Sir Ector in the middle of the Cathedral Square. All the knights from the tournament were there now.

"Listen, good knights!" cried Merlin. "One night, fifteen years ago, I took a little baby to Sir Ector and his wife. I told them to look after the child – and to call him Arthur."

"So I'm not your son?" said Arthur to Sir Ector. "But all these years I've been calling you Father and Mother. I …"

"That baby," Merlin went on, "was the son of King Uther and Queen Igrayne. They had many enemies, and so the baby's life was in danger. I promised to make the child King when the time was right."

"Arthur!" cried Sir Ector. "I've always loved you as my own son. But now the time has come …"

"Show the knights, Arthur!" said Merlin.

And when Arthur pulled the great sword out of the stone, there was a loud cheer from the crowd.

"Arthur!" called the knights. "Long live King Arthur!"

And they fell to their knees in front of him.

1 The characters and their feelings

First think of adjectives that describe feelings (e.g. angry, sorry, surprised). Then try to imagine how the characters in the story felt. Explain why you think so.

Example: 1. the knights – when they saw the sword in the stone
– I think the knights were very surprised, because the sword in the stone was a strange sight.

2. the knights – when they couldn't move the sword
3. Arthur – when the door of the inn was locked
4. Kay – when he saw the sword in Arthur's hand
5. Sir Ector – when Kay showed him the sword
6. Kay – when he couldn't put the sword back in the stone
7. Arthur – when Merlin explained who he really was
8. the knights – when they saw what Arthur could do

felt …
was/were …
couldn't …
didn't know what to …/ whether, to …

2 Kay and Arthur

Look at these statements. Do you think they are true or not? Check with the text to find out.

1. Arthur is a helpful person.
– Yes, I think that's true.
In line … he says he'll ride back to the inn and get Kay's sword.

2. Kay is a bully.
3. Arthur is a bit scared of Kay.
4. Kay only thinks of himself.
5. Sir Ector believes Kay at first.
6. Kay is jealous of Arthur.

3 Word power Families

a) *Find the words that go together. There are seven different 'families' of three words each here.*

valley golf inn route Romans village hill path
hotel rugby city road English mountain Welsh
Saxons Scottish Britons town youth hostel climbing

b) *Now make new families – with these words:*

1. sheep 2. south 3. windy 4. bus 5. king

4 Listening practice: Sir Ector remembers

Sir Ector is talking to Arthur about what happened 15 years ago.
Listen to the dialogue. Try to find out …

1. … whether Sir Ector and his wife were surprised when Merlin brought the baby;
2. … what Kay thought of the new baby;
3. … what happened to Arthur's real parents.

Let's check

1 Gosh! So long?

Ask questions with 'How long...?' Can your partner give the answer?

Example:

1. A woman is waiting at the doctor's. She sat down there nearly two hours ago. *(wait)*

   – How long has she been waiting?
   – She's been waiting for nearly two hours.

2. The Walkers are on the M6. They left the Snowdon Hotel at 9.30. Now it's nearly 4.30 in the afternoon, and they aren't back home yet. *(drive)*
3. The weather was OK when the group left the youth hostel. But now they're standing under a tree. The rain started about an hour ago. *(rain)*
4. The Browns' house is in a quiet valley. They moved there twelve years ago. *(live)*
5. Hugh started watching TV when he came home at 6 o'clock. It's quite late now. *(watch)*

2 I don't know ...

What can you say?

what to ... | which ... to ... | where to ... | how to ... | when to ... | whether to ...

Example: 1. You've got no plans for the weekend. *(do)*
– I don't know what to do at the weekend!

2. You need a new film for your camera, but you don't know the town well. *(buy)*
3. You're going to a party, but all your clothes seem 'wrong'. *(wear)*
4. The invitation card doesn't say when the party starts. *(go)*
5. Your friend asks you to come on a riding holiday, but you've never ridden before. *(ride)*
6. There's a new film on at the cinema, and some people like it, but others don't. *(see)*
7. You've got two books from the library, and they both look interesting. *(read first)*

3 Not sure

When people aren't quite sure about something, they often check – and ask someone.
Finish the sentences with question tags.

1. This is the way to Caernarvon, ...?
2. We aren't going the wrong way, ...?
3. You looked at the map, ...?
4. There's a good path to the top, ...?
5. This road goes to Cardiff, ...?
6. They haven't closed all the mines, ...?
7. The castle will be open tomorrow, ...?
8. A lot of visitors to Wales come from England, ...?

LET'S READ

1 Starting off

Roman Wall Blues

Over the heather the wet wind blows,
I've lice in my tunic and a cold in my nose.

The rain comes pattering out of the sky,
I'm a Wall soldier, I don't know why.

HADRIAN'S WALL

The Romans conquer Britain AD 43 – AD 60

In AD 43 the Roman Emperor Claudius decided to make Britain part of the Roman Empire. An army of 40,000 soldiers crossed the Channel and landed in Kent. The Britons tried to defend themselves, but the Roman army at that time was the strongest in the world and

1 The subject

The texts on these two pages are not complete – they are just the beginnings of texts. *Look at them carefully, then try to answer these questions:*

tip Think first:
- What is the text about?
- What do you expect when you read about this subject?

1. What is each text about?
2. What do you find out from the texts about the history of Britain?
3. What else do you know about the Romans? (Think of films or TV programmes you've seen, books or comics you've read, what you've learnt at school.)
4. How do you expect the texts will go on?
   Example: In the first text a Roman soldier is speaking. He doesn't sound very happy. I expect he will say more about his life as a "Wall soldier" … .

2 More clues

It isn't only from words that you can get information. *Look again.*

1. What else can you see here?
2. Look at everything carefully. What information does each part give you?
3. What did you already know? What was new to you?
   Example: I knew the Romans were in Britain, but I didn't know they built a wall in the North of England.

It was a warm evening in August when she first saw Roman soldiers. The sun was setting in the west now, and the long line of helmets shone like gold as the Romans marched past.
She stood at the door of the hut with the child in her arms. Her husband was still out with the horses, so there was no-one at home to protect them. But the line of soldiers was already on its

3 Different kinds of text

Look at each text again. Then try to answer the questions:

1. What kind of text is this? Or where could it be from?

story report brochure letter play poem history book …

2. What do you expect when you read this kind of text?

I expect to | find out … / read … | an exciting story, facts (about …), interesting things (about …) …

A … | often / usually | has … / gives … | rhymes, a lot of details about …, funny jokes/pictures …

tip Now look again:
- What kind of text is this?
- What do you expect when you see this kind of text?

4 Talk about it

1. Think of famous walls you've seen (or know about) – in Germany, and in other parts of the world. Make a list. Then try to explain why they are there.
2. Why do you think the Romans built Hadrian's Wall?

protect … from dangerous keep … out keep … in safe …

Workshop C

2 How to read a text

1 Getting the gist

'Getting the gist' of something means understanding the 'main ideas'. You can often find out what a text is about – or 'get the gist' of it – before you start to read it.

Look at this 'newspaper page'. What is it about? Make a list of the things that give you the gist.

tip You needn't always read every word of a text to find out what it's about.

Watch out for
- **headings**
- **key words**
- **pictures**
- **the beginnings of paragraphs**

BRITANNIA TODAY AD 123

EMPEROR HADRIAN HERE IN BRITAIN!
A VIP from Rome is now in this country – the Emperor Hadrian! Yesterday crowds of people (British and Roman) stood in the streets of Londinium to welcome the great man.

Plans for Wall in North
Trouble in the North with wild Celtic tribes has become a big problem. Hadrian has plans for a great wall – from coast to coast.

Border Safe at Last
The new wall will protect the Empire from these wild Celts. It will also mark the border.

• CRITIC'S CORNER •
Great roads that cut through our fields. Big houses with central heating, hot baths and toilets. New towns with straight streets, shops, even theatres! British people in togas and sandals – some with wigs and false teeth! The Latin language everywhere.
Yes, that's life in Britain today. But is it what we really want? Have we forgotten we're British?

LOOKING BACK

63 Years Ago: The Iceni Rebellion
In AD 60 Boudicca, the great Queen of the Iceni, led her tribe in the last British rebellion against the Romans.

3 Cities in Flames
They burned three cities, and killed 70,000 people. Other tribes joined the Iceni, and soon Boudicca had an army of 100,000 soldiers.

Boudicca's Unhappy End
There was a great battle, but luck was on the Romans' side.
Their army killed most of the British soldiers. Boudicca herself took poison before the Romans were able to take her prisoner.

Are you …
… young and strong?
… looking for a job?
… able to speak some Latin?
Then why not **help to build the WALL**?
Call at your nearest Roman fort for details!

B. Burton: History Project Year 9

2 Understanding the details

> **tip** To get your details right,
> - stop when you find a key word and read that part carefully
> - read it again and make notes
> - translate parts of the text if it helps you

When you want to know more about a text, you must look for details. Give your partner a test about "life in Roman Britain".
Look for interesting facts in the 'newspaper'. Make notes.
Then write down three questions and ask each other.

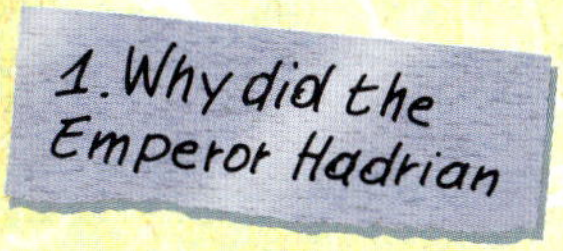

3 Picking out information

Look at this information from a brochure about Hadrian's Wall.
Find out which page of the brochure you should read if you want to know these things:

1. How many years did the Romans use the wall?
2. What was a Roman soldier's life like?
3. How did the soldiers spend their free time?
4. What happened to the wall later?
5. What happened to the British people who lived near the wall?

> **tip** **Brochures, timetables ...**
> - Only look for the information you need
> - Write down useful information

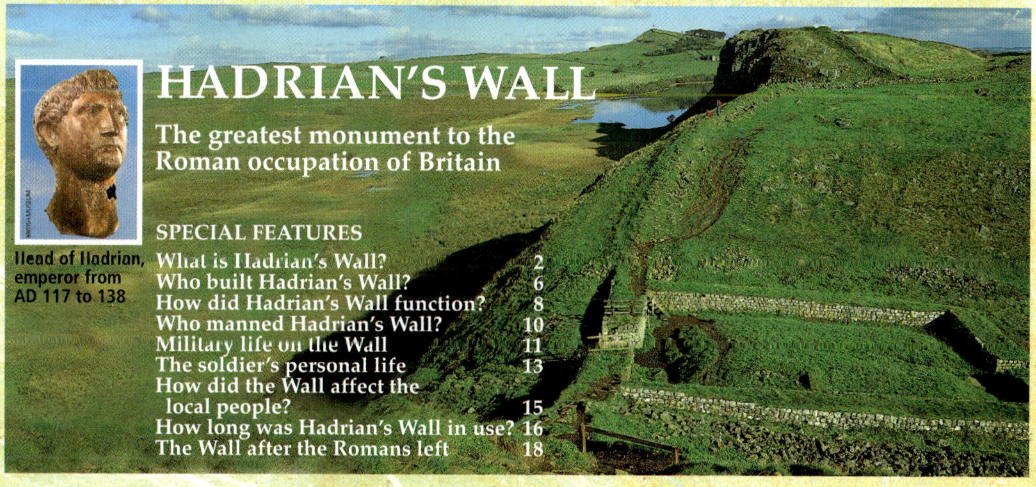
HADRIAN'S WALL

The greatest monument to the Roman occupation of Britain

Head of Hadrian, emperor from AD 117 to 138

SPECIAL FEATURES

Can you explain how you found out?

Example:
– I saw the word '...'.
That's a bit like '...'/I know the verb '...'.

4 Talk about it

1. Are there any Roman remains near your home? Talk about what you know. You can check the information about the Romans in your school history book, too!
2. Have you seen any Roman remains when you've been in other countries? Talk about where you've been, and what you've seen there.

3 Reacting to a text

1 Reacting while you read

When you read a text, there may be places where you want to stop and ask yourself:

- What do I already know about this? Does it help me to understand the text better?
- What does the author mean here? Can I 'read between the lines'?
- Do I understand any of the new words? Can I guess from the context? (Look again at the tip on page 26.)

Two worlds meet

Marcus, a Roman soldier in Britain in the 2nd century, is staying at his uncle's house, west of Londinium. In the garden one day he meets a British girl who lives in the house next door. They begin to talk together – in Latin.

She was about thirteen, Marcus imagined. A tall, thin girl with a pointed face. After a little while he said: "I have told you my name. What is yours?"
"My aunt and uncle call me Camilla, but my real name is Cottia," said the girl. "They like everything to be very Roman, you see."
"And you do not?" he said.
"I? I am of the Iceni! So is my Aunt Valaria, though she likes to forget it. – We are all horse-breeders, we of the Iceni, from the King downward – when we had a King. – My father was killed breaking a young horse, and that is why I live with my Aunt Valaria now."
"I am sorry. And your mother?"
"There was a hunter who always wanted her, but her parents gave her to my father. And when my father went West of the Sunset, she went to the hunter, and there was no room in his house for me. It was different with my brother, of course. It is always different with boys. So my mother gave me to Aunt Valaria, who has no children of her own."
"Poor Cottia," Marcus said.
"Oh no. I did not wish to live in that hunter's house. He was not my father. Only … ."
"Only?"
"Only I hate living with my aunt. I hate living in a town full of straight lines, inside brick walls. I hate being called Camilla; and I hate – hate – hate it when they try to make me pretend to be a Roman maiden and forget my own tribe! – No! I will not let them! I pretend, outside my tunic. I answer when they call me Camilla, and I speak to them in Latin. But underneath my tunic I am of the Iceni. And when I take off my tunic at night, I say, 'There! That rids me of Rome until the morning!' And I lie on my bed and think – and think – about my home … . I remember all the things that I am not supposed to remember, and talk to myself inside my head in my own tongue."
She looked at him in quick surprise. "We are talking in my tongue now! How long have we been doing that?"
"Since you told me about your real name – Cottia."
Cottia nodded. It did not seem to strike her that Marcus was himself a Roman: and it did not strike Marcus. For the moment all he knew was that Cottia, too, was in exile.

Think what you already know about this British tribe. How did they react to the Romans?

Think how a British family could make their everyday life "very Roman". What might they do differently?

What does Cottia mean here? Can you read between the lines?

Try to imagine what Cottia's life with her aunt and uncle is like. Think how **they** may feel about **her**!

What does this tell you about the Romans in Britain? Are you surprised?

Remember what you know about the changes the Romans made when they came to Britain.

2 The characters

Who are the characters in the text? (Think first about the characters in the scene itself. Then think about the people they talk about.) What do you know about them?

1. Cottia:
- 13 years old
- British
- lives with

3 Reacting to the text

1. *Which of the characters do you like or feel sorry for? Why? Talk about their situation. Would you like to be in their place? Why (not)?*
   Example: I feel sorry for Cottia/I can understand her when she says … .
   I don't feel sorry for her/I think she's silly/I can't understand her when … .
2. *Now find words or sentences in the text that give you these feelings.*
   Example: "My father was killed": When I read that, I feel sorry/unhappy/…
   The author uses these words so that the reader will feel …/because …

4 Comparing situations

Think about the situation you've read about. Does it remind you of anything in your own life – or the lives of people you know?
Think about what happens when people from different places (like Cottia and Marcus) live in the same country. What problems can they have?

strange · language · food · live with · (not) allowed to · different · difficult · religion · (not) understand · …

5 Looking at language: The Romans in Europe

TOWER · STRASSE · CASTELLUM · TAFEL · STRATA · FAMILIE · JANUARIUS · KAROTTE · TURRIS · AUGUSTUS · TABULA · JANUARY · FRUCTUS · FRUIT · TURM · VALLUM · CAROTA · WALL · FAMILIA · AUGUST · CASTLE

a) Wherever the Romans went, their language went with them. Some of the Britons learnt to speak Latin, but when the Romans left, their language died out. Only a few words lived on.

Look at these words.
Which are English, German or Latin?
Make three lists.
Try to add the English or German words if they are missing.

Latin	English	German
vallum	wall	Wall

b) *Put the English words into groups. Find names for the groups. What areas of life did the Romans change in Britain?*

The environment

Step A

A trip to a theme park

It is early Saturday morning. The Penroses want to go to Alton Towers, a theme park 39 miles west of Nottingham.

1 The way to Alton Towers

Look at the road map.
What roads should they take to get from Nottingham to Alton Towers?

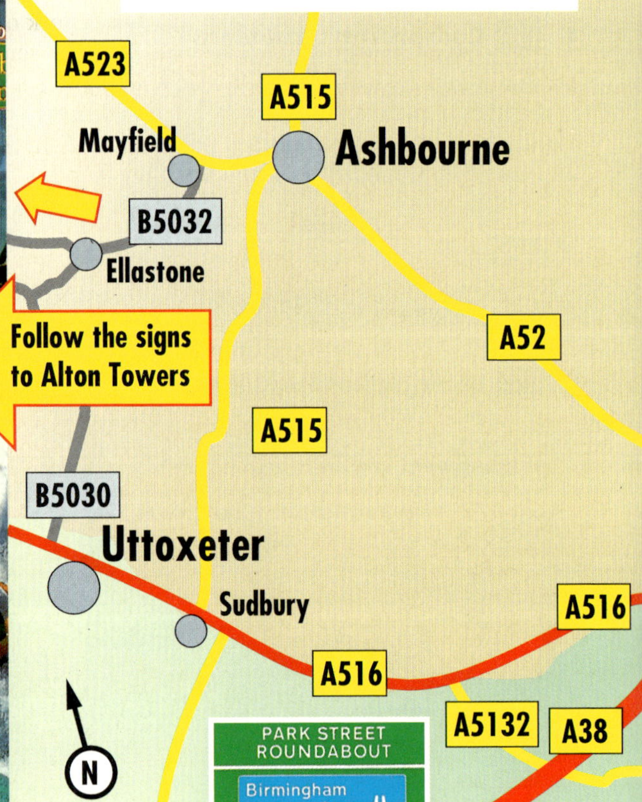

Step A

◀ There can be heavy traffic on British motorways. When there are roadworks or if there has been an accident, you could get stuck in a traffic jam.

At service stations you can get petrol. There are often shops and restaurants, too. ▶

2 Listening practice: Traffic news

a) Look at all the information on these two pages. Then listen to the traffic news with the Penroses. What does it say about the route they should take to Alton Towers? *Take notes.*

b) Now work out a route for the Penroses from Nottingham to Alton Towers.

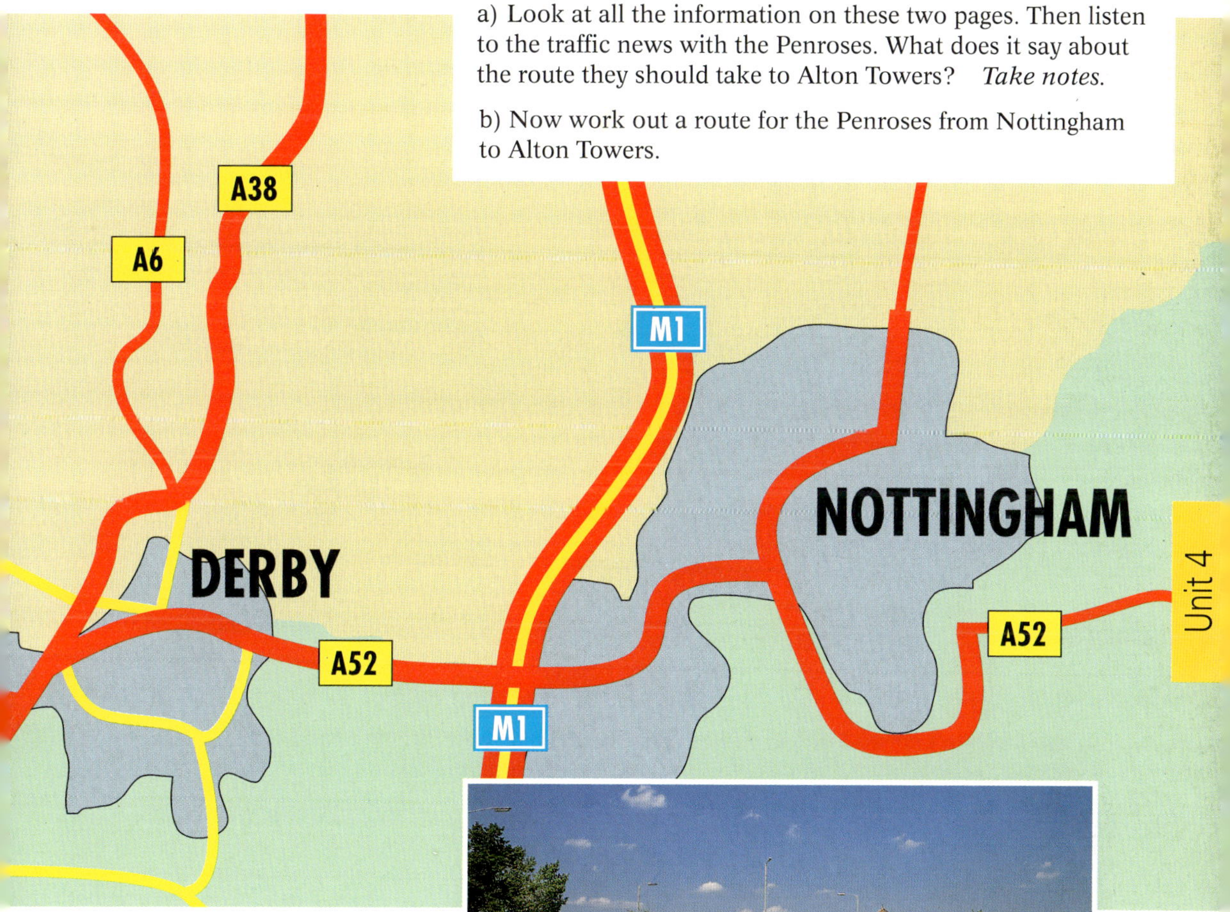

◀ There are a lot of roundabouts on British roads. So people don't have to wait at traffic lights. ▶

In the car

The Penroses are on the A52 now. David and Mark are looking at a copy of **Our Earth**, a magazine about the environment.

Mr Penrose: Look at all these cars!
David: You know, Dad, we really shouldn't use our car so often. That's what it says in this magazine.
Mark: Why not?
David: Because cars pollute everything. You know, they cause pollution.
Mark: What's that?
Mrs Penrose: That means they make the air dirty. Cars and a lot of other things do that.
David: And ours is one of the worst. It says so here.
Mark: But we can't walk to the park.
Mrs Penrose: No, sometimes you have to use a car. But we shouldn't *always* use it.
Mr Penrose: Well, with this slow traffic, walking is probably quicker.

3 What should we do?

The boys found this in their **Our Earth** *magazine.*

What should *we do?*
What shouldn't *we do?*

Use the information from the magazine to make sentences.
Examples: We should switch off the lights when we leave a room.
We shouldn't use our cars … .

Think about the radio, TV, bottles, plastic cups, cars, bikes, walking, the bus, water, paper, …

4 Word power Can you find the right words?

1. Factories often cause … .
2. The world around us is our … .
3. When we use paper and glass again, we … them.
4. Cars need … .
5. We shouldn't … energy because we don't have enough of it.
6. Industry … our world, too.
7. Doing little things like switching off the … helps the environment, too – and it … money.

Step B

An article in Our Earth magazine

Every year more and more of our lovely English countryside is destroyed. Trees are cut down, new wider roads are built, our environment is damaged. Here Mavis Brandon talks about what happened to her village.

"Greendale was always a quiet little place. I loved living there. And then last April the bulldozers came. Two fields were destroyed, some houses were pulled down and the road was moved. Then they put up traffic lights – and lots of other changes were made, too. Greendale is a very different place now, and I don't like living here any more."

1 Looking at English

Find the passive sentences in the two texts above and put them in two lists.

present tense			past tense		
subject	to be	past participle	subject	to be	past participle
... countryside	is	destroyed.	Two fields	were	destroyed.
Trees			Some ...		

Can you find a rule for making passive sentences?

2 New roads

What is done when a road is built?

Example:
1. buy land from farmers
   Land is bought from farmers.
2. build tunnels
3. pull down walls
4. bring in bulldozers
5. destroy good farm land
6. change the countryside
7. pollute the environment

3 Last year

Say what was done at Greendale last year.

Example:
1. Traffic lights were put up.

1. traffic lights to put up
2. some trees to cut down
3. road to make wider
4. car park to build
5. three houses to pull down
6. service station to build

Unit 4

Saving the environment

Last month **Our Earth** magazine had an article about doing things to save the environment. Many readers have written letters. Here are four of them.

Dear Magazine,
Of course the environment has been polluted a bit. But we just can't give up all the things that make life so easy. I don't want to live in the Stone Age. Nobody does! A lot of answers to these pollution problems have already been found, and I'm sure a clean kind of energy will be found, too. We should wait and not do anything silly now.

Paula Warren, Rugby

Dear 'Our Earth',
The air, the land, the water – everything has been polluted. If we don't do something soon, our whole environment will be destroyed. We must get rid of everything that causes pollution. We must change our laws and our way of life before it is too late.

Ricky Dart, Birmingham

Dear friends,
I think we should all use bikes instead of cars, but in my town it's too dangerous to do that. There are too many cars. I've been injured twice on my bike. So now I use my car again. I just hope that public transport will be improved soon.

Samuel Jones, York

Dear 'Earth',
I'm so upset. We've got a bottle bank and a paper bank in our town, but nobody uses them. Don't people understand that we must do everything we can to keep this earth clean for our children? In other countries people are better at that. When will laws be passed here to improve the situation?

Charles Pritchard, Bournemouth

4 What do you think?

a) 1. – What things that make life so easy is Paula Warren thinking of?
   – Do you agree with her? Say why or why not.
2. Look at Mr Jones's letter.
   – Is it better to use bikes than cars? Can you think of any problems?
   – What about public transport? Can we use it for everything?
3. What things is Ricky Dart thinking of? Do you agree with him?
4. What does Charles Pritchard mean by bottle and paper banks? Are they a good idea?

b) Your turn What can **you** do to help the environment?

5 It's up to you

a) Not all towns are like Greendale. In the village next to Greendale a lot of good changes have been made. *Make passive sentences in the present perfect.*

Public transport Special cycle paths Bottle and paper banks The town centre The pond in the park	improve put in the car park build clean make into a traffic-free zone

b) Your turn What will happen if we do nothing to save our Earth? Use the future form of the passive.

6 At Alton Towers

The Penroses are in the park now. They are waiting at the information stand.

1. This little train is great. You **will be shown** round the whole park (to show round).

2. Don't worry. I'm sure your purse … (to find). And if somebody finds it after you leave, it … to you (to send).

3. That ride … next year (to improve). It will be even better then.

4. The film … in half an hour (to show). The doors … in fifteen minutes (to open).

5. Your group … here in half an hour (to collect).

6. Yes, it's a fantastic ride. You … all the way to the top (to take). It'll be great fun.

7 Role play: Cars – or bikes and public transport?

Make two groups. One group is ***for*** *giving up cars and using bikes or public transport. One is* ***against*** *it. Here are some ideas to help you. Can you find more for each side?*

trees will die | too slow | public transport | families with small children | too expensive | old people or people who are ill | shopping | bad weather

When you have enough ideas, you could start like this:

We must give up cars or we'll be in trouble.

But think of … .

Yes, but then we must … .

8 An accident

On the way back from Alton Towers the Penroses heard this report about a car accident on the radio. *Can you put the verbs in the correct passive tenses?*

1 to kill
2 to injure
3 to take
4 to hurt
5 to damage
6 to take
7 to take
8 to find
9 to hurt
10 to improve

The accident happened twenty minutes ago, when a van hit a car on the M1. Luckily nobody ..1.., but the two people in the car ..2.. badly … . They ..3.. already … to hospital.

The driver of the van ..4.. not …, but the front of the van ..5.. . The car and the van ..6.. off the road in a few minutes now.

Accidents often happen because people drive too fast. But this one happened because a horse suddenly ran onto the motorway. It ..7.. now … off the road, but its owner ..8.. not … yet.

Police interviewed the driver of the van after the accident. Here he is now. – Can you tell us what happened?
"When the horse ran in front of my van, I drove into the car. It all happened so fast! It's a miracle that the horse ..9.. not …! I hope the people who were in the car will be all right."

Thank you. This part of the motorway ..10.. last year. But police say it is still dangerous because there is always so much traffic in this area.

9 ⟨Just for fun⟩

Police officer: Someone who drives like you shouldn't have a driving licence.
Driver: That's all right then. I haven't got one.

Step C

Tomorrow

"Tomorrow is the big day," the teacher said to his pupils. "Tomorrow you'll be allowed to see the real thing. But today we're going to get ready for it."
The teacher was taking Year 9 through the transport part of the World Museum.
They entered a room with a very interesting model. "This is the – er – famous Model T," the teacher explained. "I gave you some information on it at school. Remember, it wasn't the first car, but it was the first car from an assembly line. So we can say that it was the beginning of everything."
The children were very quiet. Then Miry asked, "It wasn't very fast, was it? Not like our air stream travel."
"No, of course not. But in its own time it was. At first many people thought that it was too fast. They thought God didn't want people to travel so fast."
The children laughed – a little.
The teacher showed his pupils other models: fantastic American cars from the 1950's, German supercars and examples of Japanese technology.
"Lots of people had a car then," he told them.
"And they all used petrol, didn't they?" Richy asked.
"Yes, that's right, and that was the problem. It was one of the problems, one of the reasons why the environment was polluted so badly."
"But why wasn't the car industry stopped?" Eddy asked.
"Nobody really wanted that. There were experiments with other kinds of energy, but they didn't really work. And then it was too late."
"Tomorrow – will we see tigers and elephants?" Lucy suddenly asked.
"Yes, Lucy," the teacher said, "but only models. But now, please look at these things. You see, people didn't want to give up their –"
"Freedom," Dordy said. He was the best pupil, and the teacher smiled at him. "Yes," he said, "it was called freedom. Dordy is right."
"But it was a big price to pay for this freedom, wasn't it?" Dordy said, and his teacher smiled again.
"Yes, a great price, but in the end it wasn't only cars, but all the stupid things that were done."
"Will we see dogs and cats, too?" Lucy asked.
"Yes, there are two cats and a dog," the teacher said. "Real animals. Special rooms have been built for them."
"Can we play with them, too?" Richy asked.
"No," the teacher did not smile now. "Children, tomorrow when we are in the biology section, you will have to be very careful. Don't touch anything – not the models and of course not the living examples."
"How many are there?" Richy asked.
"Five. Only five. They are the last examples."
"But they can ... er ... have babies," Dordy said.
"No! They are usually kept in different places. They aren't allowed to have babies and they never will be. Too dangerous," the teacher said. "These are the last five humans and when they are dead, there will be no more."

1 Looking at the story

1. Where are the teacher and his pupils?
2. What are they looking at? Why?
3. Why does the teacher think that the Model T was the beginning of everything?
4. Why does the teacher always smile when Dordy says something?
5. What animals are there in the biology part of the museum?
6. What do we find out about them?

2 Working with the text

1. When does this story take place? How do you know?
2. This story has a surprise ending. Why? What don't we know until the end?
3. What happened to all the people? Why?
4. Do you think this could happen? Say why.

3 Word power Words without plurals

Eight of these words don't have a plural form. Can you find them?

fun car water model information village
garage luck piece petrol motorway
pollution roundabout traffic human air

4 Word power How many?

a) You can count words with no plurals if you use the phrases from this box.

Example: a piece of news *Go on.*

1 x news 3 x chocolate 2 x coffee
5 x lemonade 4 x information 7 x tea
6 x water 3 x milk 2 x soap

pints of
glasses of
pieces of
cups of
bars of
bottles of
kinds of
...

b) *Now write a sentence with each of these expressions.*

Example: I heard an interesting piece of news on the radio last night. *Go on.*

A surprise

ⓐ When the Penroses came home, they got a surprise.
"Oh no!" said Mrs Penrose. "Look, that window has been broken. Burglars!"
"I hope our TV hasn't been stolen," Mark said.
"Should we call the police before we go in?" David asked.
"No," Mr Penrose said and opened the door.
"Careful," he said. "Don't touch anything."
Just then the telephone rang. David answered it. He listened for a moment, then he said, "That window wasn't broken by burglars. *Robert* broke it with a ball."
"It was broken *by Robert*?" Mrs Penrose said. "Great!"

5 All this happened the same day

1

to break

2

to hit

3

to injure

4

to wake up

5

to take

6

to catch

Example: 1. The window was broken by Robert.

ⓑ Five minutes later Robert arrived at the Penroses' house. Mark opened the door and took him into the living-room. The Penroses smiled when they saw Robert. Robert looked surprised. "I broke your window. Aren't you angry?" he asked them.

6 Looking at English

Find the verbs in text ⓑ.
Put the ones with no object in one list and the others in another one.
Which group of verbs can you use in passive sentences?

Verbs with no object	verbs with an object
arrive	open

7 ⟨A song: 2-4-6-8 Motorway⟩

Tom Robinson, © Konkwest Music Ltd./Transamerika MV KG, P. Kaminsky

1. Drive my truck midway to the motorway station
Fairlane cruiser coming up on the left hand side
Headlight shining, driving rain on the window frame
Little young Lady Stardust hitching a ride ... and it's

> 2-4-6-8 ain't never too late
> Me and my radio trucking on through the night
> 3-5-7-9 on a double white line
> Motorway sun coming up with the morning light

2. Whizz-kid sitting pretty on your two-wheel stallion
This old ten-ton lorry got a bead on you
Ain't no use setting up with a bad companion
Ain't nobody get the better of you-know-who

> 2-4-6-8 ...

3. Well there ain't no route you could choose to lose the two of us
Ain't nobody know when you're acting right or wrong
No one knows if a roadway's leading nowhere
Gonna keep on driving home on the road I'm on.

> 2-4-6-8 ...

8 Listening practice: Park-and-ride in Nottingham

Parking is always a problem.
Look at the cartoon. Then listen to a Nottingham police officer.
Can you explain how park-and-ride in Nottingham works?

Step D

Let's check

1 A new road

Can you make passive sentences?

1. The environment

for many years

2. These trees

last month

3. A house

every day

4. A new road

soon

2 An accident report

Can you put the verbs in the correct passive form?

to injure ✓ — to pull — to throw — to send — to take — to interview — to steal — to steal — to take

Three young boys **were injured** in a car accident last night. Two of the boys … out of the car by police. The third boy … out of the car when it hit a tree. All three … to hospital but … home tomorrow.

The boys … by police after that because the car … . Police say that a lot of cars … in Nottingham every month. Often they … by young people who 'just want to have some fun'. Sometimes this 'fun' finishes like this.

3 Counting things

1. Three …

2. …

3. …

4. …

4 Word power The environment

Make a 'mind map'. How many words can you find?

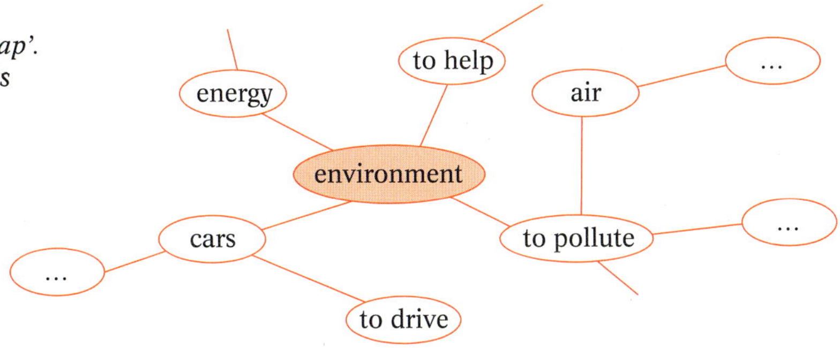

LET'S WRITE

1 Getting ideas together

Why does Mike read reviews?

1 A model text

Read this review.
Mike Jenkins wrote about a computer game for the Haywood Herald.

MERLIN'S PUPIL: An adventure game

MERLIN'S PUPIL is a video game that not only teaches you something but is also full of action and adventure.

It takes place in the past and you play the role of Arthur as a boy. Merlin the wizard is your teacher and you travel through time with him. You do quizzes on British history and geography, kill dragons and fight against your enemies.
There are five levels. You need to complete them before you can take the sword from the stone and become King. At each level you get stronger and Merlin helps you to go on to the next level.
The graphics are colourful and the sound effects are great, especially the dragon noises. The puzzles and quizzes are difficult, but on the whole you have fun while you learn.

The game costs £49.99. Although this is quite expensive, I think you get a lot for your money.

Mike Jenkins

The **title** says what the review is about.

The **introduction** tells us in a few words what kind of game it is.

The **main part** describes it in more detail, and says what is good or bad about it.

The **ending** gives a summary of the author's opinion.

3 Good or bad?

Copy the notes into your exercise book. Then complete them with the information from both reviews.

Title:	MERLIN'S PUPIL	GIRL MEETS BOY
Kind of game:	adventure game on video	
Where it takes place:		school
What you do:	travel through time, do quizzes, kill …,	
How you win:		
Good things:		no violence, …
Bad things:		
Worth buying:		

4 Word power
Review words

Collect words and phrases from the texts that are useful when you write a review or a report.

I think …

… not only … but also …

Although …

First … …

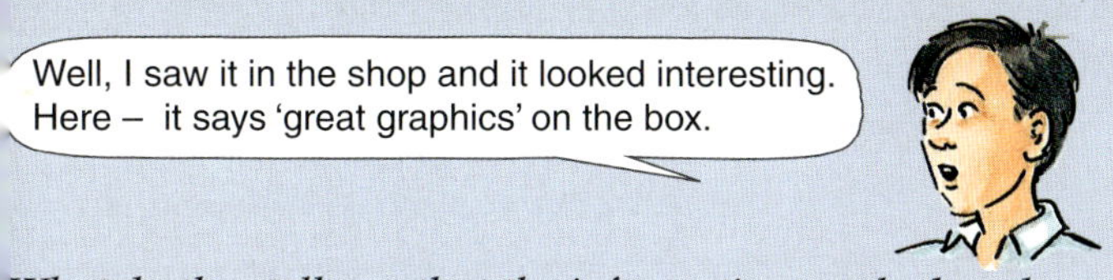

What do they tell you that the information on the box doesn't?

2 Becky's review

This is a review by Becky, but it is in the wrong order.
Say which is the title, which is the introduction, and so on. The main part has two paragraphs.

B The game is cheap (£29.99 and a free lipstick) but in my opinion it isn't worth buying. Girls aren't so stupid, and real life is more interesting!

E GIRL MEETS BOY is a game on CD for girls who want to find a boyfriend. It takes place in a school, and you can be Tammy, the drama group star, or Candy, the 'Jazz Dance Queen'.

C GIRL MEETS BOY: This game isn't a joke!

A First you meet lots of boys and click on the one you like most. Then you follow him through different places and try to talk to him. If you're lucky, he will let you ride on his motorbike. When he says "I love you", you have won the game.

D There are some great songs, but it's the silliest game I've ever played. It also made me angry because the girls are shown as stupid. There isn't any violence, but I nearly threw my mouse through the screen!

5 Brainstorming

Before you start to write, you need to think about what you want to say. Brainstorming can help you to get ideas. This is another new computer game.

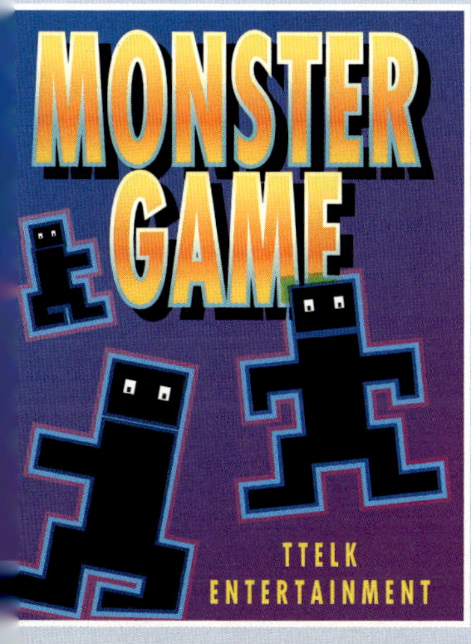

Do some brainstorming first. What words do you think of when you look at the picture? Think of nouns, adjectives, verbs, etc. and write them down as quickly as you can.

6 Organizing ideas

tip Always put your notes in a good order. Then it's easier to write a text from your notes.

You are going to write a review of a computer game. You can choose the game in exercise 5 or one you know already. Make notes on these questions:

- What kind of game is it (adventure, sport, ...)? Where does it take place?
- What happens in the game?
  Who are the characters?
  What do you (the player) have to do?
  How do you win or lose?
- What are the good and bad things about the game?
  (Your review needn't only say good things!)

2 Writing the text

1 Conjunctions

A pupil wrote this letter to 'Dear Harry' in the Haywood Herald.

Put in the conjunctions.

and | so | when | because | but | but | although

Dear Harry,
I'm writing to you ... I'm worried about my brother. Before he got his computer he was a happy, healthy boy, ... now he's a different person. He spends all his free time alone with his computer, ... he doesn't see his friends any more.
... he's only thirteen, he has already started to write his own programmes. ... he has a problem with his computer, he doesn't eat or sleep, ... last night he didn't even go to bed. I've told him it's an unhealthy way of life, ... he won't listen to me. Can you help me?
Worried, 9MD

2 Putting ideas together

a) *Think of endings for the sentences. Write them on a piece of paper, but in a different order.*

Example: 1. I got really upset yesterday because ...
... my dog ate my homework.

2. People say car races are exciting but ... .
3. Although he didn't have a ticket ... .
4. I never go outside when ... .
5. I couldn't find my key so ... .
6. As soon as we heard the news, ...
7. If I can't sleep tonight, ...

b) *Give your list of endings to your partner and look at your partner's list. Think of new ways to start sentences with your partner's endings. Use each conjunction once.*

3 Word power Interesting words

A text becomes more interesting if you use "different" adjectives. *Make lists of adjectives that you can use to describe these things. (The reviews on page 74 will give you some ideas.)*

Characters: interesting, ...
A story: funny, ...
Pictures or graphics: real, ...
A game: difficult, ...
Tips: helpful, ...

4 Writing the text

Write the review about your computer game from your notes (exercise 6, page 75). Just do a 'first copy' because you may want to change it later.

5 ⟨Just for fun⟩

3 Checking the text

1 Collecting tips for a checklist

These tips will help you when you write a review.

tip
Grammar
- 3rd person singular *s*
- pronouns
- genitive-*s*
- 'to do' in questions and negative sentences
- adjectives/adverbs

tip
Spelling and punctuation
- small or capital letters
- y → ie
- not too many commas

tip
Style
- colourful words
- conjunctions
- sentences not too long

a) *Think of words or sentences for each tip that explain the tip or show 'the right way'.*

Examples: • 3rd person singular: 'I help' but 'he/she/it help**s**'.
• Pronouns: **She** helped me and I helped **her**.

b) *Do you know any other good tips? Collect ideas with your class and make a checklist of the most useful tips.*

2 Checking your review

a) *Read through your review with your checklist. Make changes if you need to.*

b) *Give your review to a partner and read his or her review.
Tell each other about mistakes or things that aren't clear.
(A different pair of eyes can notice a lot!)*

c) *Before you give your review to your teacher, write it out again.*

3 Practising your skills

Write a review of a film, a book or a concert. Try to use the skills you have learned in this unit. The review should be about 100 words.

4 ⟨Just for fun⟩

Workshop D

Great Britain and the sea

Step A

An island country

"I must go down to the seas again,
to the lonely sea and the sky"

(From 'Sea-Fever' by John Masefield)

The sea has always played a big part in the lives of British people. If you look at British art, you will find lots of pictures of the sea. Many stories and poems have also been written about the sea.
Even today you cannot forget that Britain is an island. Fishing and North Sea oil are important industries. And because you are never more than seventy miles from the coast, it is easy to go to the sea for a day trip or a holiday.
Britain has more than 2,500 miles of coast. Some of it is flat, but in many places there are high cliffs. Especially on the east coast the cliffs are not very strong.
People who live close to the sea know how unpredictable it can be. Sometimes it is calm and then it is safe to play in the waves. But the weather can change very quickly, and in a storm the sea is made rough by the wind and the rain. Even in good weather there are always strong tides round the British coast. That is why the coastguard and lifeboat services are so important.

1 A picture and a poem

Talk about the picture. What words can you use to describe the sea in it? Do you think this is the kind of scene Masefield was imagining when he wrote the first line of the poem 'Sea-Fever'? Try to explain your answer.

2 Listening practice: People and the sea

a) *Before you listen, look at the photos. What part do you think the sea plays in these people's lives? Collect ideas.*

b) *Listen to what they say. Were you right?*

c) *Who uses these phrases? What are they talking about, and what do they mean?*
"into water sports" – "in my blood" – "as far as you can get from the coast" – "all I've done is to change ferries" – "I don't see much of it" – "no future"

A

B

C

3 Word power Sea words

a) *Collect groups of sea words – new words from page 78, and words you already know. Start with these headings.*

The weather

'Sea work'

The coast
rock, tide, beach

The coast

Fun at the seaside

b) *Find more pictures or photos of the sea (in magazines and brochures). Bring them to school and put them on a desk. Choose* **one** *of them and write a short description of it. Read your text to a partner. Can he/she guess which picture it describes?*

4 If you think about it, you won't do it!

Imagine you're at the seaside. Your friend wants to climb a cliff to look at some bird's eggs – but you don't like this idea. How can you warn your friend? Make sentences with 'if'. (Careful! The order of the clauses isn't always the same.)

Example: 1. you/go near those eggs – the mother bird/fly away
If you go near those eggs, the mother bird will fly away.

2. she/not come back again – she/be too scared
3. the eggs/become cold – the little birds in them/die
4. you/hurt yourself – you/try to climb that cliff
5. the cliff/not be strong enough – it/fall away
6. you/fall with it – you/break a leg (or worse!)
7. you/be sorry – you/not listen to me

She won't … if she … .
And if … .
Anyway, … .
Go on.

5 ⟨Just for fun⟩

There is a club for young people who are interested in the lifeboat service. This is a cartoon from the club magazine.

Unit 5

Step B

Out in the North Sea

PEOPLE AROUND BRITAIN

This week's report comes from an oil rig in the North Sea. Amy Anderson talked to Pete Cameron.

What do you do on this rig, Pete? – My job, you mean? I help to check and repair the rig itself. If the rig wasn't strong enough, it would break like a toy in this rough sea.

It looks like a hard life. – It is. If you worked on the rig, you would find out just how hard! And it can be dangerous, too.

What do you do on an oil rig when you aren't working? – Well, we eat, of course. The food is very good. And we watch films or we just sleep. Really, we don't have much free time. We work very long hours.

So why do you do this job? – Money. I wouldn't get so much if I did anything else. I have to look after my family.

But if you had a job on land, you would see your family more often. – Well, you can't have everything. But you're right. I'm always glad to get on that helicopter and fly back home for a week.

1 Would you like it?

Think how it would be if you worked on an oil rig. What would or wouldn't you like?
Example: "I wouldn't like it if the work was dangerous."

I'd like it if …

I wouldn't like it if …

I got a lot of money | the work was hard/dangerous | there were bad storms | I could fly in a helicopter | I didn't see my family very often | I could watch lots of films | I had to work very long hours | the food was good

2 Important work

a) *Put the right parts of the sentences together.*

1. If Britain had no oil to sell, ----→ the country would be much poorer.
2. If there were no fishermen,
3. If all the ferries stopped,
4. If we didn't have lifeboats,
5. If nobody made weather forecasts,

more people would die at sea.
we wouldn't know when to expect bad weather.
the country would be much poorer.
everyone would have to use the Channel Tunnel.
we wouldn't have any fish to eat.

b) *Can you finish these sentences?*

1. If we didn't have any teachers, … .
2. If I had a lot of money, … .

3 Looking at English

a) *Find the 'if' sentences in the report.*
- In sentences like these the verb in the main clause is in the conditional tense. Explain how you make the conditional tense.
- Which tense do you use in the 'if' clause? (Is it the same in German?)

b) *Can you explain when you use 'if' sentences like these? It will help if you compare them with the sentences you made in exercise 4 on page 79.*
- Which 'if' sentences are about situations which are **real** and can easily happen?
- Which sentences are about situations which are **imagined** and probably won't happen?

4 Just imagine!

Work with a partner.
Talk about what you would do if these things happened. (They won't!)

You can use these ideas.

Example:

If I saw a ghost, I would run away.

Oh, I wouldn't do that. If I saw a ghost, I would ask its name.

fight invite
say run away ask
help shout buy
wait live in take
go crazy give …

1

see

2

find

3

win

4

meet

5

get stuck

6

become

5 If I were you

a) *What advice would you give these people?*

tip When you want to give advice in English, you often start with 'If I **were** you, …'. Just learn this verb form as a phrase.

Example:
1. Hm. I'd like to go swimming, but the sea looks a bit dirty.
   – If I were you, I wouldn't swim in that water.
2. I'd like to take my boat out tomorrow, but I don't know what the weather will be like then.
3. Where can I go for a nice seaside holiday? The weather here is so unpredictable.
4. I'm planning to go to France, but I always feel ill on the ferry.
5. Hey, part of the cliff has fallen away over there – with an old house on it. I think I'll go and have a look.
6. Mm. Isn't it lovely to lie in the hot sun like this all day?

b) *Think of problem situations. Explain your problem to your partner. What advice does he/she give you?*

The lifeboat service

The coast all round Britain is looked after by hundreds of lifeboats – big and small. The lifeboat crews do not get any money for their work. The service is a charity. Every year people give, collect or make millions of pounds for it. The lifeboats are all paid for with this money. The lifeboat service means that many lives can be saved at sea. But of course it is better if the lifeboats do not have to be called out. There is a leaflet which informs people about safety in boats.

6 Tips for people in boats

a) *Read these tips, and find out which pictures from the leaflet they go with.*

A

It is important to carry extra petrol. A rope **should be carried**, too.

A radio can be useful. It **can be used** to call the coastguard or other boats for help.

Instructions how to use signals safely **must be read** before your trip – it's too late when you need to use them!

B

C

b) *Make more tips for the leaflet. Use these ideas – there is often more than one correct answer – but put them into the same passive forms as in a). (You often use the passive when you give information like this.)*

Start like this: 1. The trip **should be planned** carefully.
2. Lifejackets must be … .
3. Extra clothes … . *Go on.*

The trip
The boat
Lifejackets
Extra clothes
Tide tables
Someone on land
A pocket knife
The weather
…

can / must / should | be

check
carry
read
inform about the trip
wear
plan carefully
take
…

7 All for the lifeboats

to | of (2 x) | at | about | after | for

Read what a girl from a fishing village in Cornwall says. Find the right prepositions to finish the passive forms.

1. My dad is a lifeboatman. He is the only person whose work is paid … by the lifeboat service. 2. That's because he is the mechanic – every lifeboat has to be looked … by a mechanic. 3. Lots of people in our village make money for the lifeboat service. All kinds of crazy activities are thought … . 4. I was laughed … last year when I wanted to walk one mile on all fours. 5. But I did it, and I collected a lot of money. It was even written … in the newspaper. 6. That day I was spoken … by lots of people in the street. 7. So you see, I've been famous for a day – even if I'm never heard … again!

8 A big oil problem

In February 1996 an oil tanker hit some rocks near the south coast of Wales, and got stuck. A lot of oil from the tanker escaped into the sea, and the coast was badly polluted.

Read what people in the area said at the time.
Then explain what had to be done about the problem.

OIL POLLUTES WELSH COAST

1. It won't be easy to pull the tanker off the rocks.
2. What a terrible job to clean the beach!
3. We'll have to take away all the sand with oil on it.
4. Yes, and we need helpers to collect the oil on the rocks, too.
5. It's important to help the poor seabirds.
6. We must catch and wash the live birds.
7. Then we'll have to pick up all the dead birds. There are thousands of them!

Example: 1. The tanker **had to be pulled** off the rocks. 2. The beach had to be … . *Go on.*

SB 9 ⟨A song: Sloop John B.⟩

We come on the sloop John B.
My grandfather and me.
Around Nassau town
We did roam
Drinking all night,
Got into a fight.
Well, I feel so broke-up.
I want to go home.

Chorus:
So hoist up the John B. sail,
See how the mainsail's set.
Call for the captain ashore
Let me go home!
Let me go home, –
I want to go home!
Well, I feel so broke-up,
I want to go home.

The first mate he got drunk.
Broke in the Captain's trunk
The Constable had to come
And take him away.
Sheriff John Stone,
Why don't you leave me alone?
I feel so broke-up.
I want to go home.

Step C

Sea Rescue

1 Before you read the story

a) *Look at this leaflet and try to understand what it says. (Look back at the tips in exercise 2 on page 26.)*

If you see someone in trouble in the water tell a lifeguard if there is one on patrol, otherwise...

DIAL 999

and ask for...

COASTGUARD
The Maritime Emergency Service

The Coastguard are on call 24 hours a day to co-ordinate any search and rescue operation that may be needed. So if you see a red flare, or someone in trouble at sea or on the coast, go to the nearest telephone, dial 999 and ask for the Coastguard. Give any information you can and follow any instructions you are given. You could help to save lives.

b) *The leaflet could give you ideas about the story. Say in a few words what you think the story is about. First look at these words:*

some friends — fall — a boat — sea — a swimmer — the tide — a storm — be in trouble — some rocks — a family — ...

Examples:
"Maybe a girl is walking on the cliffs when she sees a swimmer in trouble."
"I think the story is about a family who ... ."

2 Now read the story

Find out if your ideas in exercise 1 were right.
This really happened, on the west coast of Wales. The names of the people have been changed.

"Come on, Tom! We've got to get off this beach!" "OK, Mary. You too, Sam, help to push! You other kids, stay where you are!" Again and again, fourteen-year-old Sam Jackson and his parents tried to push their boat out into the sea. But a storm was starting. They had to fight against the wind and the rain and the tide. A great wave broke over the boat. It was full of water now, and the engine was wet. There was nothing more they could do.

They went back onto the beach where Sam's younger brothers and sisters were waiting. Sam looked at the cliffs. They were too high to climb. Maybe they could escape if they went along the coast over the rocks at the bottom of the cliffs. But it was too difficult for the younger children. His father seemed to know what he was thinking. "Sam and I will go and get help," Tom Jackson told his wife Mary. "Don't worry," he added and tried to smile. But they both knew how serious it was. The tide was coming in faster now.

Sam followed his father. It was raining more than ever, and the wind was stronger, too. He thought of the beautiful sun that morning as they left Broad Haven in their boat and went up the coast to Nolton Haven in a calm sea. How quickly the weather could change! Now their perfect day on the beach was suddenly a nightmare.

The mile over the slippery rocks along the coast to Druidston seemed endless. In the village at last, Tom Jackson called the coastguard.

"My family is trapped between the sea and the cliffs at Nolton Haven. Please send a lifeboat! My son and I are going back!"

Right away the coastguard at Milford Haven called the rescue services at Broad Haven.

A few minutes later the crew was already in the lifeboat and on the way. For Sam and his father the way back was much worse than before. Now there was water over most of the rocks. They had to climb along the bottom of the cliffs, and so they went much more slowly.

At last they were near Nolton Haven again. But then they found that they were trapped themselves. They could not go back to Druidston because the tide was now too high behind them. And they could not go on because the waves were crashing angrily into the cliff in front of them. Not far away they could see Mary Jackson and the four other children. There was no beach now. They were on a rock. If help did not come right away, they would have no chance.

Suddenly, through the rain, Sam saw something out on the sea. "The lifeboat!" he shouted. "I think the crew have seen Mum and the others!" The lifeboat moved closer to the group on the rock. It was dangerous in the rough sea under the cliffs, but at last the boat was able to get close enough. One of the lifeboatmen jumped onto the rock. One by one he threw the children across, and another member of the crew caught them. While he was helping the mother, a mountain of water broke over them both. But at last they were all safely in the lifeboat.

Now the boat moved over to Sam and his father. But three huge waves hit it. It was almost turned over by the last wave. With all the water that was now in the boat it was too dangerous to try to rescue two more people. "We'll have to take the others to Druidston first. We'll be back!" shouted a lifeboatman.

It was a terrible moment when the lifeboat went away. "How high will the tide come up? How much time have we got?" Sam asked. A wave broke near their feet.

"It might be better if we tried to climb the cliff," his father said.

Slowly they began to climb up. It was very frightening. The cliff was steep and the wind was throwing the rain against them. Then the cliff suddenly became much steeper. They could not climb up or down. They were stuck.

They thought that this was the end for them. The wind and the rain made a terrible noise. But then there was another sound. Soon they could hear the sound better. It was an engine. They looked down at the sea and saw the lifeboat. "Hold on!" one of the crew shouted. "The coastguard has sent the Cliff Rescue team from Broad Haven. They'll be with you soon!"

The next few minutes seemed like hours. But at last the Cliff Rescue team were at the top of the cliff. From where they were, Sam and his father could not be pulled up to the top. So one of the team came down to them on a rope. First he took Sam, then Tom Jackson, down to the bottom of the cliff again. There they were rescued by the lifeboat and taken to Druidston. At last all the family were safe.

The brave lifeboat crew of Broad Haven won a medal for this rescue.

3 The map

a) *Find these places on the map on page 85.*
Talk about what part they play in the story.
Example: Broad Haven
– That is where the Jacksons started their boat trip.
The rescue services also came from Broad Haven.

Broad Haven | **Druidston** | **Nolton Haven** | **Milford Haven**

b) *Why didn't Mr Jackson and his son Sam stay safely at Druidston after they called the coastguard? (The text doesn't tell us – what do you think?)*

4 Writing a newspaper report

a) *First make notes about the story.*
In what order did everything happen?

morning – left Broad Haven – in boat – good weather – to Nolton Haven – day on beach – suddenly a storm – couldn't

Now go on with the notes.

b) *Check your notes. Have you got all the important facts?*
Do you want to add anything? Or leave anything out?

c) *Now use your notes and write a newspaper report about the rescue. Try to keep it short but clear. Think of a good heading, too. – Reports often start with a little summary before they tell the whole story. You can start like this:* A family of seven were rescued by the Broad Haven lifeboat yesterday. In the morning the Jacksons left … .

5 What would you do?

How would you feel if …?

What would you do if …?

Ask your partner about dangerous situations.
You can use the ideas in the story, or think of different ideas.

you/see a boat in trouble | a lifeboat/save your life | your friend/get stuck on a cliff | you/rescue someone | a swimmer/shout for help | …

6 Looking at English: Special nouns

a) *Compare these two sentences from the story.*

"My family **is** trapped." – "All the family **were** safe."

In which sentence do you think of the different members of the family? In which sentence do you think of the family as one whole group? How does the verb form show this?

b) *You can use singular or plural verb forms with a few other nouns, too.*
Look at these pairs of sentences. Which verb form would you choose? Try to explain why.

1. All the crew (lives/live) near the lifeboat. A good crew (is/are) very important.
2. There (was/were) a crowd on the beach. The crowd (was/were) all people from the area.
3. My family (is/are) Welsh. But not all my family (speaks/speak) the Welsh language.
4. Our swimming team (loses/lose) all their races. The team (needs/need) better swimmers.

Step D

Let's Check

1 Word power You know …

Can you help these people to find the right word? (All the words are new in this unit.)

1. The part of Germany where I live is – er – the land doesn't have any hills.
   – The word is **flat**.
2. Last night I had a – a terrible dream.
3. The weather is so – well, you never know what it will be like.
4. Have you ever flown in a – you know – not a plane – the thing people fly to and from oil rigs in.
5. When we came across the Channel, the sea was – er – there were no waves on it.
6. We found a lovely beach with white sand and steep – er, things like mountains.
7. How do you become a member of the – er – the team of people in the lifeboat?

2 All around Britain

What would you do in these places? You can choose the activities. Think about what you have learned about different parts of Britain.

Example: 1. stay at Fort William
If I stayed at Fort William, I would climb Ben Nevis. I would probably drive to Loch Ness and look for the monster, too!

2. visit North Wales
3. go to Caerleon
4. be in Nottingham
5. have a holiday in Cornwall
6. spend a week in London

3 A fantasy school

Imagine a fantasy school. Write down some ideas about what can/should/must/needn't be done in your school. Try to think of funny or "different" ideas.

Examples: Ice cream **should be eaten** at the end of every lesson
Uniform **must be worn** – but only by teachers!

pay pupils for their work	do homework	take pets to school
write reports about teachers	play games in lessons	make exams easy
put a TV in every classroom	organize a school trip to …	…

4 ⟨Just for fun⟩

Unit 5

⟨Extra line⟩

⟨Reading corner⟩

The Gunpowder Plot[1]

Characters

Catesby[2]
Percy[3]
Wright[4]
Winter
Guy Fawkes[5]
} *Plotters[6] against[7] the King*

Monteagle[8]
Soldier[9] 1, 2
Speaker 1, 2, 3
Chorus
House owner

Speaker 1: November 5th is Guy Fawkes' Day in Britain. On this day people light[10] big fires and burn[11] 'guys'[12] made of straw[13]. There are firework displays[14] all over the country and people come together in the streets to watch them. Why do the British do this? Who was Guy Fawkes? Watch our play and you'll learn the answer.

Speaker 2: In 1605 James I[15] was King of England. One group of people hated[16] him and his Parliament so much that they planned to kill him. This is the story of the Gunpowder Plot.

Chorus:
Remember, remember, the fifth of November,
Gunpowder, treason[17] and plot.
I see no reason[18] why gunpowder treason
Should ever be forgot[19].

Speaker 3: **Scene 1:** *A room in the house of Robert Catesby, an English Catholic[20]. Guy Fawkes has just come back to England. He is talking to Catesby, Wright, Percy and Winter.*

Catesby: Welcome back, Fawkes! It's good to see you. We heard a lot about your adventures in the war[21]. I hope you are well?

Guy Fawkes: Very well, my friend. And how is our country, England?

Winter: England is still the most beautiful country in the world, but it is not a happy place.

Catesby: I know you are a good Catholic, Fawkes. We Catholics have no peace of mind[22] now. There's a new law[23]. We must pay money if we don't go to church on Sundays – to *their* churches, of course. We can't have churches of our own[24].

Percy: My friends, we talk and talk, but we do nothing. Now is the time for action!

Catesby: You're right, Percy. It is time for action. We've got a plan. Will you join us, Fawkes?

Guy Fawkes: I will! What is your plan?

[1]Gunpowder Plot ['gʌnpaʊdə ˌplɒt] *Pulververschwörung* – [2]Catesby ['keɪtsbɪ] *Familienname* – [3]Percy ['pɜːsɪ] *Familienname* – [4]Wright [raɪt] *Familienname* – [5]Guy Fawkes [ˌgaɪ 'fɔːks] *historischer englischer Verschwörer* – [6]plotter ['plɒtə] *Verschwörer* – [7]against [ə'genst] *gegen* – [8]Monteagle [ˌmɒn'tiːgl] *Familienname* – [9]soldier ['səʊldʒə] *Soldat* – [10]to light [laɪt] *anzünden* – [11]to burn [bɜːn] *verbrennen* – [12]guy [gaɪ] *hier: Puppe* – [13]straw [strɔː] *Stroh* – [14]firework display ['faɪəwɜːk dɪsˌpleɪ] *Feuerwerksvorführung* – [15]James I [ˌdʒeɪms ðə 'fɜːst] *engl. König* – [16]to hate [heɪt] *hassen* – [17]treason ['triːzn] *Verrat* – [18]reason['riːzn] *Grund* – [19]should … be forgot [ˌʃʊd ... bɪ fə'gɒt] *sollte … vergessen werden* – [20]Catholic ['kæθəlɪk] *Katholik* – [21]war [wɔː] *Krieg* – [22]peace of mind [ˌpiːs‿əv 'maɪnd] *innere Ruhe, Seelenfrieden* – [23]law [lɔː] *Gesetz* – [24]of our own [əv‿ɑːr‿'əʊn] *unser/e eigene/r/s*

Percy: To blow up[25] the King with gunpowder when he comes to open Parliament next November.

Guy Fawkes: But that's treason and we'll die horribly[26] if they catch us! Do we really need to do that? Won't the King listen to us?

Plotters: No! The King will listen to nobody.

Guy Fawkes: But we'll kill a lot of other people, too!

Catesby: Yes, but we need to: the King must die!

Guy Fawkes: But where do we get gunpowder from? And how do we get it into the Houses of Parliament?

Wright: Well, that's all part of the plan. Just wait and see …

Chorus: Remember, remember, the fifth of November,
Gunpowder, treason and plot.
I see no reason why gunpowder treason
Should ever be forgot.

Speaker 3: **Scene 2:** *A house next to the Houses of Parliament. Catesby is talking to the owner[27] of the house.*

Owner: So you want to rent[28] my house? It's a very nice place, I'm sure you'll like living here. It's quite new and it's very cheap. Please come up here sir, and have a look out of the window. You can see the boats on the River Thames.

Catesby: Yes, it is a very nice place. And it's right next to the Houses of Parliament. Yes my friend, I think I'll take it.

Chorus: Remember, remember, the fifth of November,
Gunpowder, treason and plot.
I see no reason why gunpowder treason
Should ever be forgot.

Speaker 3: **Scene 3:** *A cellar[29] underneath[30] the Houses of Parliament.*

The five plotters come in at the left side of the stage. Each one is carrying a barrel[31].

Catesby: Barrel number one! We can't turn back now.

Winter: Number two! They're very heavy[32] – they must be really full of gunpowder.

Percy: Too full! I don't like hard work. That's number three.

Wright: And number four! What a good idea it was to rent a house next to the Houses of Parliament. But it was difficult to dig[33] this tunnel. My back and hands are still sore[34].

Guy Fawkes: There's barrel number five. We're going to need thirty-six.

Plotters: Thirty-six barrels?

Catesby: That's enough gunpowder to blow up the whole of London!

Percy: It's enough to blow up King James, anyway. You've done well, Fawkes. Where did you get them all?

[25]to blow up [ˌbləʊ ˈʌp] *sprengen* – [26]to die horribly [ˈhɒrəblɪ] *einen grausamen Tod sterben* – [27]owner [ˈəʊnə] *Besitzer*– [28]to rent [rent] *mieten* – [29]cellar [ˈselə] *Keller* – [30]underneath [ʌndəˈni:θ] *unter* – [31]barrel [ˈbærəl] Fass – [32]heavy [ˈhevɪ] *schwer* – [33]to dig [dɪg] *graben* – [34]sore [sɔ:] wund

Guy Fawkes: Ask no questions. *(looking worried)* I've got a problem. I need more money to pay some people.

Percy: Who are these people?

Guy Fawkes: You're asking questions again. Let's just say we want them to keep quiet[35].

Catesby: I know just the man to help us. He is a good Catholic and he hates the King.

Winter: Are you sure he is a friend? Will he keep quiet?

Catesby: Yes, I'm very sure. We'll get the money for you.

Chorus: Remember, remember, the fifth of November,
Gunpowder, treason and plot.
I see no reason why gunpowder treason
Should ever be forgot.

Speaker 3: **Scene 4:** *The cellars underneath the Houses of Parliament. It is the night before November 5th.*

Monteagle and two soldiers come onto the stage.

Soldier 1: You say you got a letter? Who was it from?

Monteagle: I don't know. I only know what the letter said. "Do not go to the Houses of Parliament when the King comes. Something terrible will happen." I showed the letter to a friend, and my friend showed it to the King.

Soldier 1: And the King sent us down to the cellars. What are we looking for?

Monteagle: I don't know. Gunpowder, maybe?

Soldier 2: Well, there's nothing in this cellar. Let's try through here.

The men go to one side of the stage.

Guy Fawkes: Who's that? Don't come near me! Stay away! I'll blow you all up! I will!

The soldiers run to Guy Fawkes and hold him.

Soldiers: Got you!

Monteagle (counting the barrels): … thirty-four, thirty-five, thirty-six! That's enough gunpowder to blow up the whole city! Stand up. You're going to see the King.

Speaker 2: The soldiers got the names of the other plotters out of Guy Fawkes. The plotters were all executed[36] and that was the end of the Gunpowder Plot.

Speaker 1: But to this day soldiers still search[37] the cellars of the Houses of Parliament for gunpowder every year before Parliament opens.

[35]to keep quiet [ˌkiːp ˈkwaɪət] *ruhig bleiben, den Mund halten* — [36]to be executed [ˈeksɪkjuːtɪd] *hingerichtet werden* – [37]to search [ˈsɜːtʃ] *durchsuchen*

Religious[1] festivals in Britain

Christmas is not the only religious festival in Britain. It is the most important Christian[2] festival, of course. But there are a lot of people with other religions in Britain, too – Muslims, Jews[3], Hindus, … . And they have their own special festivals.

Hannukah[4] is very important for Jewish[5] people. It's always a special time for the family when we light[6] the Menorah[7].

I can't wait till Eid[10] starts! I've got a new shalwaar kameez[11] for the mosque[12]. And we're going to have a big family party.

We get lots of cards from other Hindus at Diwali[8]. And when it gets dark, we have fireworks[9] in the garden.

Hannukah is at the beginning of December. Jews go to the synagogue[13] and celebrate[14] the fact that they are free to pray[15] in their own way. Families give presents, play games and eat together. They often make pancakes[16], or 'latkes'. A very important tradition[17] is to light candles on the Menorah – one for each day of the festival. By the end of Hannukah there are eight candles.

At **Diwali** Hindus celebrate the future. They hope it will be good for them. The festival is for two to five days in November. People decorate[18] their homes with lots of little lamps[19]. Today they often use electric lights[20], too. They eat fruit and other sweet things with their family and friends, and on the Saturday or Sunday near Diwali they worship[21] at the temple.

Eid is a happy time because it is the end of Rama-dan. (That is a month when Muslims are not allowed to eat till the sun[22] goes down.) The Muslim year has only 354 days, so Eid is on a different date every year. On the first day of the festival Muslims go to the mosque in their best clothes. There they pray and give money for the poor. There are cards, presents, and big family meals at Eid.

Eid Mubarak (Happy Festival)

Happy Hannukah!

Merry Christmas and a Happy New Year!

Subhli Diwali (Happy Diwali)

Best wishes for …

Thinking of you at …

[1]religious [rɪ'lɪdʒəs] *religiös* – [2]Christian ['krɪstʃən] *christlich* – [3]Jew [dʒu:] *Jude/Jüdin* – [4]Hannukah ['hænu:kə] *jüdischer Feiertag* – [5]Jewish ['dʒu:ɪʃ] *jüdisch* – [6]to light [laɪt] *anzünden* – [7]Menorah [mə'nɔ:rə] *traditioneller achtarmiger Leuchter* – [8]Diwali [dɪ'vɑ:lɪ] *hinduistisches Fest* – [9]fireworks ['faɪəwɜ:ks] *Feuerwerk* – [10]Eid [i:d] *moslemisches Fest* – [11]shalwaar kameeze [ʃal,wa ka'mi:z] *moslemische Kleidung* – [12]mosque [mɒsk] *Moschee*– [13]synagogue ['sɪnəgɒg] *Synagoge* – [14]to celebrate ['selɪbreɪt] *feiern* –[15]to pray [preɪ] *beten* – [16]pancake ['pænkeɪk] *Pfannkuchen* – [17]tradition [trə'dɪʃn] *Tradition* – [18]to decorate ['dekəreɪt] *dekorieren* – [19]lamp [læmp] *Lampe* – [20]lights [laɪts] *Lichter* – [21]to worship ['wɜ:ʃɪp] *Gottesdienst feiern* – [22]sun [sʌn] *Sonne*

Nathan and Lara

In the dark[1] assembly hall, almost every eye was on the young actors on the stage. They were in the middle of a funny song. Every year, a group of pupils did a play for other pupils and for parents, and this year it was a musical[2]. It was very good. Only Lara[3] and Nathan[4] at the back of the hall were not interested in the play. These two pupils were too busy with their plans. "Well, I'd like to, Nathan," Lara whispered. "Really, but I just can't – I'm sorry."

Nathan was a pupil at Nelson Comprehensive[5] in Watford[6]. Lara was not. She was from Nelson's partner school in Germany and was on a short visit with 32 other pupils.

"It's OK, no problem," Nathan said. But he wasn't happy. He liked Lara and he knew that she liked him, too. They were good friends already, even after just a week.

Their problem was the next day. Saturday was the German group's last day in England. "We're going to visit Stratford-upon-Avon[7]," Lara explained in a quiet voice, "and nobody must miss the trip. We all have to go. I'd like to stay here in Watford with you but I can't. It isn't just a holiday, you know. We have to answer more questions on worksheets. About Shakespeare[8] this time, of course."

"It's OK, I understand," Nathan said.

But Lara wasn't so sure. Did he understand? "He probably thinks I don't care for him[9]," she thought.

"Some English pupils are going to come with us tomorrow," she said. "Did you know that? We're going to use two buses. Both are full or almost full, I think, but perhaps somebody is ill. Can you be at the school car park at 8 o'clock?"

Before Nathan could say anything, the musical finished and everybody clapped. He and Lara started to clap, too. Then suddenly the lights were on again and everybody got up. After the musical, Nathan, Lara and Susan Fox[10] walked to Susan's house where Lara was a guest for the week. Susan soon said, "Good night." Then she went inside.

"Well?" Lara asked.

"I can't. I'm playing in a football match in the morning. The team needs me. It's an important game," Nathan said. "Are you sure you can't spend the day here, Lara? Perhaps *you* can get up late and miss the bus? Then you can watch our football match and after lunch we can go for a walk by the river. Or we can meet my friends and listen to music. What do you think?"

Nathan waited for Lara's answer. Lara thought for a moment. She needed a good idea now. She wasn't very interested in football – but the river was pretty, and of course she wanted to see Nathan again. But then, school was important to her, too. That was why she was here. She wanted to find out more about England. She really wanted to visit Stratford.

[1]dark [dɑ:k] *dunkel* – [2]musical [ˈmju:zɪkl] *Musical* – [3]Lara [ˈlɑ:rə] *Mädchenname* – [4]Nathan[ˈneɪθən] *Jungenname* – [5]Nelson Comprehensive [ˈnelsn kɒmprɪˌhensɪv] *Name einer engl. Schule* – [6]Watford [ˈwɒtfəd] *Stadt in Südengland* – [7]Stratford-upon-Avon [ˈstrætfəd‿əˌpɒn‿ˈeɪvn] *Stadt in Mittelengland* – [8]Shakespeare [ˈʃeɪkˌspɪə] *engl. Dramatiker, geboren in Stratford-upon-Avon* – [9]to care for s.o. [ˈkeə fə‿ˌsʌmwʌn] *jdn. mögen* – [10]Fox [ˈfɒks] *Familienname* – [11]excuse [ɪkˈskju:s] *Ausrede, Entschuldigung*

And she didn't want to get into trouble with her teachers. "No, I can't," Lara said. "I don't usually miss lessons at home and I'm not going to start now, I'm sorry."

"Then I won't see you again?" Nathan said. "It will be late when you get back from Stratford tomorrow. And your bus back to Germany leaves early on Sunday morning, doesn't it?"

Lara laughed. Or she tried to laugh. "Well, you might get up early and come to the bus and say goodbye to me. And you can see me in Germany when your group comes to our school."

"Mm," Nathan said.

After Lara went inside she thought of an excuse[11] for not going to Stratford. She called a friend and told her that she didn't feel well and couldn't go on the trip.

She felt terrible because she didn't usually tell lies, but all she could think about was seeing Nathan on her last day in England.

So, the next morning she didn't go to the buses but went to watch the football match.

It was an exciting game, but Nelson lost 4 : 3. Worse still, she didn't see Nathan. He wasn't in the team.

"Where's Nathan?" she asked one of the players right after the game.

"Don't ask me, I don't know and I don't want to talk about him," was the answer.

Lara asked another boy. "I'm looking for Nathan. Have you seen him?"

"Perhaps he's still in bed. He hates getting up early in the morning. He likes playing football in the afternoon. We had to play with ten men."

Lara had a lot of free time now, so she went to Nathan's house. Perhaps he was ill?

"No," his mother said. "He left the house this morning without any breakfast. He said he was late for a bus to Stratford."

Nathan's mother was right. That morning he ran to the school car park and got there just in time. He jumped on the nearest bus and hoped that Lara was on the other which was just leaving.

A week later, Lara got a postcard from England. On one side, there were pictures of Shakespeare's Stratford-upon-Avon. On the other side, it said:

The killing[1] of a god

James Cook[2] was the most famous sea captain[3] of the 18th century. In 1776 he set off[4] for the Pacific Ocean[5], to find a way round Canada[6] into the Atlantic[7]. On his way north from Tahiti[8], Cook discovered[9] the Hawaiian islands[10]. First he made maps of the islands, then he found a good bay[11] and stayed for five weeks.
Now, on February 4th 1779, his ships were leaving the island again …

The old sailor[12] blew smoke[13] into the warm air. "Funny thing about the natives[14] and the Captain," he said. "They really think he's a god." "Yes," said his young friend, "he's lucky. Everything is so beautiful here – the birds, the trees, the flowers, the girls, … and a whole pig costs just one nail[15] – it's paradise[16]!" The old man thought for a moment. Today the natives were especially friendly. But they had often stolen things; they had even taken some nails from the bottom of the boats, under water. And the Captain didn't want to be a god. "Paradise?" said the old man. "I'm not so sure."

On the beach the Hawaiian King shook his head. He respected[17] Cook, but he was happier now that the ships were sailing[18] away. Twice he had given them food, pigs, fruits and vegetables, and presents. The sailors had given them knives, nails and mirrors – useful, but not things you could eat. They had hardly[19] a pig left[20], it was good that the white gods – or men – were going.

The priests[21] said that these strange white men were gods. When the great boats first arrived it was at the time of Orono's[22] feast[23]. They sailed round the island, then stopped at Orono's temple – just as in the Hawaiian legend[24].
When Orono came onto the beach they got down on their knees in front of him. Sometimes smoke came out of the mouths of other white gods – they must be the gods of the volcanoes[25]. But after a time the people said, "These gods can cut themselves. Their blood is red like ours. We have given them all our food, but what do they give us? – a few nails. Why don't they go back to their own land and leave us alone?" The gods had stayed too long.

A few days later a bad storm broke off Cook's masts[26]. He decided to sail back to the island to repair them.

Suddenly the Hawaiians did not treat[27] Cook like a god any more. A second visit wasn't in the legend. One pig now cost five knives.

Early the next morning the sailors saw that the natives had taken their largest boat. Cook was very angry, so he decided to go and see the King. He wanted to take the King and his sons back to his ship and keep

[1]killing ['kılıŋ] *Töten* – [2]James Cook [ˌdʒeımz 'kʊk] *engl. Entdecker und Seefahrer* – [3]captain ['kæptın] *Kapitän* – [4]to set off [ˌset‿'ɒf] *starten, losfahren* – [5]the Pacific Ocean [ðə pəˌsıfık 'əʊʃn] *der Pazifik* – [6]Canada ['kænədə] *Kanada* – [7]the Atlantic [ði:‿ət'læntık] *der Atlantik* – [8]Tahiti [tɑ:'hi:tı] *Tahiti* – [9]to discover [dı'skʌvə] *entdecken* – [10]Hawaiian islands [həˌwaııən 'aıləndz] *Hawaii* – [11]bay [beı] *Bucht* – [12]sailor ['seılə] *Seemann* – [13]smoke [sməʊk] *Rauch* – [14]native ['neıtıv] *Eingeborene/r* – [15]nail [neıl] *Nagel* – [16]paradise ['pærədaıs] *Paradies* – [17]to respect s.o. [rı'spekt] *jdn. respektieren* – [18]to sail [seıl] *segeln* – [19]hardly ['hɑ:dlı] *kaum* – [20]left [left] *übrig* – [21]priest [pri:st] *Priester* – [22]Orono [ə'rəʊnəʊ] *hawaiianischer Gott* – [23]feast [fi:st] *Festmahl* – [24]legend ['ledʒənd] *Legende* – [25]volcano [vɒl'keınəʊ] *Vulkan* – [26]mast [mɑ:st] *Mast* – [27]to treat s.o. [tri:t] *jdn. behandeln* – [28]gun [gʌn] *Gewehr* – [29]to spread like wildfire [ˌspred laık 'waıldˌfaıə] *sich wie ein Lauffeuer verbreiten* – [30]iron ['aıən] *Eisen* – [31]stick [stık] *Stock, Stab* – [32]back [bæk] *Rücken* – [33]bone [bəʊn] *Knochen* – [34]to bury ['berı] *beerdigen* – [35]Staithes ['steıðz] *engl. Küstenort* – [36]Whitby ['wıtbı] *engl. Küstenort* – [37]Royal Navy [ˌrɔıəl 'neıvı] *königliche Marine* – [38]voyage ['vɔııdʒ] *Schiffsreise*

them there until the natives gave the boat back. They needed the boat to get food, perhaps even as a lifeboat.
Cook walked through a crowd on the beach to the King's house with nine soldiers. They heard a gun[28] in the bay. The King was friendly and came out of his house with Cook. Just at that moment a man brought the news that sailors had killed some natives. The news spread like wildfire[29] through the crowd. How could these white men kill their people with their iron[30] sticks[31]? The women pulled the King back, they shouted that he mustn't go onto the ship. Cook walked slowly through the crowd to the beach. It was only forty steps to the boats. The natives started to throw stones, so the soldiers on the beach all fired their guns, but the natives didn't stop. The soldiers turned and ran for their lives now but not all of them got away. Natives killed four of them with knives and stones and the beach was red with blood.
Then the sailors in the boats also shot at the crowd. Cook turned to them – but at that moment a native hit him from behind. Another native pushed a knife into Cook's back[32]. Then a whole crowd jumped on him, angry with this man who wasn't a god. They pulled his body up the beach, cut it into pieces and gave the pieces to the most important families. The sailors quickly rowed back to the ships. Suddenly, everything was very quiet.

Later, Cook's men used the ships' big guns, burned the village and killed about 200 more natives. The King then collected Cook's bones[33] and brought them back. The sailors buried[34] them at sea, then sailed away as quickly as they could.

Captain James Cook (1728–1779)

1737 His father works on a farm. James is clever at school.

1745 Cook works in a shop at Staithes[35], North Yorkshire. He wants to go to sea.

1746 He moves to Whitby[36] to work on a ship. He works hard and learns Maths in the evenings. For many years he takes ships down the dangerous east coast to London.

1755–1766 He joins the Royal Navy[37] and makes good maps of the East of Canada.

1768–1771 The Navy sends Cook to look for land in the Pacific. He sails round the world for the first time, makes good maps of New Zealand and discovers the east coast of Australia.

1772–1775 Second great voyage[38], this time round the world from East to West.

1776–1779 Third voyage to the Pacific. Cook dies on a Hawaiian beach (14th February 1779). The ships return in October 1780.

Christmas

A song: The little drummer[1] boy

Come, they told me
Pa rumpa pum pum
A new born[2] king to see
Pa rumpa pum pum
Our finest gifts[3] we bring
Pa rumpa pum pum
To set[4] before the king
Pa rumpa pum pum
Rumpa pum pum
Rumpa pum pum
So to honour[5] him
Pa rumpa pum pum
When we come

Little baby
Pa rumpa pum pum
I am a poor boy too
Pa rumpa pum pum
I have no gift to bring
Pa rumpa pum pum
That's fit[6] to give a king
Pa rumpa pum pum
Rumpa pum pum
Rumpa pum pum
Shall I play for you
Pa rumpa pum pum
On my drum[7]

Then he nodded[8]
Pa rumpa pum pum
The ox[9] and lamb kept time[10]
Pa rumpa pum pum
I played my drum for him
Pa rumpa pum pum
I played my best for him
Pa rumpa pum pum
Rumpa pum pum
Rumpa pum pum
Then he smiled at me
Pa rumpa pum pum
Me and my drum

A recipe: Make a gingerbread[11] man

This is an original[12] English recipe for a gingerbread man – or a gingerbread woman.

You need

- 125 g[13] butter
- 125 g sugar
- 250 g flour[14]
- 1 small egg
- 1 teaspoon ground ginger[15]
- 1 teaspoon ground cinnamon[16]
- 1 teaspoon baking powder[17]
- a pinch of salt[18]

1. Mix[19] the butter and the sugar.
2. Mix in the egg.
3. Mix in the flour, the baking powder, the ginger, cinnamon and salt.

4. Roll[20] out on a table with flour.

5. Cut out a gingerbread man or a gingerbread woman. Make eyes, a nose and a mouth with raisins[21].

6. Bake[22] in the oven[23] for ten minutes at 200° C[24].

[1]drummer ['drʌmə] *Trommler* – [2]new born ['nju: bɔ:n] *neu geboren* – [3]gift [gɪft] *Geschenk* – [4]to set [set] hier: *niederlegen* – [5]to honour ['ɒnə] *ehren* – [6]fit [fɪt] *passend*– [7]drum [drʌm] *Trommel* – [8]to nod [nɒd] *nicken* – [9]ox [ɒks] *Ochse* – [10]kept time [ˌkept 'taɪm] *schlugen den Takt* – [11]gingerbread ['dʒɪndʒəbred] *Lebkuchen* – [12]original [ə'rɪdʒənl] *echt*– [13]g = gram [græm] *Gramm* – [14]flour ['flaʊə] *Mehl* – [15]ground ginger [ˌgraʊnd 'dʒɪndʒə] *gemahlener Ingwer* – [16]cinnamon ['sɪnəmən] *Zimt* – [17]baking powder ['beɪkɪŋ ˌpaʊdə] *Backpulver* – [18]pinch of salt [ˌpɪntʃ‿əv 'sɔ:lt] Prise Salz – [19]to mix [mɪks] *mischen* – [20]to roll [rəʊl] *rollen* – [21]raisins ['reɪznz] *Rosinen*– [22]to bake [beɪk] *backen* – [23]oven [ʌvn] *Ofen* – [24]200 ° C ['tu: ˌhʌndrəd dɪˌgri:z 'sentɪgreɪd] *200 Grad Celsius*

⟨Translation practice⟩

Achte ganz besonders auf folgende Dinge:

- Wörter haben oft verschiedene Bedeutungen, z. B. *to change – (sich) verändern, wechseln* oder auch *umsteigen*;
- die Wortstellung ist im Englischen oft ganz anders als im Deutschen, z. B. *In the evening we went to bed early, because we were tired.*
  Am Abend gingen wir früh ins Bett, weil wir müde waren.
- Redewendungen werden in der anderen Sprache häufig ganz anders ausgedrückt, z. B. *What's wrong with you? – Was fehlt dir?*
- Oft sind verschiedene Übersetzungen gleich gut: z. B. *Be careful! – Sei vorsichtig!/Pass auf!/Achtung!*

Unit 1 A trip to London

a) – How can we get to the Tower from here?
– We can go by underground. We must change at Victoria, and then take the Circle Line and get off at Tower Hill.
– Maybe we could go to the London Dungeon in the afternoon?
– Yes, I'd like to do that. It's only a short walk from the Tower. Or are you tired of walking?
– No, that's all right. I like walking.

b) *What's that in English?*
1. – Was machst du gern in deiner Freizeit?
– Ich lese gern. Und ich spiele gern Tischtennis.
– Schwimmst du auch gern?
– Nein, ich bin nicht so gut im Schwimmen!
2. – Sieh dir dieses Rezept an: 'Indisches Huhn mit Curry und Bananen'. Das hört sich gut an.
– Vielleicht schmeckt es auch gut.

Unit 2 Trouble at school

a) *Edward:* Does anyone want to see my photos?
David: Are they photos you took in India?
Edward: No, I just thought you'd like to see some pictures of the boarding school I went to. Look, this is a photo my father took at the end of term.
David: Gosh! Is that the uniform you had to wear? It looks even worse than ours! – Hey, and who's that girl?
Edward: That's a girl whose brother was in my tutor group. There weren't any girls at St John's.
David: No girls? What a strange school!

b) *Becky:* My purse is missing! What shall I do?
Edward: Don't worry. I'll pay for those crisps for you! Shall I buy you a drink, too?
Becky: Thanks! – Do you think Wayne could be the person who took my purse? You know what he's like!

c) *Jenny:* What are you doing tonight, Edward?
Edward: I'm not doing anything special.
Jenny: Well, perhaps you'd like to come to my house. Becky and Robert are coming, too. Robert's bringing the video of 'Romeo and Juliet'.
Edward: Yes, of course I'll come. Thanks!

d) *What's that in English?*
1. Hast du das Buch gelesen, das ich dir letzte Woche ausgeliehen habe?
2. Kennst du das Mädchen, das gerade mit Edward redet?
3. Ich mag gern Lehrer, die im Unterricht Witze erzählen.
4. Leute, die lügen, kann ich nicht ausstehen.

Unit 3 Welcome to Wales

a) – Good evening. Have you got two double rooms? We haven't booked.
– Just a moment. Ah yes, you are lucky. Someone has cancelled.
– Are the rooms next to each other?
– No, but they're both on the same floor. Here are the keys. The lift's over there.
– Thank you. ... We aren't too late for an evening meal, are we?
– No, of course not. The restaurant's open till half past nine.

b) – What's wrong? You don't look very happy today.
– I don't know what to do. I've lost Sam! Mrs Lee's dog! I told you about Mrs Lee, didn't I? She's visiting her sister in America, and I've been looking after Sam for a week now. I took him for a walk near the river yesterday, and suddenly he was gone!
– Cheer up! I'll help you to look for him.
– But I don't know where to look! I've been worrying about him all day and I've been everywhere now.

c) *What's that in English?*
1. Warum kommst du denn so spät? Ich warte schon seit 20 Minuten auf dich!
2. Wie lange wohnt ihr schon in Wales? – Seit Februar.
3. „Ein Wunder ist geschehen!" sagte Merlin. „Seit vielen Jahren träume ich von diesem Tag. Nun hat Arthur uns allen gezeigt, dass er unser wahrer König ist."

Unit 4 The environment

a) – This slow traffic is terrible. Maybe there's been an accident.
– No, look, we're coming to some roadworks.
– What on earth are they doing to the road this time? Only last year this part was made wider, and all those lovely old trees were cut down. Do you remember?
– Yes, I do! So many changes have been made in this area, I've almost forgotten what it was like when we moved here!

b) *How to help the environment:*

1. **Give up your car and go by public transport. If this isn't possible, only use the car when you really have to.**
2. **Save energy and don't have the heating on at night.**
3. **Don't get drinks in plastic bottles. Keep plastic bags – you can use them again.**
5. **Take old newspapers and magazines to a paper bank. If they are recycled, forests will be saved!**
6. **Eat fruit and vegetables that grow in your area. Remember how much energy is wasted when food is sent from one side of the world to the other!**

c) *What's that in English?*
1. Ich habe gerade eine interessante Nachricht gehört.
2. Einige Informationen sind falsch.
3. Jeden Tag wird Energie verschwendet. Neue Straßen werden gebaut. Die Umwelt wird verschmutzt, und unsere schöne Landschaft wird verändert. Wenn nichts getan wird, um die Situation zu verbessern, wird unsere Welt langsam zerstört.

Unit 5 Great Britain and the sea

a) *The Müllers see this article about themselves in the newspaper. Sven's parents aren't very good at English. But they want to know what the article says! How does Sven explain – in German of course – the parts they don't understand?*

Herr Müller: 'Was trapped …' Was heißt denn das?
Sven: …

LIFEBOATMEN SAVE GERMAN FAMILY

A German family of four was trapped at the west end of White Sands beach yesterday. In the morning they walked all the way to the other end of the beach, over Black Dog Rocks, when the tide was out. Five hours later their day out changed into a nightmare. The tide was coming in fast and the rocks were under water, so there was no way back. They saw at once how serious the situation was. At first they wondered whether to try to swim back, but the sea was too rough. When the waves came up higher over the beach, they bravely tried to climb the cliffs, but they are steep and dangerous in that area. Luckily for them, Mrs Ann Wood of Cliff Road was out with her dog on the coast path and heard the family's calls for help. When she saw they were in trouble, she called the coastguard and a lifeboat went out to rescue them.

"This is our first seaside holiday in England," said Sven Müller, 14. "We had no idea about the strong tides round the coast."

b) *What's that in German?*

1. If the weather's good, we'll go to the beach tomorrow.
2. If we lived close to the sea, we'd buy a boat.
3. I wouldn't swim in that pond if I were you!
4. The coast round Britain has to be looked after by coastguards.
5. When people are in trouble at sea, lifeboats have to be called out.

c) *What's that in English?*

1. Wenn der Sommer dieses Jahr schön ist, gehe ich jeden Tag schwimmen.
2. Wenn Peter mehr Freizeit hätte, hätte er nicht so viel Geld!
3. – Habt ihr keine Schwimmwesten?
   – Nein, aber der Wetterbericht ist gut. Es wird wohl nichts schiefgehen, wenn wir mit dem Boot rausfahren.
   – Das würde ich an eurer Stelle nicht tun!

⟨Extra line⟩

Grammar revision

Hallo, wenn du bisher mit *Orange Line New* gelernt hast, findest du auf den folgenden beiden Seiten ein paar Grammatikregeln, die du noch nicht kennst. Sieh sie dir am besten zum Schuljahresanfang an.

1 ‚Can/could' und die Ersatzform ‚be able to'
'Can/could' and the substitute form 'be able to'

Can ist wie *must* ein unvollständiges Hilfsverb, mit dem man nicht alle Zeiten bilden kann. Für die Zeitformen, die mit *can* oder *could* nicht gebildet werden können, nimmt man eine Form von *be able to*.

simple present	simple past	future
can	**could**	
David can play the guitar.	Last year he could only play easy songs.	
can't	**couldn't**	
I can't go to work today.	My grandpa couldn't play the piano.	
am/is/are able to	**was/were able to**	**will be able to**
Jenny is able to write in German and English.	Last summer her parents were able to visit her.	Next summer they'll be able to visit Berlin.
am not/isn't/aren't able to	**wasn't/weren't able to**	**won't be able to**
She isn't able to sing this song.	Yesterday I wasn't able to do my homework.	They won't be able to come. They're ill.

2 Adverbien der Art und Weise Adverbs of manner

adjective		adverb	
John is very **quiet.** John is a **quiet** boy.	… ist sehr ruhig. … ist ein ruhiger …	John speaks **quietly.**	… spricht ruhig.

- Adjektive geben an, wie eine Person oder Sache ist.
  What** is he **like**? – He is **quiet.
- Sie stehen vor einem Substantiv *(quiet boy)* oder nach dem Verb *to be (is quiet)*.

- Adverbien der Art und Weise *(adverbs of manner)* geben an, wie etwas geschieht.
  How** does he speak? – He speaks **quietly.
- Sie werden meistens aus Adjektiven gebildet, indem man *-ly* anhängt:
  quiet + ly *quietly*
- Sie stehen meistens am Satzende.

- Im Deutschen haben Adjektive und Adverbien die gleiche Form.

- **Besondere Formen**

adjective	**adverb**
good	well
fast	fast
hard	hard

- **Beachte beim Schreiben:**

adjective		**adverb**
careful	→	careful**ly**
hungry	→	hungr**ily**
terrible	→	terrib**ly**

3 Die Steigerung des Adverbs The comparison of adverbs of manner

Die Steigerung dieser Adverbien wird nach den gleichen Regeln gebildet wie die Steigerung der Adjektive.

My brother plays the guitar **beautifully.**	… spielt schön.
My father can play it **more beautifully.**	… spielt schöner.
But my mother plays it **most beautifully.**	… spielt am schönsten.

- Adverbien mit der Endung *-ly* werden, so wie mehrsilbige Adjektive, mit *more* und *most* gesteigert.

I work **hard.**
My friend works **harder.**
But my dad works **hardest.**

- Einsilbige Adverbien werden wie die einsilbigen Adjektive mit *-er* und *-est* gesteigert.

Wie bei den Adjektiven gibt es bei den Adverbien zwei unregelmäßige Formen. Nur die Grundformen sind unterschiedlich, die Steigerungsformen sind gleich:

Adjektiv	good	better	best
Adverb	well	better	best

Adjektiv	bad	worse	worst
Adverb	badly	worse	worst

4 Vergleiche mit Adverbien Comparisons with adverbs

Wie bei den Adjektiven gibt es bei den Adverbien drei verschiedene Möglichkeiten, Gleichheit oder Ungleichheit auszudrücken.

Gleichheit	as … as	My mother works **as hard as** my father. Mark can do puzzles **as quickly as** Becky.
Ungleichheit	… than …	Sarah plays cards **more cleverly than** Robert. My brother can run **faster than** everyone else.
	not as … as	Robert ca**n't** play cards **as cleverly as** Sarah. I **can't** run **as fast as** my brother.

Grammar

Hallo,

hier ist die Grammatik noch einmal zusammengefasst.
Die Regeln helfen dir nachzuschlagen, wenn du dir mal nicht ganz sicher bist.
Außerdem helfen sie dir bei den Hausaufgaben und zur Vorbereitung auf Klassenarbeiten.
In der Übersicht auf Seite 116 findest du eine alphabetische Grammatikliste mit den deutschen und englischen Begriffen und Beispielen zu jeder Regel.

Manchmal kann man Grammatik besser lernen, wenn man sich Hilfen bastelt, z. B. ein großes Poster mit Merkregeln oder Zeichnungen macht. Das kann man dann zu Hause oder im Klassenzimmer aufhängen.

Workshop A | 1

§ 1 Verben mit Objekt + Ergänzung
Verbs with object + complement

	verb	**object + complement**	
My name is Thomas. You can	call	me	Tom.
Take this map. You'll	find	it	useful.
Don't laugh at Dad's French. You'll	make	him	angry.

- Manche Verben haben neben ihrer normalen auch eine weitere Bedeutung:

to call	(= rufen)	*Please*	***call***	***the police.***	
	(= nennen)	*You can*	***call***	***me***	*Tom.*

In der weiteren Bedeutung braucht das Objekt noch eine Ergänzung.
Diese Ergänzung kann ein Substantiv oder ein Adjektiv sein.

Unit 1 Step B

§ 2 Das Gerundium The gerund

Sieh dir mal die folgenden Sätze an: Tom likes **books.**
Tom likes **reading.**

Du siehst, dass statt des Substantivs *(books)* nach dem Verb eine *ing*-Form *(reading)* stehen kann. Diese *ing*-Form heißt im Englischen *gerund.*
Die Form wird gebildet aus einem Verb + *ing:* read + *ing* = *reading.*
Das *gerund* kann sowohl Subjekt als auch Objekt eines Satzes sein.

1 Das Gerundium als Subjekt The gerund as subject

subject		
Dancing	can be	great.
Swimming	is	my favourite sport.
Playing football	can be	fun.
Going to the cinema	is	exciting.

- Das *gerund* hat ähnliche Eigenschaften wie ein Substantiv. Deshalb kann es auch Subjekt eines Satzes sein. Es kann
  - allein stehen **(dancing, swimming)**
  - mit einem weiteren Substantiv stehen (**playing** *football*)
  - mit einer adverbialen Bestimmung stehen (**going** *to the cinema*)

2 Das Gerundium als Objekt The gerund as object

			object
	I	enjoy	**reading.**
	What do you	like	**doing** at weekends?
	We	love	**playing** games.
	My friend	doesn't like	**running.**
	She	hates	**working** in the garden.
	I	can't stand	**doing** homework.

Das *gerund* als Objekt steht sehr oft nach Verben der Vorliebe *(enjoy, like, love)* oder der Abneigung *(not like, hate, can't stand)*.

Das *gerund* darf nicht mit der *progressive form* (*be + verb + ing*) verwechselt werden:

He is watching TV. = Er sieht gerade fern.
He likes watching TV. = Er sieht gern fern.

§3 Das Gerundium nach Adjektiv + Präposition
The gerund after adjective + preposition

	adjective + prep.		gerund	
I'm	interested	in	**looking** at museums.	Ich interessiere mich für Museen.
She's	good	at	**reading** maps.	Sie ist gut im Kartenlesen.
He isn't	good	at	**taking** photos.	Er kann nicht gut fotografieren.
I'm	tired	of	**standing** in queues.	Ich bin es leid Schlange zu stehen.

- Es gibt Adjektive, die immer mit einer bestimmten Präposition benutzt werden (z. B. *interested in* etc.). Sie bilden eine feste Einheit, die man sich als Paar einprägen muss. Nach solchen Paaren (adj. + prep.) folgt immer das *gerund* oder ein Substantiv:
  Vergleiche: *She's good at reading maps.*
  She's good at Geography.

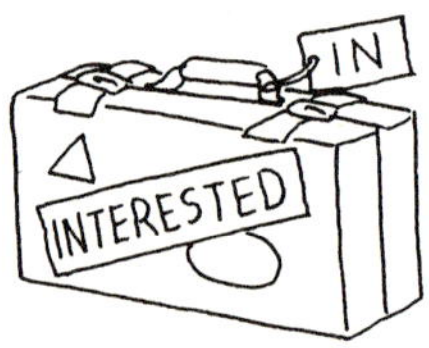

Vielleicht kannst du selbst eine kleine Zeichnung machen, die dir beim Lernen hilft.

§4 Das Adjektiv nach bestimmten Verben
Adjectives after certain verbs

Something to eat? That	**sounds**	great.
This soup	**looks**	nice
and it	**smells**	good.
I really	**feel**	hungry.
Oh, it	**tastes**	wonderful.

- Wenn die Verben *sound, look, smell, feel, taste* den Klang, das Aussehen, den Geruch, das Gefühl, den Geschmack von etwas beschreiben (Verben der Wahrnehmung), dann folgt ihnen ein **Adjektiv** und kein Adverb.
- Auch das Wort *seem* verhält sich wie die Verben der Wahrnehmung, weil es immer eine persönliche Wahrnehmung ausdrückt: *This idea **seems** great.*

Beachte den Unterschied:

Sinneswahrnehmung + Adjektiv	**Tätigkeit + Adverb**
The cyclist looked angry.	The cyclist looked angrily at Christoph.
Der Radfahrer **sah** ärgerlich **aus.**	Der Radfahrer **sah** Christoph ärgerlich **an.**

Workshop B 4

§ 5 Reflexivpronomen
Reflexive pronouns

Die Formen der Reflexivpronomen lauten:

singular	myself	yourself	himself herself itself
plural	ourselves	yourselves	themselves

1. Verstärkender Gebrauch

You needn't help me. I can easily do it	**myself.**
Darren can repair his bike	**himself.**
The Penroses painted their house	**themselves.**

- Mit dem Reflexivpronomen kann man eine Person besonders hervorheben. Das Pronomen entspricht dann dem deutschen ‚selbst/allein'.

2. Reflexiver Gebrauch

Have you hurt	**yourself?**	
She often talks to	**herself.**	
Why do budgies always look at	**themselves**	in the mirror?

- Das Reflexivpronomen kann Objekt im Satz sein und sich reflexiv (rückbezüglich) auf das Subjekt beziehen. In diesem Fall entspricht es den deutschen Pronomen ‚mich/mir, dich/dir, sich' usw.

Das Reflexivpronomen wird im Englischen wesentlich seltener gebraucht als im Deutschen. Viele Verben, die im Deutschen reflexiv sind, sind im Englischen nicht reflexiv.

Vergleiche: She has changed a lot. Sie hat sich sehr verändert.

to change	sich (ver)ändern
to concentrate	sich konzentrieren
to feel	sich fühlen
to happen	sich ereignen
to hurry	sich beeilen
to meet	sich treffen
to remember	sich erinnern
to sit down	sich (hin)setzen

§ 6 Das reziproke Pronomen ‚each other'
The reciprocal pronoun 'each other'

Monny and Monna love **each other.**	… sich …
They often talk to **each other.**	… miteinander …
They often help **each other.**	… sich (gegenseitig) …

- Das reziproke Pronomen *each other* drückt aus, dass zwischen Personen eine wechselseitige Beziehung besteht.

Im Deutschen wird es meist mit ‚sich / einander / gegenseitig' wiedergegeben.
Statt *each other* kann man auch *one another* verwenden, besonders wenn es sich um mehr als zwei Personen handelt: *David, Robert and Sarah know one another well.*

He is looking at ***her.***

They are looking at ***themselves.***

They are looking at ***each other.***

Unit 2 Step B

§ 7 Bestimmende Relativsätze   Defining relative clauses

Ein bestimmender Relativsatz (auch: „Einschränkender Relativsatz") ist manchmal notwendig um einen Hauptsatz verständlich zu machen. Es gibt zwei Arten von bestimmenden Relativsätzen:

1 Bestimmende Relativsätze ohne Relativpronomen   Contact clauses

Vergleiche:

	bestimmender Relativsatz	
Oh, that's the pullover.		Hier ist unklar, welcher Pullover gemeint ist.
Oh, that's the pullover	you got for your birthday.	Nun ist klar, welcher Pullover gemeint ist.

- Wenn man den zweiten Satz ins Deutsche übersetzt, benutzt man ein Relativpronomen (… der Pullover, **den** …). Im Englischen braucht man kein Relativpronomen, wenn ein neues Subjekt (hier: *you*) im Relativsatz folgt. Solche Sätze nennt man *contact clauses.*
- *Contact clauses* sind vor allem in der Umgangssprache sehr gebräuchlich.
- Anders als im Deutschen schreibt man kein Komma zwischen Hauptsatz und Relativsatz, und beim Sprechen macht man auch keine Pause dazwischen.
- Beachte die Stellung von Verb und Präposition:
  The house we **live in** … (Das Haus, in dem wir wohnen, …)

2 Bestimmende Relativsätze mit Relativpronomen
Defining relative clauses with relative pronouns

Vergleiche den zweiten Satz mit dem *contact clause.*

Oh, that's the pullover		you got for your birthday.
Oh, that's the pullover	**which**	was your birthday present.

Die Relativpronomen *who, which, that* können Subjekt oder Objekt des Relativsatzes sein. Ist das Relativpronomen Objekt des Relativsatzes, wird es in der Regel ausgelassen (siehe *contact clauses*). Man kann es jedoch auch hier benutzen:
Oh, that's the pullover ***which*** *you got for your birthday.*
Als Subjekt im Relativsatz sind die Relativpronomen aber unbedingt notwendig:

Mrs Benson was the teacher	**who/that**	saw the graffiti first.	... die Lehrerin, die ...
A dictionary is a book	**which/that**	explains words.	... ein Buch, das ...
Where are the magazines	**which/that**	were on my desk?	... die Zeitschriften, die ...

- *Who* bezieht sich nur auf Personen.
- *Which* bezieht sich nur auf Dinge.
- *That* bezieht sich auf Personen oder Dinge.
- *Whom* ist ein weiteres Relativpronomen, das als Objekt im Relativsatz stehen kann. Es wird meistens in der Schriftsprache benutzt, ist aber kaum noch gebräuchlich. Statt dessen benutzt man einen *contact clause* oder gebraucht *who.*
  Is he the boy you got the present from?
  Is he the boy who you got the present from? } Ist das der Junge, von dem du das ... ?
  Is he the boy from whom you got the present?

§ 8 whose

Relativsätze können auch durch das Relativpronomen *whose* + Substantiv eingeleitet werden.

What's the name of the boy	**whose**	**bike you repaired?**	**... dessen Fahrrad ...**
Those are the people	**whose**	**dog** always barks at me.	... deren Hund ...
We found a poor cat	**whose**	**leg** was broken.	... deren Bein ...

- *whose* wird meistens für Personen oder Tiere gebraucht und drückt Besitz oder Zugehörigkeit aus.

§ 9 Das present progressive zur Wiedergabe der Zukunft
The present progressive with a future meaning

- What **are** you **doing** tomorrow, Robert?
- **I'm meeting** Jenny in the evening.
- And on Tuesday?
- **I'm playing** tennis with Edward.
  Uncle Arthur **is coming** on Wednesday.
  But on Thursday **I'm** not **doing** anything special.

- Neben dem *will-future* und dem *going-to-future* kann man auch das *present progressive* verwenden um zukünftige Handlungen auszudrücken.
- Das *present progressive* betont, dass etwas für die Zukunft fest geplant oder vereinbart ist.
- Damit es keine Verwechslungen mit gegenwärtigen Handlungen gibt, werden oft Zeitbestimmungen der Zukunft verwendet wie: *tomorrow, next week, on Tuesday, ...*

I'm helping Robert with his homework.	Ich helfe ihm gerade ...
I'm helping Robert with his homework tomorrow.	Ich helfe ihm morgen ... (es ist vereinbart.)

§ 10 Shall I? Shall we?

It's very hot in here. **Shall I** open the window?	Soll ich …?
The weather's lovely today. **Shall we** go for a bike ride?	Sollen wir …?
Where **shall we** go?	Wohin sollen wir …?

- Mit *Shall I …?* oder *Shall we …?* kann man einen Vorschlag machen oder den Wunsch eines Gesprächspartners erfragen.

§ 11 Will you?

Will you	open the window, please?	Öffnest du bitte …?
Will you	pass me the sugar, please?	Reichst du mir bitte …?
Will you	please be quiet? I can't hear anything.	Sei/Seid bitte ruhig. …

- Mit *will you … (please)…* kann man einen Wunsch oder eine Bitte aussprechen.
- Wenn man noch höflicher sein möchte, kann man auch *would you …* verwenden:
  ***Would you** help me to carry these things, please?*

Unit 3 Step B

§ 12 Die Verlaufsform des present perfect The present perfect progressive

past	present	future
It began to rain at two o'clock. 	Now it's five o'clock. It's still raining. 	?

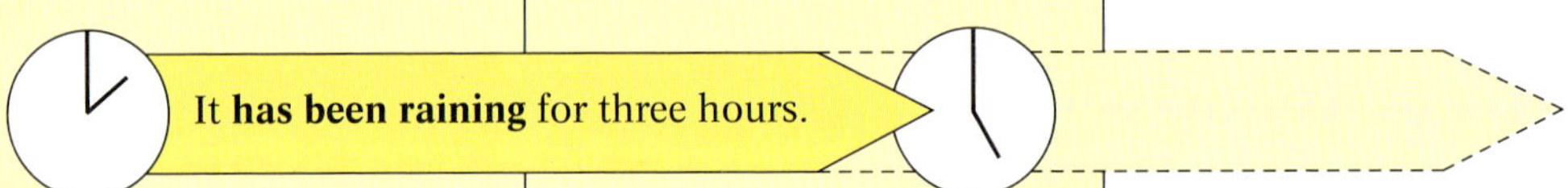

- Das *present perfect progressive* wird gebildet aus *have been/has been* und der *-ing*-Form:
  I/you/we/they have been waiting…
  He/she/it has been waiting…
- Mit dem *present perfect progressive* kann man etwas beschreiben, das in der Vergangenheit anfing und noch nicht beendet ist.
- Im Deutschen benutzen wir meist das Präsens und betonen die Dauer des Vorgangs mit **„schon":**
  It has been raining for hours.
  Es regnet **schon** stundenlang.

‚for' und ‚since'

For und *since* werden häufig mit dem *present perfect progressive* verwendet.

How long?

The Pritchards **have been living** in North Wales **for a few months.**	… wohnen (schon) seit einigen Monaten …
Gwen **has been learning** Welsh **for three years.**	… lernt (schon) seit drei Jahren …

Since when?

Mr Pritchard **has been working** at the Snowdon Hotel **since September.**	… arbeitet (schon) seit September …
Gwen and Hugh **have been watching** TV **since they came home from school.**	… sehen schon fern, seit sie nach Hause gekommen sind.

- ***For*** bezieht sich auf den **Zeitraum**, den eine Handlung bereits andauert:
  for two hours, a long time, years, twenty minutes, …
- ***Since*** bezieht sich auf den **Zeitpunkt**, an dem die Handlung begann:
  since three o'clock, last week, I was little, 1996, May, …

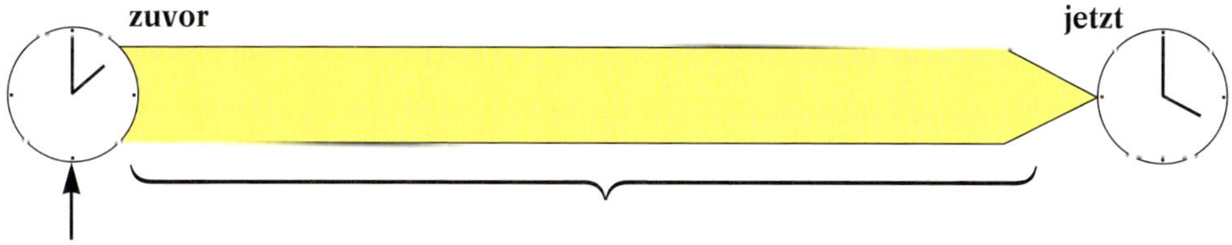

since two o'clock
seit 2 Uhr
|
Zeit**punkt** des Beginns

for two hours
seit 2 Stunden
|
Zeit**raum**

Ich wohne hier seit einem Jahr (= ein Jahr lang).
I've been living here for a year.

§ 13 Der Infinitiv nach Fragewörtern
The infinitive after question words

... where to buy ... – ... wo ich ... kaufen kann.
... how to get back ... – ... wie ich zurückkommen soll.
... when to be ... – ... wann ich ... sein muss.

- Fragewörter wie *where, what, which* usw. + Infinitiv mit *to* werden oft nach den Verben *know, tell, wonder, remember* usw. verwendet.
- Dies gilt auch für das indirekte Fragewort *whether,* das man mit „ob" übersetzt:
  *I don't know **whether to** go or to stay.* – Ich weiß nicht, **ob** ich gehen oder bleiben soll.
- Der Infinitiv mit *to* kann anstelle von indirekten Fragen mit *can, must* oder *should* gebraucht werden. Vergleiche:

We aren't sure whether	*we should go*	*by car or by train.*	Wir sind nicht sicher, ob wir ...
We aren't sure whether	*to go*	*by car or by train.*	

§ 14 Bestätigungsfragen Question tags

Wenn man im Deutschen eine Bestätigung oder Zustimmung zu einer Aussage erwartet, verwendet man Ausdrücke wie „nicht wahr?/nicht?/oder?". Im Englischen hängt man in solchen Fällen ein *question tag* an den Aussagesatz an.

⊕ **Bejahter Aussagesatz**	⊖	⊖ **Verneinter Aussagesatz**	⊕
Gwen **can** speak Welsh,	can't she?	Mrs Pritchard **can't** speak German,	can she?
She**'s** got a French penfriend,	hasn't she?	She **hasn't** got a German penfriend,	has she?
Hugh **is** doing his homework,	isn't he?	He **isn't** watching TV,	is he?
The Pritchards **live** in Wales,	don't they?	They **don't** live in England,	do they?
They **moved** there last year,	didn't they?	At first they **didn't** like it there,	did they?
Hugh **plays** rugby at school,	doesn't he?	But he **doesn't** play tennis,	does he?

- Die Bestätigungsfrage greift das Hilfsverb und das Subjekt des Aussagesatzes wieder auf. Das Subjekt erscheint immer als Personalpronomen.
- Wenn es im Aussagesatz kein Hilfsverb gibt, wird das Vollverb in der Bestätigungsfrage durch *do/does* oder *did* ersetzt.
- Ist der Aussagesatz bejaht, so ist die Bestätigungsfrage verneint.
  Ist der Aussagesatz verneint, so ist die Bestätigungsfrage bejaht.

Die Intonation (Satzmelodie) in Bestätigungsfragen

Hugh can't play on Saturday, **can he?** – Of course he can.	It's a lovely day today, **isn't it?**
The Pritchards come from Nottingham, **don't they?** – No, they don't. They come from South Wales.	Her new haircut doesn't look very good, **does it?**

- Man spricht Bestätigungsfragen mit steigender Satzmelodie, wenn man nicht ganz sicher ist, ob die Aussage stimmt und man vom Gesprächspartner Zustimmung oder Ablehnung erwartet.
- Man spricht mit fallender Satzmelodie, wenn man eine Meinung äußern will. Man erwartet in diesem Fall Zustimmung.

Unit 4 Step B

§ 15 Aktiv und Passiv
Active voice and passive voice

Passivsätze stellen eine Handlung aus anderer Sicht dar. Sie betonen, **was** gemacht wird. So steht die Handlung selbst im Mittelpunkt. In Aktivsätzen hingegen wird betont, **wer** etwas macht. Man benutzt Passivsätze vor allem dann, wenn man nicht genau weiß, wer die Handlung ausgeführt hat, oder wenn es unwichtig ist.

active voice	passive voice
An **ambulance** took the man to hospital.	The man **was taken** to hospital.

- In diesem Satz ist *ambulance* **Subjekt** und steht damit im Vordergrund.
- In diesem Satz liegt die Betonung auf der **Handlung.** Wer den Mann ins Krankenhaus bringt, ist unwichtig.

a) Simple present passive

When a road **is built**, fields **are destroyed.** — **am/is/are + past participle**

b) Simple past passive

Last year a service station **was built** at Greendale. — **was/were + past participle**

c) Present perfect passive

Look, the road **has been changed** here.
But the roundabout **hasn't been moved.**

d) Future passive

Next year the new car park **will be opened.**
Then the old one **won't be needed** any more.

Das *present perfect passive* wird mit *have/has been + past participle* gebildet.
Das *future passive* wird mit *will be + past participle* gebildet.

- Passivsätze kann man nur mit transitiven Verben bilden, also Verben, die ein Objekt haben, z. B. *to open (a door), to cut down (a tree), to destroy (the countryside), etc.*
  Intransitive Verben können kein Objekt haben und deshalb nicht im Passiv stehen:
  The train arrives at 12.55.

§ 16 Passivsätze mit by-agent
Passive sentences with by-agent

Auch im Passivsatz kann man den Verursacher einer Handlung mit Hilfe des *by-agent* nennen:

	by-agent
In England the milk is brought	by the milkman.
Yesterday our car was hit	by a van.
Every morning I am woken up	by my cat.

- Wenn man also im Passiv betonen will, **wer** etwas getan hat, muss man einen *by-agent* verwenden.
- Das Objekt des Aktivsatzes wird zum Subjekt des Passivsatzes.
- Das Subjekt des Aktivsatzes erscheint als *by-agent* im Passivsatz.
  Vergleiche:

	subject		**object**
active voice	*The milkman*	*brings*	*the milk.*
passive voice	*The milk*	*is brought*	*by the milkman.*
	subject		**by-agent**

Unit 5 Step B

§ 17 Bedingungssätze
Conditional sentences

Der Bedingungssatz besteht aus einem *if*-Satz und einem Hauptsatz:

If people pollute the sea, a lot of birds will die.

Bedingungssatz Typ II

if-Satz: **past tense**	Hauptsatz: **would + infinitive** (= *conditional*)
If the rig **wasn't** strong enough,	it **would break** like a toy in this rough sea.
If Pete **had** a job on land,	he **would see** his family more often.
If he **didn't work** so hard,	he **wouldn't get** so much money.
If the sea **was** always calm,	his job **wouldn't be** so dangerous.

- Das *past tense* im *if*-Satz drückt aus, dass es unwahrscheinlich oder sogar unmöglich ist, die Bedingung zu erfüllen.
- Im Hauptsatz steht das Konditional: *would + infinitive*.
- Obwohl das *past tense* von *I am* eigentlich *I was* heißt, wird im if-Satz sehr oft *I were* verwendet:
  *If **I were** a good tennis player, I would make a lot of money.*
- Bedingungssätze können entweder mit dem *if*-Satz oder dem Hauptsatz beginnen:
  If I spent a week in London, I would go and see the Tower.
  I would go and see the Tower if I spent a week in London.
- Im Deutschen verwendet man für die Übersetzung des *if*-Satzes den Konjunktiv:
  Wenn ich eine Woche in London verbrächte/verbringen würde, ...
  Im Englischen wird *would* im *if*-Satz in der Regel aber nicht gebraucht.

§ 18 Das Passiv bei Verben mit Präpositionen
The passive of verbs with prepositions

active voice	Hundreds of lifeboats **look after** the coast all round Britain.
passive voice	The coast all round Britain **is looked after** by hundreds of lifeboats.

- Verb und Präposition gehören im Englischen so eng zusammen, dass sie auch im Passivsatz nicht getrennt werden.

§ 19 Der Infinitiv des Passivs
The passive infinitive

active voice			**passive voice**		
	modal	infinitive		modal	passive infinitive
You	can	use the radio.	The radio	can	be used.
You	must	check the lifejackets.	The lifejackets	must	be checked.
You	should	carry enough petrol.	Enough petrol	should	be carried.

- Wie du weißt, steht im Aktivsatz nach Hilfsverben der Infinitiv *(use, check, carry)*. Im Passivsatz steht der *passive infinitive (be used, be checked, be carried)*.
- Der *passive infinitive* ist sehr nützlich, wenn man Empfehlungen geben oder Regeln aufstellen möchte. Man kann ihn auch negativ gebrauchen:
*"Would" should **not** be used in if-clauses!*

ORANGE GREEN

Übungen zu den Adverbien

1 How do they do it? *Put in the adverbs. (see p. 100 [2])*

1. Dad has got a headache, so Mark must play … .
2. David ran to school very … but he still arrived late.
3. Becky's clothes are usually on the floor, but today she is putting them … in the cupboard.
4. Simon heard a strange noise outside. He opened the back door … .
5. Robert laughed … at Sarah's new joke.
6. Maxi is looking … at the meat on the kitchen table.

hungry nervous tidy fast quiet loud

2 David and Robert *Adjective or adverb?*

1. David likes … music. He often plays his guitar … . (loud) 2. Then his mum is … . She shouts … , (angry) 3. "Can't you play that thing …? It's never … in this house!" (quiet) 4. David can draw … . His dad has put his most … pictures up in the living-room. (beautiful) 5. Sarah loves … jokes. And she can tell jokes …, too. (good) 6. She isn't usually a … worker, but sometimes she does her homework very … . (fast)

Übersicht: Die Zeiten The tenses

1. Active

tense	positive statements	negative statements/questions
simple present	I call She call**s**/he write**s**	She doesn't call **Do** you call? **Does** he write?
simple past	I call**ed**/he **wrote**	I **didn't** call/write **Did** you call/write?

- Beachte das -s in der 3. Person Singular des *simple present*!
- Fragen und verneinte Aussagen werden im *simple present* und im *simple past* mit einer Form von *to do* gebildet.

will-future	**I'll** (will) call	She **won't** (will not) call **Will** you call?
conditional	**I'd** (would) call	She **wouldn't** call **Would** they call?
present perfect	**I've** (have) call**ed** She**'s** (has) **written**	You **haven't called** **Has** she written?

- Alle übrigen Zeiten werden mit einem Hilfsverb gebildet. Eine Form von *to do* darf hier nicht gebraucht werden.
- Dem Hilfsverb folgt je nach Zeit eine bestimmte Verbform:
nach *will/would* steht der Infinitiv; nach *have/had* folgt das *past participle* (*infinitive* + *(e)d* oder eine unregelmäßige Form).

present progressive	I **am** call**ing**
past progressive	I **was** call**ing**
present perfect progressive	I **have been** call**ing**

- Die Verlaufsformen werden mit einer Form von *to be* und dem *present participle* (*infinitive* + *ing*) gebildet.

2. Passive

(simple) present passive	I am called/told
(simple) past passive	I was called/told
future passive	I will be called/told
present perfect passive	I have been called/told

- Das Passiv wird mit einer Form von *to be* und dem *past participle* (*infinitive* + *ed* oder eine unregelmäßige Form) gebildet.

Grammar list

German	English	§
Adjektive nach bestimmten Verben	adjectives after certain verbs	4
This soup smells good and tastes wonderful.		
Adverbien der Art und Weise	adverbs of manner	**R2**, R3, R4
John speaks quietly.		
Steigerung des Adverbs der Art und Weise	comparison of adverbs of manner	R3
Bob speaks more quietly, but my sister speaks most quietly.		
Vergleiche mit Adverbien	comparisons with adverbs	R4
Peter speaks German as well as John, better than Sarah, but not as well as Mr Cooper.		
Bedingungssätze	conditional sentences	17
If she didn't work so hard, she wouldn't get so much money.		
Bestätigungsfragen	question tags	14
You live in London, don't you?		
***Can**/could* und die Ersatzform *be able to*	*can/could* and the substitute form *be able to*	R1
Dan can play the guitar. Last year he could only play easy songs. Soon he'll be able to play in a band.		
Gerundium	gerund	**2**, 3
Dancing can be great, but I also enjoy reading a book.		
Gerundium nach Adjektiv und Präposition	gerund after adjective and preposition	3
I'm good at taking photos.		
Infinitiv nach Fragewörtern	infinitive after question words	13
I wonder how to get back to my hotel.		
Aktiv und **Passiv**	active voice and passive voice	**15**, 16, 18, 19
The man was taken to hospital.		
Passivsätze mit *by-agent*	passive sentences with *by-agent*	16
In England the milk is brought by the milkman.		
Passiv bei Verben mit Präpositionen	passive of verbs with prepositions	18
The coast all round Britain is looked after by thousands of lifeboats.		
Infinitiv des Passivs	passive infinitive	19
The computer can be used easily.		

German	English	§
Verlaufsform des **present perfect**	present perfect progressive	12
He has been living in Wales for three years/since 1994.		
Present progressive zur Wiedergabe der Zukunft	present progressive with a future meaning	9
What are you doing tonight, Jane? – I'm going to the cinema with Bob.		
Reziprokes **Pronomen** *each other*	reciprocal pronoun each other	6
Susan and Sarah like each other. They talk to each other a lot.		
Reflexivpronomen	reflexive pronouns	5
myself, yourself, himself, herself, itself, ourselves, yourselves, themselves		
Bestimmende **Relativsätze mit Relativpronomen**	defining relative clauses with relative pronoun	**7**, 8
That's the teacher who saw the graffiti. Where are the books which were on my desk?		
Bestimmende **Relativsätze ohne Relativpronomen**	*Contact clauses*	**7**
That's the pullover you got for your birthday.		
Relativpronomen *whose*	relative pronoun *whose*	8
I saw a man whose dog only had three legs.		
Shall	*Shall*	10
Shall I open the window?/Shall we go to the concert?		
Verben mit Objekt + Ergänzung	verbs with object + complement	1
My name is Thomas. You can call me Tom.		
Verlaufsform des present perfect	present perfect progressive	12
He has been living in Wales for three years/since 1994.		
***Will* you?**	*Will you?*	11
Will you pass me the sugar, please?		

Vocabulary

Englische Lautschrift

Vokale

[ɑː] car, father
[ʌ] number, bus, mother
[e] yes, pen, friend
[ə] a sister
[ɜː] girl, her, turn
[æ] bag, cat, that
[ɪ] it, a bit, six
[iː] she, see, please
[ɒ] on, dog, what
[ɔː] door, four, morning
[ʊ] put, look
[uː] you, two, blue

Konsonanten

[j] yes, you
[l] let's, blue, school
[ŋ] morning, sing
[ŋg] English
[r] radio, red
[s] see, sister, class
[z] is, dogs, cars
[ʒ] television
[dʒ] German, Jenny
[ʃ] she, fish
[tʃ] teacher, child
[ð] the, this, mother
[θ] thank you, thing
[v] vet, of
[w] one, what, sandwich

Doppellaute

[aɪ] nice, five, bye
[aʊ] now, pound
[eə] there, chair, their
[eɪ] name, say, table
[ɪə] here, clear
[ɔɪ] boy
[əʊ] no, go, show
[ʊə] you're

[ː] bedeutet, dass der vorangehende Laut lang ist, z. B. blue [bluː]

[ˈ] bedeutet, dass auf der folgenden Silbe die Hauptbetonung liegt, z. B. hello [həˈləʊ]

[ˌ] bedeutet, dass auf der folgenden Silbe die Nebenbetonung liegt, z. B. washing up [ˌwɒʃɪŋ‿ˈʌp]

[‿] zwischen zwei Wörtern bedeutet, dass man den letzten Laut des ersten Wortes zum nächsten Wort hinüberzieht, z. B. come on [kʌm‿ˈɒn]

a) Aufbau des Vokabulars

Das Vokabular ist genau wie in deinem Buch vom letzten Schuljahr aufgebaut:
In der linken Spalte findest du die englischen Wörter in der Reihenfolge, in der sie in der *Unit* vorkommen. Dahinter steht die Lautschrift in eckigen Klammern. Wie du die Lautschrift lesen musst, steht oben auf dieser Seite.

In der mittleren Spalte stehen Beispielsätze oder kleine Zeichnungen sowie wichtige Hinweise, die dir beim Lernen helfen.

In der rechten Spalte findest du eine deutsche Übersetzung des englischen Wortes. Vergiss aber nicht, dass sich Wörter aus einer Sprache nicht einfach in die andere übersetzen lassen. Deshalb werden manchmal mehrere deutsche Übersetzungsmöglichkeiten angeboten.
Wie im Buch vom Vorjahr findest du Tipps zum Vokabellernen in den Kästchen vor den ersten *Units* und *Workshops*. Außerdem findest du *vocabulary boxes*, die Wörter und Wendungen wiederholen und zusammenfassen. Du lernst sie am besten in Gruppen.

b) Abkürzungen und Zeichen

(pl) Plural, Mehrzahl
(sg) Singular, Einzahl
(s.th.) something
(s.o.) someone, somebody
(s.b.) somebody

= ist gleich
⟷ ist das Gegenteil von
→ siehe auch

° Bei Wörtern mit diesem Zeichen frag bitte deine Lehrerin oder deinen Lehrer, ob du sie lernen musst. (Erläuterungen hierzu finden sich auf Seite 156.)

Vocabulary

In den ersten zwei Bänden hast du schon einige Vokabellerntipps kennengelernt, die dir auch in diesem Schuljahr eine Hilfe beim Wörterlernen sein können.

Also, denk daran:

- **Kleine Lernportionen** von 10–15 Wörtern lernen sich am besten, wenn du dir diese Portionen **mehrmals am Tag** zwischen anderen Aufgaben vornimmst und sie **nur jeweils 5–10 Minuten** „bearbeitest".
- Die **Vokabelkartei** hilft dir dabei, die schwer zu lernenden Wörter herauszufinden und gezielt zu wiederholen. Genauso können **Lernplakate** mit „schwierigen Fällen" dich beim Hinsehen immer wieder daran erinnern.
- Versuche, für jedes neue Wort **Zusammenhänge** herzustellen, die das Erinnern erleichtern.
- Falls du jetzt anfängst weitere Sprachen zu lernen, solltest du versuchen, Verwechslungen zwischen den Sprachen zu vermeiden. **Halte sie auseinander!** Also erst die neuen Englisch-Vokabeln, dann die Mathematik-Hausaufgaben und dann erst die neuen Wörter für Französisch oder Latein lernen. Und dazwischen sind auch die **Lernpausen** wichtig.

Workshop A Let's Talk

ORANGE GREEN

Graue Boxen wird es vor jeder neuen Unit geben. Wenn du früher mit Orange Line New gearbeitet hast, kennst du diese Vokabeln noch nicht und solltest sie vor Beginn der Unit lernen. Ansonsten kannst du die graue Box zur Wiederholung nutzen.

address [ə'dres]	Adresse	**long** [lɒŋ]	lang
alone [ə'ləʊn]	allein	**lovely** ['lʌvlɪ]	schön, herrlich
to answer ['ɑːnsə]	antworten	**to mind** [maɪnd]	jdm. etwas ausmachen
brochure ['brəʊʃə]	Broschüre	**moment** ['məʊmənt]	Moment
conjunction [kən'dʒʌŋkʃn]	Konjunktion	**the Netherlands** [ðə 'neðələndz]	die Niederlande
country ['kʌntrɪ]	Land	**to make notes** [ˌmeɪk 'nəʊts]	sich Notizen machen
else [els]	sonst (noch)	**to take notes** [ˌteɪk 'nəʊts]	sich Notizen machen
everywhere ['evrɪweə]	überall	**pocket** ['pɒkɪt]	Tasche (bei Kleidung)
to fall [fɔːl]	fallen	**Poland** ['pəʊlənd]	Polen
famous ['feɪməs]	berühmt	**side** [saɪd]	Seite
high [haɪ]	hoch	**situation** [sɪtjʊ'eɪʃn]	Situation
like [laɪk]	wie	**sound** [saʊnd]	Klang, Geräusch
travel agent's ['trævl ˌeɪdʒənts]	Reisebüro	**to be surprised** [sə'praɪzd]	überrascht sein
home [həʊm]	nach Hause	**text** [tekst]	Text
lake [leɪk]	See		
to let [let]	lassen		
list [lɪst]	Liste		

Vocabulary

Part 1: **New friends**

Around the world

People in	speak	I like
America [ə'merɪkə]	**English**. ['ɪŋglɪʃ]	**American films**. [ə'merɪkən]
Australia [ɒ'streɪljə]	**English**. ['ɪŋglɪʃ]	**Australian jokes**. [ɒ'streɪljən]
Austria ['ɒstrɪə]	**German**. ['dʒɜ:mən]	**Austrian sweets**.
Belgium ['beldʒəm]	**French and Dutch**. [frentʃ, dʌtʃ]	**Belgian chocolate**. ['beldʒən]
Britain ['brɪtn]	**English**. ['ɪŋglɪʃ]	**British weather**. ['brɪtɪʃ]
China ['tʃaɪnə]	**Chinese**. [ˌtʃaɪ'ni:z]	**Chinese meals**.
Denmark ['denmɑ:k]	**Danish**. ['deɪnɪʃ]	**Danish ham**.
England ['ɪŋglənd]	**English**. ['ɪŋglɪʃ]	**English lessons**.
France [frɑ:ns]	**French**. [frentʃ]	**French bread**.
Germany ['dʒɜ:mənɪ]	**German**. ['dʒɜ:mən]	**German comics**.
Greece [gri:s]	**Greek**. [gri:k]	**Greek salad**.
India ['ɪndjə]	**a lot of different languages**.	**Indian curries**. ['ɪndjən]
Ireland ['aɪələnd]	**English**. ['ɪŋglɪʃ]	**Irish music**. ['aɪrɪʃ]
Italy ['ɪtəlɪ]	**Italian**. [ɪ'tæljən]	**Italian pizzas**.
the Netherlands [ðə 'neðələndz]	**Dutch**. [dʌtʃ]	**Dutch cheese**.
Poland ['pəʊlənd]	**Polish**. ['pəʊlɪʃ]	**Polish sausages**.
Russia ['rʌʃə]	**Russian**. ['rʌʃən]	**Russian songs**.
Scotland ['skɒtlənd]	**English**. ['ɪŋglɪʃ]	**Scottish lochs**. ['skɒtɪʃ]
Spain [speɪn]	**Spanish**. ['ʃpænɪʃ]	**Spanish holidays**.
Switzerland ['swɪtsələnd]	**French**. [frentʃ] **German**. ['dʒɜ:mən] **Italian**. [ɪ'tæljən]	**Swiss clocks**. [swɪs]
Turkey ['tɜ:kɪ]	**Turkish**. ['tɜ:kɪʃ]	**Turkish dancing**.
Wales [weɪlz]	**Welsh**. [welʃ]	**Welsh hills**.

Vergiss die Großbuchstaben nicht!

workshop ['wɜ:kʃɒp] — Werkstatt, Kurs, Schulung

crossing ['krɒsɪŋ] — A sea ~ in windy weather can be exciting! — Überfahrt mit der Fähre

Rotterdam [rɒtə'dæm] — *Hafenstadt im Norden der Niederlande*

Hull [hʌl] — *Hafenstadt im Nordosten Englands*

Phew! [fju:] — ~! We've arrived at last! — *Ausruf*

alive [ə'laɪv] — *alive* ⟷ dead — lebendig, am Leben

to **meet, met, met** [mi:t, met, met] — Have you *met* my friend John? – No, I haven't. — (sich) kennen lernen

international [ˌɪntə'næʃənl] — Achte auf die Betonung! — international

1a) **typical** ['tɪpɪkl] — Curry is a ~ Indian meal. — typisch

b) to **revise** [rɪ'vaɪz] — If you want to be good at English, you must sometimes ~ your grammar and vocabulary. — überarbeiten, korrigieren, den Stoff wiederholen

tense [tens] — – Zeit, die vergeht: **time** – The simple present and the simple past are ***tenses*** — (grammatische) Zeit

c) to **imagine** [ɪ'mædʒɪn] — *Imagine* what life was like in the Middle Ages! — sich vorstellen

2	**language** ['læŋgwɪdʒ]	How many ~s can you speak?	Sprache
a)	**lots of** ['lɒts‿əv]	***lots of*/ a lot of** in positiven Sätzen **many** in verneinten Sätzen und Fragen	viele
	tip [tɪp]	Monny gives you a lot of good ~s, because nobody is *perfect*.	Tipp
	perfect ['pɜ:fɪkt]	Achte auf die Betonung!	perfekt

Part 2: **The right words**

The British Isles

England Scotland + Wales	Great Britain + Northern Ireland [ˌnɔ:ðən 'aɪələnd] Nordirland	the United Kingdom + the Republic of Ireland [ðə rɪˌpʌblɪk‿ɒv‿'aɪələnd] die Republik Irland
= Great Britain [ˌgreɪt ˌbrɪtn] Großbritannien	= the United Kingdom = the UK	= the British Isles [ðə ˌbrɪtɪʃ‿'aɪlz]

	deck [dek]	*deck* → 	(Schiffs-)Deck
	on deck [ˌɒn 'dek]	In the summer it is nice to stay ~ during a crossing.	an Deck
	Edinburgh ['edɪnbrə]		*Hauptstadt von Schottland*
	round [raʊnd]	When you go ~ Great Britain you can see places like London, Edinburgh or Hull.	rund um ..., durch ganz ...
	to **go crazy** [ˌgəʊ 'kreɪzɪ]	I could ~! Tabby has eaten my ice cream!	verrückt werden
	to **call** [kɔ:l]	What do you ~ people from the Netherlands?	nennen
	to **upset s.b.** [ʌp'set ˌsʌmbədɪ]	You *upset* a Scottish person if you *call* him or her English.	jdn. ärgern, kränken
	object ['ɒbdʒɪkt]	The sentence "Call me Tom" has two ~s.	Objekt, Gegenstand
1b)	**See you tomorrow!** [ˌsi: ju: tə'mɒrəʊ]		Bis morgen!
	°**formal** ['fɔ:ml]	"Hello!" is more ~ than "Hi!"	formal, formell
	situation [sɪtjʊ'eɪʃn]		Situation
	difference ['dɪfrəns]	What's the ~ between Great Britain and England? Just look at the box 'The British Isles'.	Unterschied
4	**accent** ['æksent]	People from Hamburg and Leipzig have different ~s.	Akzent
	recording [rɪ'kɔ:dɪŋ]		Aufnahme
	Snowdon ['snəʊdn]		*Berg in Wales*
b)	**Luton** ['lu:tn]		*Stadt nördl. von London*
	Glenarm [glen'a:m]		*Kleinstadt in Nordirland*

Vocabulary

Part 3: **On the telephone**

1a)	**face to face** [ˌfeɪs tə ˈfeɪs]		persönlich, direkt, vis-a-vis
	message [ˈmesɪdʒ]	Sorry, Mary isn't at home. Can I give her a ~?	Nachricht, Mitteilung
	answering machine [ˈɑːnsərɪŋ məˌʃiːn]	You can leave a message on an ~.	Anrufbeantworter
	machine [məˈʃiːn]		Maschine, Gerät
	°**tone** [təʊn]	= sound	Ton
c)	**call** [kɔːl]	Mr Dixon can't go out. He is waiting for a ~.	Anruf
	to **make a call** [ˌmeɪk‿ə ˈkɔːl]	to phone s.o.	jdn. anrufen
2	to **take a message** [ˌteɪk‿ə ˈmesɪdʒ]	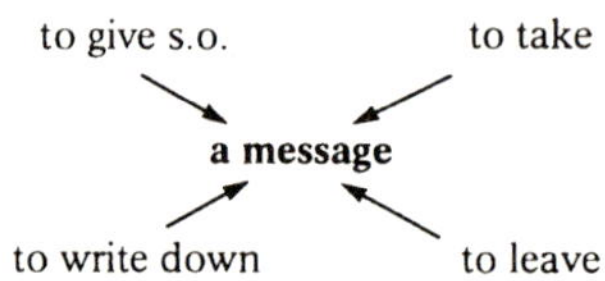	eine Nachricht entgegennehmen
4	**the Lake District** [ðə ˈleɪk ˌdɪstrɪkt]		*Landschaft im Nordwesten Englands*
	Ambleside [ˈæmblsaɪd]		*Kleinstadt im Nordwesten Englands*
	youth hostel [ˈjuːθ ˌhɒstl]	Achte auf die Aussprache: *hostel* [ˈhɒstl] ABER: hotel [həʊˈtel]	Jugendherberge
	to **book** [bʊk]	You can ~ a bed in a youth hostel or tickets for a pop concert.	buchen, reservieren
	°**warden** [ˈwɔːdn]	A ~ looks after a youth hostel.	Herbergsvater/-mutter, Leiter/in
	°to **cancel** [ˈkænsl]	*to cancel* ⟷ to book	absagen, abbestellen, stornieren
	to **check in** [ˌtʃek‿ˈɪn]		sich anmelden, einchecken
5a)	**Lake Windermere** [ˌleɪk ˈwɪndəˌmɪə]		*See im Nordwesten Englands*
	Scarborough [ˈskɑːbrə]	English people sometimes spend their holidays at ~.	*Küstenstadt in Ostengland*
	York [jɔːk]		*Stadt in Yorkshire*
	Malham [ˈmæləm]		*Dorf in Yorkshire*

Part 4: **A short talk**

	talk [tɔːk]	to talk → *a talk*	Referat, Rede, Gespräch
	to **give a talk** [ˌgɪv‿ə ˈtɔːk]	At school pupils sometimes ~ about interesting things.	eine Rede/ein Referat halten
	experience [ɪkˈspɪərɪəns]	What's the strangest ~ you've ever had?	Erlebnis, Erfahrung
	key [kiː]	With a ~ you can *lock* a house, a room, a cupboard.	Schlüssel
	to **lock** [lɒk]	*to lock* ⟷ *to **un**lock*	abschließen
	to **lose, lost, lost** [luːz, lɒst, lɒst]	*to lose* ⟷ to find	verlieren
1a)	**full** [fʊl]	In the summer youth hostels in the Lake District are often ~.	voll, ausgebucht

2a)	to **cycle** ['saɪkl]	to ride a bike	Rad fahren
	°**picnic** ['pɪknɪk]		Picknick
	rainstorm ['reɪnstɔːm]	~ + thunder = thunderstorm	Unwetter, Regenguss
	bus shelter ['bʌs ˌʃeltə]	At a bus stop there is often a ~.	überdachte Bushaltestelle
	Newstead Abbey [ˌnjuːstɪd‿'æbɪ]		*Kloster in der Nähe von Nottingham*
3	**own** [əʊn]	Becky and Simon have got their ~ rooms.	eigen
	to **divide** [dɪ'vaɪd]	For group work you must ~ into groups.	teilen, sich aufteilen

Part 5: ⟨**Practice page**⟩

2	to make s.o. welcome [ˌmeɪk sʌmwʌn 'welkəm]	jdn. mit offenen Armen aufnehmen
3a)	one day ['wʌn ˌdeɪ]	eines Tages, an einem Tag
	dragon ['drægən]	Drache

The weather

winter	bad weather	summer
cold	cloud	sunny
wet	rainstorm	nice
nasty	to rain	warm
snow	rainy ['reɪnɪ] regnerisch	hot
to snow [snəʊ] schneien	thunderstorm	
ice [aɪs] Eis	thunder	
	lightning	

Die Vokabel-Kartei – für „schwere Fälle“

Die Arbeit mit der Vokabel-Kartei kennst du ja schon lange, und dennoch gibt es noch weitere Möglichkeiten, sie als Lern- und Erinnerungshilfe einzusetzen. So kannst du mit ihr speziell „schwierige Fälle“ bearbeiten. (Erinnere dich an besonders ärgerliche Fehler bei den letzten Arbeiten.) Das können Wörter oder Wendungen sein:

- die du dir nur schwer oder auch gar nicht merken kannst,
- die du immer wieder falsch schreibst,
- deren Aussprache dir Schwierigkeiten bereitet oder
- bei denen du die falsche Präposition verwendet hast.

Markiere die obere rechte Ecke jeder Vokabelkarte aus einer dieser Gruppen mit einer Farbe, z.B.

- grün: schwer zu lernende Wörter,
- blau: Wörter mit schwieriger Rechtschreibung,
- gelb: Wörter mit schwieriger Aussprache,
- rot: Wörter mit einer Präposition, die nicht die gleiche wie im Deutschen ist.

Schau dir die Karten mit gleicher Sortierfarbe öfters – und besonders vor Arbeiten – an und präge dir die Wörter ein. Bilde kleine Sätze mit ihnen, versuche, sie auswendig zu schreiben, sprich sie laut. Damit kannst du die Zahl der lästigen „Problemwörter“ verringern.

Unit 1 Welcome to London

ORANGE GREEN

above [ə'bʌv]	über	**may** [meɪ]	darf/dürfen, könnte /könnten
Africa ['æfrɪkə]	Afrika	**meaning** ['mi:nɪŋ]	Bedeutung
although [ɔ:l'ðəʊ]	obwohl	**nationality** [næʃə'nælɪtɪ]	Nationalität
body [bɒdɪ]	Körper	**nose** [nəʊz]	Nase
Christmas ['krɪsməs]	Weihnachten	**Paris** ['pærɪs]	Paris
down [daʊn]	hinunter, herunter	**past** [pɑ:st]	Vergangenheit
end [end]	Ende	**questionnaire** [kwestʃə'neə]	Fragebogen
far [fɑ:]	weit	**to seem** [si:m]	scheinen
hobby ['hɒbɪ]	Hobby	**slow** [sləʊ]	langsam
idiot ['ɪdɪət]	Idiot/in	**straight** [streɪt]	direkt, gerade(wegs)
ill [ɪl]	krank	**Turkish** ['tɜ:kɪʃ]	türkisch, Türkisch
lace [leɪs]	Spitze	**zoo** [zu:]	Zoo
live [laɪv]	live, direkt		
line [laɪn]	Linie		
to get lost [get 'lɒst]	sich verirren, verlorengehen		

Step A **Famous sights**

London Places

Baker Street ['beɪkə ˌstri:t]
Bethnal Green [ˌbeθnəl 'gri:n]
Big Ben [ˌbɪg 'ben]
Bond Street ['bɒnd ˌstri:t]
the British Museum [ðə ˌbrɪtɪʃ mju:ˌzɪəm]
Buckingham Palace [ˌbʌkɪŋəm 'pælɪs]
the Central Line [ðə 'sentrəl ˌlaɪn]
the Circle Line [ðə 'sɜ:kl ˌlaɪn]
Covent Garden [ˌkɒvənt 'gɑ:dn]
the District Line [ðə 'dɪstrɪkt ˌlaɪn]
Embankment [ɪm'bæŋkmənt]
Green Park [ˌgri:n 'pɑ:k]
Harrod's ['hærədz]
the Houses of Parliament [ðə ˌhaʊzɪz‿əv 'pɑ:ləmənt]
Hyde Park [ˌhaɪd 'pɑ:k]
the Jubilee Line [ðə 'dʒu:bɪli: ˌlaɪn]
Knightsbridge ['naɪtsbrɪdʒ]
Leicester Square [ˌlestə 'skweə]
London Bridge [ˌlʌndən 'brɪdʒ]
the London Dungeon [ðə ˌlʌndən 'dʌnʒən]
London Zoo [ˌlʌndən 'zu:]
Madame Tussaud's [ˌmædəm tə'sɔ:dz]
the Museum of the Moving Image [ðə mju:ˌzɪəm‿əv‿ðə ˌmu:vɪŋ‿ɪmɪdʒ]
the Northern Line [ðə 'nɔ:ðn ˌlaɪn]
Notting Hill Gate [ˌnɒtɪŋhɪl 'geɪt]
Paddington ['pædɪŋtən]
Piccadilly Circus [ˌpɪkədɪlɪ 'sɜ:kəs]
Regent's Park [ˌri:dʒənts 'pɑ:k]
the River Thames [ðə ˌrɪvə 'temz]
the Rock Circus [ðə ˌrɒk 'sɜ:kəs]
St Paul's Cathedral [sənt ˌpɔ:lz kə'θi:drəl]
Tower Bridge [ˌtaʊə 'brɪdʒ]
Tower Hill [ˌtaʊə 'hɪl]
the Tower of London [ðə ˌtaʊər‿əv 'lʌndən]
Trafalgar Square [trəˌfælgə 'skweə]
Victoria [vɪk'tɔ:rɪə]
Waterloo Bridge [ˌwɔ:təlu: 'brɪdʒ]
Waterloo Station [ˌwɔ:təlu: 'steɪʃn]
Wembley Stadium [ˌwemblɪ 'steɪdjəm]
Westminster Abbey [ˌwestmɪnstər‿'æbɪ]
Westminster Bridge [ˌwestmɪnstə 'brɪdʒ]
the White Tower [ðə ˌwaɪt 'taʊə]

sight [saɪt]	Tourists usually want to see the ~s of London.	Sehenswürdigkeit, Anblick
queue [kju:]	In London you can often see ~s **for** buses.	(Warte-)Schlange
°**carnival** ['kɑ:nɪvl]	Notting Hill ~ is in August, not in February or March.	Karneval, Volksfest

Vocabulary

square [skweə]	There are a lot of stalls in the market ~.	Platz, Quadrat
palace ['pælɪs]	Achte auf die Betonung.	Palast
queen [kwi:n]		Königin
the Queen [ðə 'kwi:n]	~ of England lives in Buckingham Palace.	die Königin
circus ['sɜ:kəs]		Zirkus, Ring
taxi ['tæksɪ]		Taxi
°**attraction** [ə'trækʃn]	Achte auf die Betonung.	Attraktion
Egyptian [ɪ'dʒɪpʃn]		ägyptisch, Ägyptisch, Ägypter/in
°**Roman** ['rəʊmən]		römisch, Römer/in
pigeon ['pɪdʒɪn]	There are often a lot of ~s in towns.	Taube
double decker bus [ˌdʌbl ˌdekə 'bʌs]		Doppeldecker (*Bus*)
cathedral [kə'θi:drəl]	A ~ is a very big church.	Kathedrale, Dom
tower ['taʊə]	A castle often has lots of ~s.	Turm
bridge [brɪdʒ]		Brücke
bit [bɪt]	Can I have a ~ of your chocolate?	Teil, Stück
°**Hindu** ['hɪndu:]	A lot of ~s come from India.	hinduistisch, Hindu
°**temple** ['templ]	Hindus don't go to church, they go to the ~.	Tempel

Step A **The exchange visit**

exchange visit [ɪks'tʃeɪndʒ ˌvɪzɪt]	Have you ever been on an ~?	(Schüler-)Austausch
flight [flaɪt]	*flight* → to fly	Flug
2 to **land** [lænd]	The plane ~ed at Heathrow Airport at 9.40.	landen, an Land gehen
3 **Bethnal Green** [ˌbeθnəl 'gri:n]		*Stadtteil von London*
°**African** ['æfrɪkən]	Africa → *African*	afrikanisch, Afrikaner/in
most of them ['məʊst‿ɒv ˌðəm]	Anders als im Deutschen braucht man hier im Englischen keinen bestimmten Artikel.	die meisten von ihnen
to **take place** [ˌteɪk 'pleɪs]	Our school fete *took place* in July. ABER: Please **sit down**. 	stattfinden
°**West Indian** [ˌwest‿'ɪndjən]	People from the West Indies are ~.	westindisch, Westinder/in
India ['ɪndjə]	*India* → Indian	Indien
West Indies [ˌwest‿'ɪndɪz]		die karibischen Inseln
°**Caribbean** [ˌkærɪ'bi:ən]	Achte auf die Schreibung!	die Karibik
Pakistan [ˌpɑ:kɪ'stɑ:n]		Pakistan
She was born … [ˌʃi: wəz 'bɔ:n]	And where *were you born*?	Sie ist … geboren.
Coventry ['kɒvəntrɪ]		*Stadt in England*
Muslim ['mʊslɪm]	My friend is Turkish. She's **a** ~.	islamisch, Moslem/Moslime
°**festival** ['festəvl]	Festivals **take place** – – people **take part in** festivals.	Fest(ival)
to **take part in s.th.** [ˌteɪk 'pɑ:t‿ɪn]		mitmachen bei, teilnehmen an
Londoner ['lʌndənə]	A lot of ~s are Hindus or Muslims.	Londoner/in
4 **Ramadan** [ræmə'dæn]		Ramadan *(islamischer Fastenmonat)*

Step A **What you can see in London**

	disappointed [ˌdɪsəˈpɔɪntɪd]	I'm so ~! The exchange visit won't take place!	enttäuscht
	°**Ugh!** [ɜːh]		*Ausruf des Ekels*
	whole [həʊl]	the ~ book = all the parts of the book	ganz
5	**underground** [ˈʌndəgraʊnd]	Did you go to Harrod's by ~?	U-Bahn
	°**waxwork** [ˈwæksw3ːk]		Wachsfigur
	king [kɪŋ]	*king* ←→ queen	König
	°**They are crowned.** [ˌðeɪ ɑː ˈkraʊnd]		Sie werden gekrönt.
	°**royal** [ˈrɔɪəl]	The King and the Queen are members of the *Royal* Family.	königlich
	prison [ˈprɪzən]	*prison* → prisoner	Gefängnis
6	°**eastbound** [ˈiːstbaʊnd]	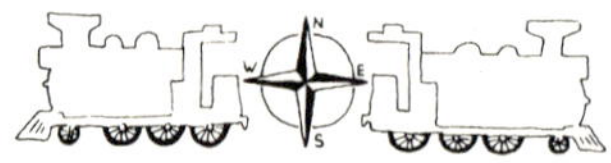	Richtung Osten
	°**westbound** [ˈwestbaʊnd]		Richtung Westen
	stop [stɒp]		Haltestelle
7	**Paddington** [ˈpædɪŋtən]		*Bahnhof in London*
	to **change** [tʃeɪndʒ]	Where must I ~ onto the Central Line?	umsteigen, wechseln
	Victoria [vɪkˈtɔːrɪə]		*Bahnhof in London*
	northbound [ˈnɔːθbaʊnd]		Richtung Norden
8	**trip** [trɪp]	Achtung! Als Verb bedeutet dieses Wort etwas ganz Anderes: stolpern.	Fahrt, Ausflug, Reise

Step A **At the Tower**

	to **go sightseeing** [gəʊ ˈsaɪtˌsiːɪŋ]		auf Besichtigungstour gehen
	°**Beefeater** [ˈbiːfˌiːtə]	~s are famous for their uniforms.	*Wächter im Tower*
	guard [gɑːd]	There are ~s in front of Buckingham Palace.	Wächter
	the White Tower [ðə ˈwaɪt ˌtaʊə]		*Teil des Tower of London*
	William the Conqueror [ˌwɪljəm ðə ˈkɒŋkərə]		Wilhelm der Eroberer
	to **build, built, built** [bɪld, bɪlt, bɪlt]	*William the Conqueror built* a lot of castles in England.	bauen
9	**Edward the Confessor** [ˌedwəd ðə kənˈfesə]		Edward der Bekenner
	however [haʊˈevə]	Peter is clever. ~, he isn't good at school.	jedoch
	Normandy [ˈnɔːməndɪ]	*Normandy* → Norman	Normandie
	to **become, became, become** [bɪˈkʌm, bɪˈkeɪm, bɪˈkʌm]	Achtung! Verwechsle *to become* nicht mit *to get* = bekommen!	werden
	Norman [ˈnɔːmən]		normannisch, Normanne/Normannin
	army [ˈɑːmɪ]	The Normans fought the English ~.	Armee
	Hastings [ˈheɪstɪŋz]	The Battle of ~ took place on October 14th, 1066.	*Kleinstadt an der Südküste Englands*
	coast [kəʊst]	The UK has got a much longer ~ than Germany.	Küste
	battle [ˈbætl]		Kampf, Schlacht
	Christmas Day [ˌkrɪsməs ˈdeɪ]	~ is on 25th December.	1. Weihnachtsfeiertag
	to **fight, fought, fought** [faɪt, fɔːt, fɔːt]		(be)kämpfen, kämpfen (gegen)

10	**religion** [rɪˈlɪdʒən]	The Hindu ~ is very important in India.	Religion
	°**spy** [spaɪ]		Spion

Step B **What do you like doing?**

	stupid [ˈstjuːpɪd]	silly, not clever, not good	dumm, doof
	to **ski** [skiː]	A lot of people love *skiing*.	Ski fahren
	to **dance** [dɑːns]	Would you like *to dance* with me?	tanzen
	to **hate** [heɪt]	– No, thanks! I *hate dancing*.	hassen
	past [pɑːst]		die Vergangenheit
1a)	°**gerund** [ˈdʒerənd]		Gerundium
	subject [ˈsʌbdʒɪkt]		Subjekt
2	to **agree** [əˈgriː]	Football is great! – No, I don't ~ (with you).	zustimmen, der gleichen Meinung sein

Step B **Getting around**

	to **be interested in s.th.** [ˌbɪ ˈɪntrəstɪd‿ɪn]	Achte auf die Schreibung und die Präposition **in**.	sich für etw. interessieren
	°**clown** [klaʊn]		Clown
	waiter [ˈweɪtə]	A ~ works in a restaurant.	Ober, Kellner
	fly [flaɪ]	*a fly* → to fly	Fliege
	soup [suːp]		Suppe
	to **be tired of s.th.** [bɪ ˈtaɪəd‿ɒv]	I'm ~ playing this game. Can't we do something else?	genug von etw. haben
	Crown Jewels [ˌkraʊn ˈdʒuːəlz]	You can see the ~ in the Tower of London.	Kronjuwelen
	°**crown** [kraʊn]	Kings and queens wear ~s.	Krone
4	to **fill in s.th.** [ˌfɪl‿ˈɪn]		etw. einsetzen, ausfüllen
	Wembley Stadium [ˌwemblɪ ˈsteɪdjəm]		*Sportstadion in London*
5	to **paint** [peɪnt]		malen, anstreichen

Step B **Going out for a meal**

	to **go out for a meal** [gəʊ ˌaʊt fɒr‿ə ˈmiːl]		essen gehen
	murgh [ˈmɜːg]		*indisches Currygericht*
	to **smell, smelt, smelt** [smel, smelt, smelt]	This curry ~s lovely.	riechen, duften
	hot [hɒt]		*hier:* scharf (gewürzt)

Step C **A trip to the British Museum**

	to **whisper** [ˈwɪspə]	Can you speak louder? I can't hear you when you ~.	flüstern
	Pardon? [ˈpɑːdn]	*Pardon*? = Sorry? What did you say? **Excuse me** wird dagegen verwendet, wenn man jemanden stört oder unterbricht: Excuse me, could you tell me the way to Wembley Stadium?	Wie bitte?

Cheer up! [ˌtʃɪər‿ˈʌp]		Kopf hoch!
all the way [ˌɔːl ðə ˈweɪ]		den ganzen Weg
afterwards [ˈɑːftəwədz]	before ⟷ *afterwards*	nachher, später, danach
worksheet [ˈwɜːkʃiːt]	You often fill in ~s at school.	Arbeitsblatt
to **go inside** [ˌgəʊ ɪnˈsaɪd]		hineingehen
quite [kwaɪt]	£5 for a ticket? That's ~ expensive.	ziemlich
°**mummy** [ˈmʌmɪ]	 ← an Egyptian *mummy*	Mumie
Hurry up! [ˌhʌrɪ ˈʌp]	~! We mustn't be late again!	Beeil dich!
across [əˈkrɒs]	 *across* the road	(quer) über
cyclist [ˈsaɪklɪst]	*cyclist* → to cycle	Radfahrer
to **cross** [krɒs]	*to cross* → across	überqueren
to **fall off s.th.** [ˌfɔːl ˈɒf sʌmθɪŋ]		von etw. herunterfallen
front [frʌnt]	*front* wheel ⟷ back wheel	Vorder-
to **bend, bent, bent** [bend, bent, bent]		beugen, (ver)biegen
along [əˈlɒŋ]	 *along* the road	entlang
to **catch up with s.o.** [ˌkætʃ ˈʌp wɪð ˌsʌmwʌn]	 He's *catching up with* her.	jdn. einholen
scarf, scarves (*pl*) [skɑːf, skɑːvz]		Schal
to **act normal** [ˌækt ˈnɔːml]		sich normal verhalten
to **act** [ækt]		*hier:* sich verhalten
normal [ˈnɔːml]	*normal* ⟷ special	normal
to **copy** [ˈkɒpɪ]	I've lost my timetable. Can I ~ yours?	kopieren, abschreiben
husband [ˈhʌzbənd]	Mr Kasim is Mrs Kasim's ~.	Ehemann
to **notice** [ˈnəʊtɪs]	*to notice* → a notice → a notice board	bemerken
4 **checklist** [ˈtʃeklɪst]		Kontrollliste
5 **missing** [ˈmɪsɪŋ]	Who is ~? Darren is. He's ill.	fehlend, nicht da

Mit Computer lernen? Na klar!

Auch dein Computer kann dir beim Vokabellernen helfen.
Du kannst ihn auch ganz vielseitig einsetzen:

- statt einer handgeschriebenen Vokabel-Kartei: Mit Farben oder selbst ausgedachten Symbolen kannst du besondere Problemfälle kennzeichnen;
- du kannst deine Vokabellisten alphabetisch sortieren;
- außerdem kannst du Vokabeldateien nach verschiedenen Schwerpunkten anlegen, z.B. Vokabeln mit schwieriger Rechtschreibung;
- es gibt auch zusätzlich Programme zum Vokabellernen, die dich testen und auch deine Fehler korrigieren.

Let's play with words

1 A game with car signs

Do you know signs like these?
Write as many as you know on little cards.
Then turn all the cards over and put them on the table.
The first player takes a card and gives information about this country.

For example: A car with an "F" on it is from France.
It must be French then.
People speak French there.
Paris is the biggest city.

He or she gets a point for every correct sentence.*
If you aren't sure, your teacher will tell you how you say the names in English.

*point ['pɔɪnt] = Punkt

2 What you can say about people

a) Look at the examples and draw more faces for the adjectives on the right and make puzzles for your partner.

VORUSEN

DRECAS

RUSPISDER

YPAPH
NRAGY
EITRD
DLAG
NPAUPYH

b) Find the missing vowels (a, e ,i, o, u) in these adjectives and explain their meaning with a short sentence.

For example:
boring: A boring thing isn't interesting.

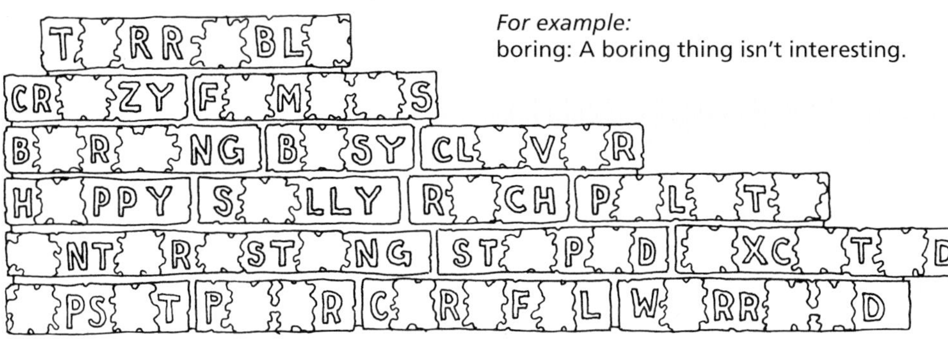

Workshop B Working with words

Vocabulary

ORANGE GREEN

to be able to [bɪ‿'eɪbl tə]	können	**to describe** [dɪ'skraɪb]	beschreiben
to add [æd]	hinzufügen	**housework** ['haʊswɜːk]	Hausarbeit
baby ['beɪbɪ]	Baby	**kind** [kaɪnd]	Art
champion ['tʃæmpjən]	Champion-, Meister-	**mirror** ['mɪrə]	Spiegel
		to organize ['ɔːgənaɪz]	organisieren

Part 1: **Understanding new words**

1	**Selby School** ['selbɪ ˌskuːl]		*Schule in London*
	Sports Day ['spɔːts deɪ]	Our ~ is on July 3rd.	Sportfest
	°**court** [kɔːt]	I'll never play on Centre ~ at Wimbledon!	(Tennis-)Platz
	to **compete in s.th.** [kəm'piːt]	*to compete* → competition	an einem Wettbewerb teilnehmen
	to **mend** [mend]	= to repair	reparieren
	°**goalkeeper** ['gəʊlˌkiːpə]		Torwart
	match [mætʃ]	The ~ between Leeds and Schalke was really exciting. aber: 'Memory' is an interesting game.	Spiel
	sportsfield ['spɔːtsfiːld]		Sportplatz
	athletics [æθ'letɪks]		Leichtathletik
	high jump ['haɪ dʒʌmp]	And what is *long jump* then?	Hochsprung
	gym (= gymnasium) [dʒɪm = dʒɪm'neɪzjəm]	Das englische Wort hat eine ganz andere Bedeutung als das deutsche.	Turnhalle, Sporthalle
	jazz dance ['dʒæz ˌdɑːns]	*dance* → to dance	Jazztanz
	rugby ['rʌgbɪ]	~ is popular in the UK.	*englischer Rasensport*
	to **train** [treɪn]	You must ~ a lot, if you want to win the 100 metres.	trainieren
	metre ['miːtə]	Achte auf die Schreibung.	Meter
	°to **jog** [dʒɒg]	*to jog* → jogging	joggen
2	to **guess** [ges]	Beachte die Aussprache, das 'u' wird nicht gesprochen.	vermuten, (er)raten
	context ['kɒntekst]		Zusammenhang

Part 2: **Organizing words**

New Zealand [ˌnjuː 'ziːlənd]	There are more sheep than people in ~.	Neuseeland
express [ɪk'spres]	An ~ train goes very fast.	Express(zug)
Tonga ['tɒŋgə]		*Inselgruppe in der Südsee*
national ['næʃənl]	*national* ⟷ international	national, National-
All Blacks [ˌɔːl 'blæks]		*Name der Rugby-Nationalmannschaft von Neuseeland*

World Cup [ˌwɜːld ˈkʌp] — Weltmeisterschaft
South Africa [ˌsaʊθ‿ˈæfrɪkə] — Südafrika
°**pitch** [pɪtʃ] — a rugby *pitch* / ABER: a tennis *court* — Spielfeld, Platz
to **weigh** [weɪ] — Beachte: gleiche Aussprache, zwei Wörter *weigh* – way — wiegen
kilo [ˈkiːləʊ] — One ~ **of** potatoes, please. — Kilo
tall [tɔːl] — groß

size [saɪz] — He takes ~ 7 in shoes. — Größe
°to **tackle** [tækl] — angreifen *(beim Sport)*
to **move** [muːv] — sich bewegen

second [ˈsekənd] — Sixty ~s make one minute. — Sekunde
past [pɑːst] — Go ~ the post office and then turn left. — an ... vorbei
°**opponent** [əˈpəʊnənt] — The people in the other team are your ~s. — Gegner

1 **vocabulary** [vəʊˈkæbjʊlərɪ] — Words, words, words! — Wortschatz, Vokabular
2 **star** [stɑː] — Stern, Star, Idol
fact [fækt] — It's a ~ that the earth is round. — Tatsache
3a) °**event** [ɪˈvent] — Where did this sports ~ take place? — Ereignis, Veranstaltung
b) **board** [bɔːd] — *board* → notice board — (Schul-)Tafel
6 to **try harder** [ˌtraɪ ˈhɑːdə] — sich mehr anstrengen
cup [kʌp] — All these are cups! — Pokal, Becher

Part 3: **Saying things in different ways**

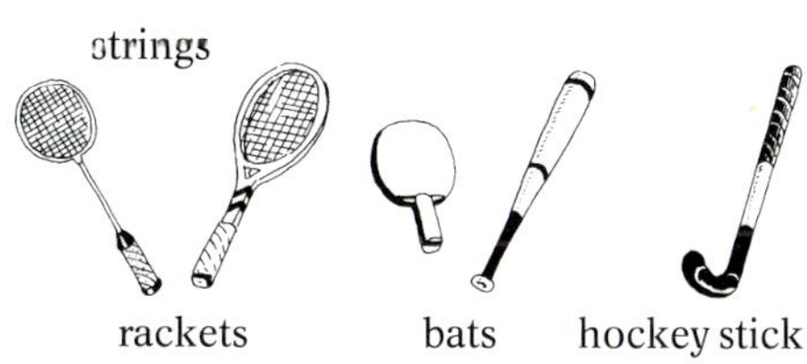

racket [ˈrækɪt] — Schläger *(für Tennis, Squash u. Ä.)*
bat [bæt] — Schläger *(für Tischtennis)*
string [strɪŋ] — Saite, Bindfaden
hockey stick [ˈhɒkɪ ˌstɪk] — Hockeyschläger

2 **changing room** [ˈtʃeɪndʒɪŋ ˌruːm] — Sports people change their clothes in the ~. — Umkleideraum
°**referee** [ˌrefəˈriː] — Beachte Schreibung **und** Betonung. — Schiedsrichter
to **dive** [daɪv] — einen Kopfsprung machen; tauchen

1.)  2.) 

⟨3⟩ champion [ˈtʃæmpjən] — Weltmeister
dues *(pl)* [djuːz] — Lehrgeld
time after time [ˈtaɪm‿ˌɑːftə‿ˈtaɪm] — immer wieder
to commit a crime [kəˌmɪt‿ə ˈkraɪm] — ein Verbrechen begehen
share [ʃeə] — Anteil
to keep on doing s.th. [ˈkiːp‿ˌɒn ˈduːɪŋ ˌsʌmθɪŋ] — etwas weitermachen

till = until [tɪl]	bis
loser ['lu:zə]	Verlierer/in
'cause (= because) [kɒz]	weil
I've taken my bows. [aɪv 'teɪkən maɪ 'baʊz]	*etwa*: Ich habe viel Applaus bekommen.
I've taken my curtain calls. [aɪv 'teɪkən maɪ 'kɜ:tn ˌkɔ:lz]	*etwa:* Ich habe viele Zugaben gegeben.
curtain ['kɜ:tn]	Vorhang, Gardine
fame [feɪm]	Ruhm
fortune ['fɔ:tʃu:n]	Glück, Schicksal
rose [rəʊz]	Rose
pleasure cruise ['pleʒə ˌkru:z]	Vergnügungsfahrt
to consider [kən'sɪdə]	betrachten als
challenge ['tʃælɪndʒ]	Herausforderung
human race ['hju:mən 'reɪs]	die Menschheit
I ain't gonna lose. [aɪ 'eɪnt ˌgɒnə 'lu:z]	Ich werde nicht verlieren.
refrain [rɪ'freɪn]	Refrain

Part 4: **Words in grammar**

ⓐ **myself** [maɪ'self] — (mich/mir) selbst
yourself [jɔ:'self] — (dich/dir) selbst
himself [hɪm'self] — (ihn/ihm) selbst
herself [hɜ:'self] — (sie/ihr) selbst
itself [ɪt'self] — (es/ihm) selbst
ourselves [ˌaʊə'selvz] — (uns) selbst
yourselves [jɔ:'selvz] — (euch) selbst
themselves [ðəm'selvz] — (sich) selbst

We can see ourselves.

I can see ~.

each other [ˌi:tʃ‿'ʌðə] — einander

1 °**reflexive verb** [rɪˌfleksɪv 'vɜ:b] — reflexives (rückbezügliches) Verb

ⓑ to **concentrate** ['kɒnsəntreɪt] — sich konzentrieren

> Es gibt einige Verben, die nur im Deutschen reflexiv sind. Siehe Tipp S. 30.

to **scream** [skri:m] — When they saw the ghost, everybody on the ghost train ~ed. — schreien, kreischen

Part 5: **Word building**

°**word building** ['wɜ:dˌbɪldɪŋ] — Wortbildung
newspaper ['nju:sˌpeɪpə] — Zeitung
article ['ɑ:tɪkl] — Artikel
Elf Row [ˌelf 'rəʊ] — *Straßenname*
Shadwell ['ʃædwəl] — *Stadtteil von London*
thief, thieves (*pl*) [θi:f, θi:vz] — knife – knives, shelf – shelves, calf – calves — Dieb/in, Diebe

bench [bentʃ] — a bench

a bank

— Bank (*zum Sitzen*)

ground [graʊnd] — Boden
°**Ms** [mɪz] — Frau *(Anrede für Frauen)*

	East Cheam [ˌiːst ˈtʃiːm]		*Stadtteil von London*
	careless [ˈkeəlɪs]	*careless* ⟷ careful; → to care	nachlässig
	helpful [ˈhelpfʊl]	*helpful* → to help, helper, help!	hilfsbereit
2	**helpless** [ˈhelplɪs]	*helpless* ⟷ helpful	hilflos
	useless [ˈjuːslɪs]	*useless* ⟷ useful → to use	nutzlos
	sleepless [ˈsliːplɪs]	*sleepless* → to sleep	schlaflos
3	**worker** [ˈwɜːkə]	*worker* → to work, workbook, worksheet	Arbeiter/in
	rider [ˈraɪdə]	*rider* → to ride, riding school	Reiter/in
	runner [ˈrʌnə]	*runner* → to run	Läufer/in
	learner [ˈlɜːnə]	*learner* → to learn	Lernende/r
	swimmer [ˈswɪmə]	*swimmer* → to swim, swimming pool	Schwimmer/in
	dancer [ˈdɑːnsə]	*dancer* → to dance	Tänzer/in
	writer [ˈraɪtə]	*writer* → to write	Schriftsteller/in, Schreiber/in
	reader [ˈriːdə]	*reader* → to read	Leser/in
4	**washable** [ˈwɒʃəbl]	= you can wash it	waschbar
	washing machine [ˈwɒʃɪŋ‿məˌʃiːn]	You wash your clothes in a ~.	Waschmaschine
	breakable [ˈbreɪkəbl]	And what is *unbreakable* then?	zerbrechlich
	understandable [ˌʌndəˈstændəbl]		verständlich
	readable [ˈriːdəbl]	Is the book boring? No, it's very ~.	lesbar
	changeable [ˈtʃeɪndʒəbl]	 Achte auf die Schreibung.	wechselhaft

Wörterlernen – am besten im Zusammenhang

Wörter nur als Wortgleichung zu lernen ist nicht die wirkungsvollste Art, neue Vokabeln zu behalten. Wenn du dir beim Lernen für ein Wort möglichst mehrere dazugehörige Wörter einprägst, machst du damit dieses Wort für dein Gedächtnis besser „merkwürdig". Das Gedächtnis hat dann einfach mehr Erinnerungswege zu diesem Wort. Die Mittelspalte des Vokabulars gibt dir oft Anregungen dazu.

Beispiele:

neues Wort	**Erinnerungsweg für das Gedächtnis**
to compete	Welches Worte kenne ich noch aus dieser Wortfamilie? → *competition*
to mend	Welches Wort hat die gleiche Bedeutung? = *to repair*
useless	Welches Wort bedeutet das Gegenteil? ⟷ *useful*
past	Wie unterscheiden sich die beiden Bedeutungen dieses Wortes im Deutschen?
to l***ie*** or to l***ay***	Wie kann ich mir solche kniffligen Unterscheidungen besser merken? Hier hilft einfach eine Eselsbrücke: to ***lie*** heißt **lie**gen, die Wörter haben ja den gleichen Anfang. Auch Reime helfen beim Merken. *t**all*** ⟷ *sm**all***
each other	Auch ein Wortbild oder eine Zeichnung kann die Bedeutung festigen.
athletics	In welches Thema lässt sich das Wort einordnen? → *sport* *Welche Wörter fallen mir noch zu diesem Thema ein? → sports centre, trainers, sportsfield, high jump, football, PE*
gymnasium	Mit welchem deutschen Wort darf ich dieses Wort nicht verwechseln?

Unit 2 Trouble at school

ORANGE GREEN

to be allowed to [bɪ‿ə'laʊd tə]	dürfen	**life** [laɪf]	Leben
Asia ['eɪʃə]	Asien	**to match** [mætʃ]	das Dazupassende finden
beginning [bɪ'gɪnɪŋ]	Anfang	**miserable** ['mɪzrəbl]	unglücklich, elend
to bother s.o. ['bɒðə ˌsʌmwʌn]	jdn. stören	**office** ['ɒfɪs]	Büro, Amt
both [bəʊθ]	beide	**row** [rəʊ]	Reihe
carefully ['keəflɪ]	vorsichtig, sorgfältig	**snake** [sneɪk]	Schlange
correct [kə'rekt]	richtig, korrekt	**top** [tɒp]	oberste/oberster/oberstes
during ['djʊərɪŋ]	während	**to play tricks on s.o.** [ˌpleɪ 'trɪks ɒn sʌmwʌn]	jdm. Streiche spielen
to escape [ɪ'skeɪp]	fliehen, entkommen	**tutor** ['tju:tə]	Klassenlehrer/in
to excuse [ɪks'kju:z]	entschuldigen	**tutor group** ['tju:tə ˌgru:p]	Klasse (in einer engl. Schule)
haircut ['heəkʌt]	Haarschnitt		
headteacher [ˌhed'ti:tʃə]	Schuldirektor/in		

Step A **The video conference**

	trouble ['trʌbl]	Bullies sometimes make ~ at school.	Ärger, Probleme
	conference ['kɒnfərəns]	Beachte die Betonung.	Konferenz
	course [kɔ:s]	Mark is going on a swimming ~ this term.	Kurs(us)
	in town [ˌɪn 'taʊn]	= in the city centre	in der Stadt
1a)	**library** ['laɪbrərɪ]	A place where you can read books. And they also lend you the books.	Bibliothek, Bücherei
	°**detention** [dɪ'tenʃn]		Nachsitzen, Arrest
	packed lunch [ˌpækt 'lʌntʃ]	You take a ~ to school.	Pausenbrot, Lunchpaket
2	°**e-mail (= electronic mail)** ['i:meɪl = ˌɪlek'trɒnɪk ˌmeɪl]	You can send messages very quickly by ~.	*elektronischer Briefverkehr*
	exam [ɪg'zæm]	A test of what you know or what you can do.	Prüfung, Examen
	to **take an exam** [ˌteɪk ən ɪg'zæm]	*to take an exam* – eine Prüfung machen	eine Prüfung machen, ablegen
	to **test s.b. on s.th.** ['test sʌmbədɪ ɒn ˌsʌmθɪŋ]	*to test* → a test	jemanden auf einem Gebiet prüfen
	primary school ['praɪmərɪ ˌsku:l]	After nursery school Mark started at *primary school.*	Grundschule
	secondary school ['sekəndərɪ ˌsku:l]	When British children are about 11 they go to ~.	*weiterführende Schule in GB*
	°**comprehensive school** [ˌkɒmprɪ'hensɪv ˌsku:l]	A *comprehensive school* is a kind of *secondary school.*	*Gesamtschule in GB*
	°**GCSE (= General Certificate of Secondary Education)** [ˌdʒi: si: es 'i: = ˌdʒenərəl sə'tɪfɪkət‿əv 'sekəndərɪ ˌedʒʊ'keɪʃn]	Most British children take ~s when they are 16.	*allgemeiner Abschluss der weiterführenden Schulen in GB*

°**general** ['dʒenərəl]		allgemeine/r/s
°**certificate** [sə'tɪfɪkət]	Beachte die Betonung.	Zeugnis, Urkunde
'A' level ['eɪ ˌlevl]	Most British children only take ~s in two or three subjects.	*britische Abiturprüfung*
mark [mɑːk]	British pupils usually get ~s from A (the best) to E.	Note *(in der Schule)*
special help [ˌspeʃl 'help]	A pupil with problems at school can get ~.	Förderunterricht
to **repeat a year** [rɪ'piːt‿ə jɪə]		eine Klasse wiederholen
to **repeat** [rɪ'piːt]		wiederholen
grammar school ['græmə skuːl]	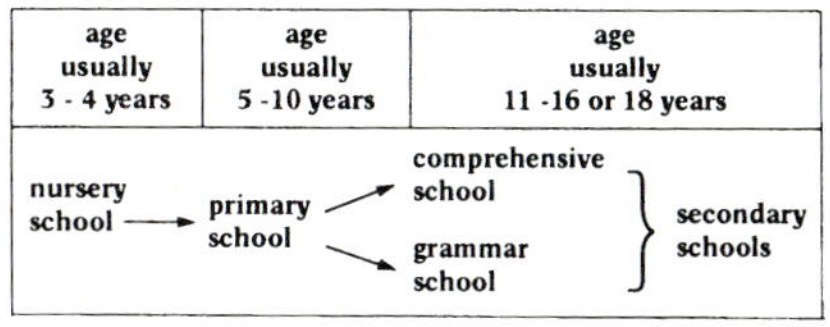	*Gymnasium in GB*
boarding school ['bɔːdɪŋ skuːl]	Pupils at ~ only go home for the holidays.	Internat
⟨4⟩ to be excused [ˌbɪ ɪk'skjuːzd]		*hier:* den Unterricht verlassen
brain [breɪn]		Gehirn
6 **St. John's School for Boys** [snt ˌdʒɒnz skuːl fə 'bɔɪz]		*Name eines Internats*
school report ['skuːl rɪˌpɔːt]	You get a ~ at the end of term.	Schulzeugnis
weak [wiːk]	2 Wörter – eine Aussprache a week – very *weak*	schwach
comment ['kɒment]	Achte auf die Betonung.	Kommentar
to **do well** [ˌduː 'wel]	*to do well* ←→ to do badly	Erfolg haben, gut sein
to **be pleased with** [ˌbɪ 'pliːzd ˌwɪð]	= to be glad or happy about s.th.	mit etwas zufrieden sein, sich über etwas freuen
progress *(no pl)* ['prəʊgres]	Anders als im Deutschen gibt es von *progress* keinen Plural: Lucy is making good ~ at school – Lucy macht gute Fortschritte in der Schule.	Fortschritt
experiment [ɪk'sperɪmənt]	Beachte die Betonung.	Experiment
lazy ['leɪzɪ]	A ~ person doesn't work enough.	faul
interest in s.th. ['ɪntrəst]	*interest* → interesting	Interesse an etwas
project ['prɒdʒekt]	We're doing an interesting history ~ now.	Projekt
to **put work into s.th.** [ˌpʊt 'wɜːk ɪntʊ ˌsʌmθɪŋ]	= to work hard	Arbeit in etwas hineinstecken
to **get better** [ˌget 'betə]	Can you remember all these? 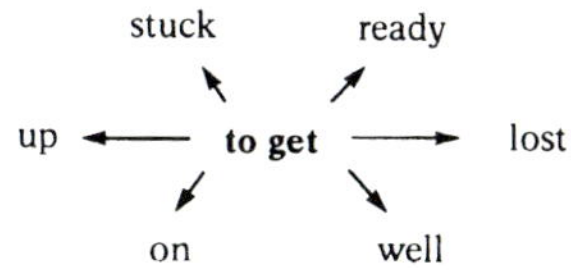	besser werden

Step B **The new boy**

°**show-off** ['ʃəʊ ɒf]	A ~ wants to show other people how fantastic he/she is.	Angeber/in
Dracula ['drækjʊlə]		Dracula

Step B **Wayne gets into trouble**

	to **get into trouble** [ˌget intʊ ˈtrʌbl]	He *got into trouble* and so he's got a problem now.	in Schwierigkeiten geraten
	back [bæk]	*back* (door) ⟷ front (door)	hintere/r/s, Hinter-
	to **spray** [spreɪ]		sprühen
	graffiti [grəˈfi:tɪ]	Some young people like spraying walls with ~.	Graffiti
	wall [wɔ:l]	Jenny's got a lot of posters on the ~s of her room.	Wand, Mauer
	spray [spreɪ]	*spray* → to spray	Spray
	to **get rid of s.th.** [ˌget ˈrɪd‿ɒf ˌsʌmθɪŋ]	It can be difficult to *get rid of* mice.	etwas loswerden
	case [keɪs]	Are thieves in the school a ~ for the police?	Fall
	chance [tʃɑ:ns]		Chance
	to **settle s.th.** [ˈsetl ˌsʌmθɪŋ]	What's the trouble? Let's try to ~ it.	etwas erledigen, in Ordnung bringen
	to **shut, shut, shut** [ʃʌt, ʃʌt, ʃʌt]	Can you remember six more irregular verbs where all three forms are the same?	schließen
	Shut up! [ˌʃʌt ˈʌp]	It isn't very polite to say *"Shut up!"*	Halt den Mund!
3	**writing** [ˈraɪtɪŋ]	*writing* → to write	Schrift
4	°**relative pronoun** [ˌrelətɪv ˈprəʊnaʊn]		Relativpronomen

Step B **A meeting on the stairs**

	stairs (*pl*) [steəz]	Watch out! These ~ are very steep!	Treppe, Treppenhaus
	to **steal, stole, stolen** [sti:l, stəʊl, ˈstəʊlən]	Thieves ~ things.	stehlen
6	°**clause** [klɔ:z]	= part of a sentence	(Teil-)Satz
	relative clause [ˌrelətɪv ˈklɔ:z]	She's the girl who comes from Wales. (who = relative pronoun; who comes from Wales = relative clause)	Relativsatz
7	to **think of s.th.** [ˈθɪŋk ˌɒv ˌsʌmθɪŋ]	I can't *think of* a grammar rule. I'm *thinking of* our holiday.	sich etwas ausdenken, an etwas denken
⟨8⟩	limerick [ˈlɪmərɪk]		*gereimter brit. Witz mit 5 Zeilen*
	creature [ˈkri:tʃə]		Kreatur, Wesen
	whom [hu:m]		welche, die

Step B **A busy week**

tonight [təˈnaɪt]	this morning – this afternoon – this evening – *tonight*	heute Abend/Nacht
"Romeo and Juliet" [ˌrəʊmɪəʊ ən ˈdʒu:ljət]		*berühmtes Theaterstück von William Shakespeare*

11	°**arrangement** [ə'reɪndʒmənt]	= plan	Plan
	flower ['flaʊə]		Blume
12	**fantasy** ['fæntəsɪ]	A ~ only happens in your head.	Phantasie
a)	°**V.I.P. (= very important person)** [ˌviː aɪ 'piː]		wichtige Persönlichkeit
	to **leave free** [ˌliːv 'friː]	= to leave out	frei lassen, offen lassen

Step B **Emma**

	So do you! ['səʊ ˌduː 'juː]	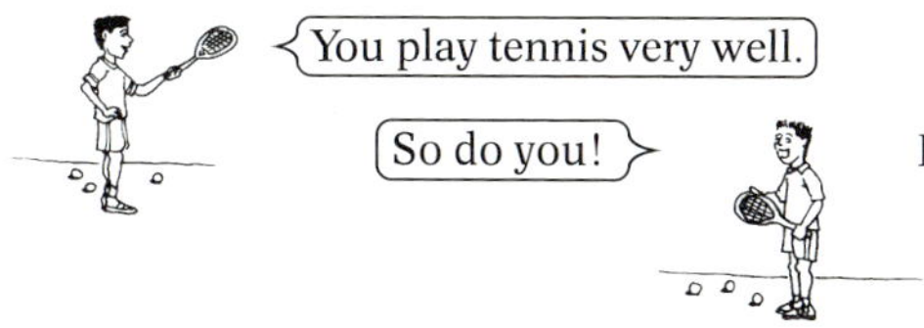	Du auch!
	shall [ʃəl]		soll
	way [weɪ]	Edward likes the ~ Jenny smiles.	Art und Weise
14	**noisy** ['nɔɪsɪ]	noise → *noisy* ⟷ quiet	laut

Step C **A thief in the school**

1	**advice** *(no pl)* [əd'vaɪs]	*advice* ist wie *progress* unzählbar. Es kann nicht im Plural stehen und auch **nie** ein ***an*** vor sich haben. He gave us a lot of advice. – Er gab uns viele Ratschläge.	Rat(schlag)
2	**clue** [kluː]	 Sherlock Holmes was looking for ~s.	Anhaltspunkt, Spur
	to **appear** [ə'pɪə]		erscheinen
	to **be in a hurry** [ˌbɪ ɪn‿ə 'hʌrɪ]	*to be in a hurry* → to hurry	es eilig haben
	to **pay s.o. back** [ˌpeɪ sʌmwʌn 'bæk]	= to give s.o. his/her money back	jemandem etwas zurückzahlen
	to **promise** ['prɒmɪs]	Robert ~d to do the washing-up, but he forgot.	versprechen
	to **be annoyed** [ˌbɪ ə'nɔɪd]	= to be angry	verärgert sein
	free [friː]	When you get s.th. ~ you don't pay for it.	gratis
	°**dinner lady** ['dɪnə ˌleɪdɪ]		*Dame an der Essensausgabe*
	dinner ['dɪnə]	You usually have hot food for ~.	warmes Mittagessen, Abendessen
	tomato, tomatoes *(pl)* [tə'mɑːtəʊ, tə'mɑːtəʊz]	*tomat**oes***, aber: photo**s** potat***oes*** radio**s** piano**s**	Tomate
	after all [ˌɑːftər‿ɔːl]		trotz allem, doch
	to **push** [pʊʃ]	*to push* ⟷ to pull	drücken, schubsen, schieben
	against [ə'genst]		gegen

	to **cry, cried, cried** [kraɪ, kraɪd, kraɪd]		schreien, weinen
	jealous of s.th/s.o. ['dʒeləs ɒv ˌsʌmθɪŋ/ˌsʌmwʌn]	FAMOUS DANGEROUS JEALOUS	eifersüchtig auf
	to **tell lies** [ˌtel 'laɪz]		lügen
	lie [laɪ]		Lüge
	safe [seɪf]	*safe* ⟷ dangerous	sicher
	°**bell** [bel]	The school *bell* is *ringing*.	Glocke, Klingel
	to **ring, rang, rung** [rɪŋ, ræŋ, rʌŋ]		klingeln, läuten
	while [waɪl]	for a *while* = for some time	Weile
5	**possible** ['pɒsəbl]	Come back as soon as ~.	möglich
⟨6⟩	Can't buy me love. ['kɑːnt ˌbaɪ miː 'lʌv]		*etwa:* Liebe kann man nicht kaufen.
	diamond ['daɪmənd]		Diamant
	to care for ['keə ˌfɔː]		gerne mögen
	satisfied ['sætɪsfaɪd]		zufrieden
8	**definition** [defɪ'nɪʃn]	Achte auf die Betonung.	Definition

Oh Schreck! Ein langes Wort!
Wie spricht man das nur aus?

Bei längeren Wörtern ist die Betonung besonders wichtig. Mit der Lautschrift kann man auch die richtige Betonung herausfinden und lernen.

Beispiel:
Schau dir das neue Wort *comprehensive school* [ˌkɒmprɪ'hensɪv ˌskuːl] an. Bei der Lautschrift steht vor der Silbe mit der Hauptbetonung dieses Zeichen ['].

- Beginne die Aussprache mit dieser Silbe und der nachfolgenden unbetonten Silbe ['hensɪv]. Sprich diesen Wortteil mehrmals laut und klopfe bei der betonten Silbe auf den Tisch.
- Füge dann die davor stehende Silbe dazu. Das Zeichen [ˌ] soll zeigen, dass die folgende Silbe die Nebenbetonung trägt. Sprich beide Teile zusammen aus.
- Sprich das ganze Wort anfangs mit überdeutlicher Unterscheidung zwischen betonten und unbetonten Silben aus.
- Markiere auf deinen Wörterkarten für Wörter mit schwieriger Aussprache die Betonung mit einem Markierstift. *comprehensive school*
- Bei englischen Wörten, die deutschen ähnlich sind, ist die Betonung manchmal tückisch: *experiment* *comment* *conference* *interest*
- Vorsicht auch bei Substantiven, Adjektiven und Verben, die sich ähneln! Die Betonung liegt nicht immer auf der gleichen Silbe. *progress* *progressive*

Unit 3 Welcome to Wales

ORANGE GREEN

Cornwall ['kɔːnwəl]	*engl. Grafschaft*	**Gosh!** [gɒʃ]	*Ausruf des Erstaunens*
crowd [kraʊd]	Menschenmenge	**knee** [niː]	Knie

Step A Country and people

Places in Wales

Aberystwyth [ˌæbəˈrɪstwɪθ]	**Cardiff** [ˈkɑːdɪf]	**Snowdonia National Park** [snəʊˈdəʊnjə ˌnæʃənl ˈpɑːk]
Caerleon [kɑːˈliːən]	**Fishguard** [ˈfɪʃgɑːd]	**Swansea** [ˈswɒnzɪ]
Caernarvon [kəˈnɑːvən]	**Holyhead** [ˈhɒlɪhed]	**Tenby** [ˈtenbɪ]

1	to **go with** [ˈgəʊ ˌwɪð]	That jacket *goes* well *with* your jeans.	passen zu, gehören zu
	strong [strɒŋ]		stark
	to **conquer** [ˈkɒŋkə]	William the Conqueror ~ed Britain in 1066.	erobern
	°**century** [ˈsentʃʊrɪ]	= one hundred years	Jahrhundert
	prince [ˈprɪns]	The son of a king or queen is a ~.	Prinz
	capital [ˈkæpɪtl]		Hauptstadt
	heavy [ˈhevɪ]	A school bag full of books can be very ~.	schwer
	industry [ˈɪndəstrɪ]		Industrie
	million [ˈmɪljən]	1,000,000 = a/one ~	Million
	video recorder [ˈvɪdɪəʊ rɪˌkɔːdə]		Videorekorder
	factory [ˈfæktərɪ]		Fabrik
	railway [ˈreɪlweɪ]	a mountain ~, a toy ~, …	Eisenbahn
	°**choir** [ˈkwaɪə]	You must have a good voice if you want to sing in a ~.	Chor
	valley [ˈvælɪ]	*valley* ⟷ hill	Tal
	coal [kəʊl]	You can make a good fire with ~.	Kohle
	mine [maɪn]	You get coal from ~s.	Bergwerk, Mine
	visitor [ˈvɪzɪtə]	Museums and adventure centres get a lot of ~s.	Besucher/in
	B&B (= bed and breakfast) [ˌbiː‿ən‿ˈbiː]	A ~ is usually cheaper than a hotel.	Privatpension (Zimmer mit Frühstück)
	village [ˈvɪlɪdʒ]	*village* → town → city	Dorf
	one in five [ˌwʌn‿ɪn ˈfaɪv]		jeder Fünfte
	°**camp** [kæmp]		(Heer-)Lager
	King Arthur [ˌkɪŋ ˈɑːθə]		*sagenhafter engl. König*
	Camelot [ˈkæmɪlɒt]		*Schloss von König Arthur*
	wild [waɪld]		wild
	countryside [ˈkʌntrɪsaɪd]	Wales has a lot of beautiful ~.	Landschaft

2	**for short** [ˌfə ˈʃɔːt]	I'm Catherine, but you can call me Kate ~.	abgekürzt
3	**mind** [maɪnd] °**mind map** [ˈmaɪnd ˌmæp]	Achtung! Als Verb bedeutet dieses Wort etwas ganz anderes: jdm. etwas ausmachen	Verstand, Gedanken *Wörternetz zur Gedächtnisstütze*
4	**area** [ˈeərɪə] **inside** [ɪnˈsaɪd] **huge** [hjuːdʒ]	In this ~ there is no heavy industry. *inside* ⟷ outside *huge* ⟷ very small	Gegend, Gebiet hinein, in(nerhalb von) groß, riesig

Step B **The Pritchards**

	penfriend [ˈpenfrend]	My ~ and I write to each other every month.	Brieffreund/in
	since [sɪns]	I have been living here ~ July.	seit
	out of work [ˌaʊt‿əv ˈwɜːk]	If you haven't got a job you are ~.	arbeitslos
	to **move** [muːv]	Jenny Leinert ~d from Berlin to Nottingham.	umziehen
1	**up here** [ˌʌp ˈhɪə]		hier oben
	to **teach, taught, taught** [tiːtʃ, tɔːt, tɔːt]	*to teach* → teacher	unterrichten, lehren
2	°**present perfect progressive** [ˌpreznt ˌpɜːfɪkt prəʊˈgresɪv]		*Verlaufsform des Perfekt*
4	**instrument** [ˈɪnstrʊmənt]	Achte auf die Betonung!	Instrument
	to **interview s.o.** [ˈɪntəvjuː ˌsʌmwʌn]	Mrs Croft often ~s famous people for Radio Nottingham.	jdn. interviewen
5	**sir** [sɜː]	Sorry, ~.	(mein) Herr

Step B **Tips for visitors**

	to **wonder** [ˈwʌndə]	I ~ what the weather will be like tomorrow.	sich etw. überlegen, sich etw. fragen
	whether [ˈweðə]	Eine Aussprache, zwei Bedeutungen: *whether* = ob, weather = Wetter	ob
	roadside [ˈrəʊdsaɪd]	You can *park* your car at the ~	Straßenrand
	to **park** [pɑːk]	but it is safer to *park* it in a garage.	parken
	service [ˈsɜːvɪs]	The ~ in this hotel is very good.	Dienst, Bedienung
	choice [tʃɔɪs]	to choose → *choice*	Wahl
	to **fish** [fɪʃ]	fish → *to fish*	fischen, angeln
	golf [gɒlf]		Golf
	route [ruːt]		Weg, Route
6a)	to **milk** [mɪlk]	milk → *to milk*	melken
	farmer [ˈfɑːmə]	farm → *farmer*	Bauer

Step B **The Celts and their language**

	°**Celts** (*pl*) [kelts]	**BC ⟷ AD** BEFORE AFTER	die Kelten
	°**Celtic** [ˈkeltɪk]		keltisch
	°**BC** [ˌbiː ˈsiː]		vor Christus
	°**AD** [ˌeɪ ˈdiː]		nach Christus

	Angles *(pl)* ['æŋglz]	The *Angles* and the *Saxons* came from an area in the north of Germany.	die Angeln
	Saxons *(pl)* ['sæksnz]		die Sachsen
	to **invade** [ɪn'veɪd]		besetzen, einmarschieren in
	Britons *(pl)* ['brɪtnz]	You can still call people who live in Britain '~'!	die Briten
	to **settle** ['setl]		sich ansiedeln
	to **exist** [ɪg'zɪst]	Ghosts don't really ~.	existieren
	official [ə'fɪʃl]	GCSE is the ~ name for the exam English pupils take when they are 16.	offiziell
	status ['steɪtəs]		Status, Anerkennung
	land [lænd]	to land → *land*	Land
⟨8⟩	tinker ['tɪŋkə]		herumziehender Kesselflicker
	lad [læd]		Junge, junger Mann
	slung [slʌŋ]		geschlungen
	hammer ['hæmə]		Hammer
	trifle ['traɪfl]		*etwa:* ein paar Pfennige
	pipe [paɪp]		Pfeife
	whiskers ['wɪskəz]		Schnurrbart, Barthaar
	'neath (= beneath) ['ni:θ = bɪ'ni:θ]		unter
	pitcher ['pɪtʃə]		Becher
	pot [pɒt]		Topf
	frying pan ['fraɪɪŋ ˌpæn]		Pfanne
	to heat [hi:t]		erhitzen, heiß machen
	iron ['aɪən]		Eisen
	to cover ['kʌvə]		bedecken
	solder ['sɒldə]		Lötzinn
	flaw [flɔ:]		Fehler, Loch
	none [nʌn]		niemand
	to seek, sought, sought [si:k, sɔ:t, sɔ:t]		suchen
	to vanish ['vænɪʃ]		verschwinden
	to miss [mɪs]		vermissen
	on every hand [ɒn 'evrɪ ˌhænd]		überall

Step B **Plans for the weekend**

10	°**knight** [naɪt]	a *knight* 	Ritter
	°**question tag** ['kwestʃən ˌtæg]		*nachgestellte Fragepartikel*

Step C **The sword in the stone**

°**sword** [sɔ:d]	A long time ago, people fought with ~s.	Schwert
King Uther [kɪŋ ju:θə]		*sagenhafter engl. König*
to **follow** ['fɒləʊ]	Please ~ me, I'll show you the way.	folgen, befolgen
to **take over** [ˌteɪk 'əʊvə]		übernehmen, wegnehmen
kingdom ['kɪŋdəm]		Königreich
handle ['hændl]	Use the ~ if you want to open the door.	(Hand-)Griff
true [tru:]	I'm not sure whether this story is ~ or not.	wahr, wirklich

	Merlin [ˈmɜːlɪn]		*sagenhafter Zauberer*
	°**wizard** [ˈwɪzəd]	~s can do fantastic tricks.	Zauberer
	°**miracle** [ˈmɪrəkl]		Wunder
	New Year's Day [ˌnjuː jɪəz ˈdeɪ]	On ~ a lot of people go to parties.	Neujahrstag
	tournament [ˈtɔːnəmənt]	There is only one winner in a ~.	Wettkampf, Turnier
	Sir Ector [ˌsɜːr‿ˈektə]		*sagenhafter engl. Edelmann*
	inn [ɪn]	A hotel at the roadside is often called an ~.	Gasthaus, Wirtshaus
	What a piece of luck! [ˈwɒt‿ə ˌpiːs‿ɒv ˈlʌk]	I've found ten pounds. ~!	Was für ein Glück!
	luck [lʌk]	Good ~ in your exams!	Glück
	till (= until) [tɪl = ənˈtɪl]	On Sundays I stay in bed ~ 11 o'clock.	bis
	look [lʊk]	He gave me an angry ~.	Blick
	to **miss** [mɪs]	This morning I got up late and ~ed the bus.	verpassen, vermissen
	to **fetch** [fetʃ]	There's been an accident. ~ the doctor!	holen
	to **believe** [bɪˈliːv]	Don't ~ him. He's telling lies.	glauben
	wife [waɪf]	husband ←→ *wife*	Ehefrau
	Queen Igrayne [ˌkwiːn ɪˈgreɪn]		*sagenhafte engl. Königin*
	danger [ˈdeɪndʒə]	dangerous → *danger*	Gefahr
	cheer [ˈtʃɪə]	There were ~s from the crowd when John won the tennis match.	Jubel(ruf)
1	**feeling** [ˈfiːlɪŋ]	If you are happy or frightened or worried you have different ~s.	Gefühl
2	**statement** [ˈsteɪtmənt]		Aussage
4	**real** [rɪəl]	Things that happen in a dream are not ~.	wirklich, echt

Klein und manchmal gemein

Jeder hat beim Lernen seine starken und schwachen Seiten.

Machst du öfters Fehler bei Wendungen mit Präpositionen, kannst du dir für jede der Präpositionen eine Liste von Wendungen anfertigen, die du nach jeder Unit erweitern kannst.

Oder leg eine Liste für ein Verb an, das mit vielen verschiedenen Präpositionen stehen kann.

Durch gezielte Wiederholung mit Hilfe solcher Listen sind die Präpositionen bald keine „schwierigen Fälle" mehr.

Let's play with words

1 Change one letter only

How do you get from **MEAT** *to* **SELL** *?*

M	E	A	T
S	E	A	T
S	E	A	L
S	E	L	L

Can you change

WALL *to* **FEEL**

RACE *to* **TAKE**

HOLD *to* **RULE**

2 Which words sound the same?

Make a list for your exercise book. *Example:* **HEAR → HERE**

ERHA	EERH	EONS	NWSOK	YB	UYB	ON	WNOK
NOE	OWN	HIRCT	HRTEE	ERD	EDAR	WOT	OTO
OERD	DORA	ESA	ESE	ETAM	ETME	HLWEO	EOLH
RTIEW	IHGTR	HREWE	ERAW	URO	ORUH	GEIHW	AYW

3 Add or take away letters

Example: **NIGHT.** This man lived in the Middle Ages → **KNIGHT** (+ 1 letter)
TOWER. A number → **TWO** (- 2 letters)

Sometimes you have to change the order of the letters.

BELIEVE	Opposite of die	**MATCH**	An animal.
CHAIR	You can drive it.	**SOLDIER**	Opposite of win.
PERSON	Part of your face.	**SCREAM**	You put it into your coffee.
DIVE	You can do it with a car.	**NOW**	You can see it in the winter.
PLACE	A house for a king.	**JEALOUS**	An animal in the sea.
BEEFEATER	You have got two of them.	**MARK**	You can buy things there.
TROUBLE	A colour.	**LEARNER**	Not far.
SHOUT	2 irregular past participles.	**RAIN**	You can go to school by it.
BOW	A colour.	**VIDEO**	To swim under water.

Workshop C Let's read

ORANGE GREEN

bath [bɑːθ]	Bad, Badewanne
the Channel [ðə 'tʃænl]	der Ärmelkanal
Europe ['jʊərəp]	Europa
to kill [kɪl]	töten
wig [wɪg]	Perücke

Part 1: **Starting off**

In dieser Unit erfährst du viel über die Römer in England. Hier sind einige nicht alltägliche Wörter, die dir beim Lesen helfen können. Du brauchst sie aber nicht zu lernen.

to affect [ə'fekt]	beeinflussen, sich auswirken auf
to be in use [ˌbɪ ɪn 'juːz]	in Gebrauch sein
blues [bluːz]	deprimierte Stimmung
Boudicca [bəʊ'dɪkə]	*keltische Königin*
to break a horse [ˌbreɪk‿ə 'hɔːs]	ein Pferd zureiten
brick [brɪk]	Ziegel
Britannia [brɪ'tænjə]	*röm. Name für das Land der Briten*
Camilla [kə'mɪlə]	*weibl. Vorname*
central heating [ˌsentrəl 'hiːtɪŋ]	Zentralheizung
children of her own ['tʃɪldrən ɒv hər‿'əʊn]	ihre eigenen Kinder
Claudius ['klɔːdjəs]	*röm. Kaiser*
Cottia ['kɒtɪə]	*weibl. Vorname*
critic ['krɪtɪk]	Kritiker/in
downward ['daʊnwəd]	abwärts
eagle ['iːgl]	Adler
emperor ['empərə]	Kaiser, Herrscher
empire ['empaɪə]	Kaiserreich
exile ['eksaɪl]	Exil
feature ['fiːtʃə]	Sonderbeitrag
flame [fleɪm]	Flamme
Hadrian ['heɪdrɪən]	*röm. Kaiser*
heather ['heðə]	Heidekraut
horse-breeder ['hɔːs ˌbriːdər]	Pferdezüchter
hunter ['hʌntə]	Jäger/in
hut [hʌt]	Hütte
I am of the Iceni. [ˌaɪ əm ˌɒv ðɪ aɪ'siːnɪ]	Ich gehöre zum Stamm der Iceni.
I'm (not) supposed to … [ˌaɪm nɒt sə'pəʊzd tə]	Ich soll (nicht) …
Iceni [aɪ'siːnɪ]	*keltischer Volksstamm*
Latin ['lætɪn]	lateinisch, Latein
legion ['liːdʒn]	Legion, Regiment
lice (*pl*) [laɪs]	Läuse
local ['ləʊkl]	einheimisch
Londinium [lʌn'dɪnjəm]	*röm. Name für das spätere London*
maiden ['meɪdn]	junges, unverheiratetes Mädchen
to make s.o. do s.th. ['meɪk ˌsʌmwʌn 'duː ˌsʌmθɪŋ]	jemanden dazu bringen, etw. zu tun
to man [mæn]	besetzen
to march [mɑːtʃ]	marschieren
Marcus ['mɑːkəs]	*männl. Vorname*
Mediterranean Sea [ˌmedɪtə'reɪnjən 'siː]	das Mittelmeer
military ['mɪlɪtərɪ]	militärisch
monument ['mɒnjʊmənt]	Monument, Bauwerk
the ninth [ˌðə 'naɪnθ]	das Neunte (*hier:* Regiment)
to nod [nɒd]	nicken
occupation [ˌɒkjʊ'peɪʃn]	Besetzung
to patter down [ˌpætə 'daʊn]	herunterprasseln
pointed face ['pɔɪntɪd ˌfeɪs]	spitzes Gesicht
poison ['pɔɪzn]	Gift
Rosemary Sutcliff [ˌrəʊzmərɪ 'sʌtklɪf]	*brit. Schriftstellerin*
sandal [sændl]	Sandale
to strike s. o. ['straɪk sʌmwʌn]	jdm. auffallen
The sun is setting. [ðə 'sʌn‿ɪz 'setɪŋ]	Die Sonne geht unter.
toga ['təʊgə]	Toga *(röm. Kleidungsstück)*
tribe [traɪb]	Volksstamm
tunic ['tjuːnɪk]	Tunika *(röm. Kleidungsstück)*
underneath [ˌʌndə'niːθ]	unter
You see … [ˌjʊ 'siː]	Weißt du, …
Valaria [və'leərɪə]	*weibl. Vorname*
West of the Sunset [ˌwest‿ɒv ðə 'sʌnset]	*etwa:* im Totenreich

	to **start off** ['stɑ:t ˌɒf]	We've got a lot of housework. Let's ~ with the bathroom.	beginnen, anfangen
	wind [wɪnd]		Wind
	to **blow, blew, blown** [bləʊ, blu:, bləʊn]	The *wind* is *blowing* hard today.	blasen
	to **have a cold** [ˌhæv ə 'kəʊld]	You can *have a cold*, have a bath, have a ride, have a break …	erkältet sein
	sky [skaɪ]	There are clouds in the ~.	Himmel
	soldier ['səʊldʒə]		Soldat
	to **decide** [dɪ'saɪd]	Have you ~d which film you want to watch?	(sich) entscheiden
	Kent [kent]		*Grafschaft in England*
	to **defend s.th./s.o.** [dɪ'fend ˌsʌmθɪŋ/ˌsʌmwʌn]	You need soldiers to ~ your country.	etw./jdn. verteidigen
	Rome [rəʊm]	*Rome* → Roman	Rom
	sun [sʌn]		Sonne
	to **shine, shone, shone** [ʃaɪn, ʃɒn, ʃɒn]	*to shine* darf man nicht verwechseln mit *to seem* – scheinen, den Anschein haben!	scheinen, leuchten
	gold [gəʊld]		Gold
	no-one ['nəʊˌwʌn]	= nobody	niemand
	to **protect** [prə'tekt]	Clothes can ~ us **from** cold weather.	(be)schützen
1	**complete** [kəm'pli:t]	*complete* → to complete	komplett, vollständig
	to **expect** [ɪk'spekt]	to think that s.th. will happen	erwarten
	subject ['səbdʒekt]	Do you remember the other meaning of this word?	Thema

Part 2: **How to read a text**

1	°to **get the gist** [ˌget ðə 'dʒɪst]	= to understand the main idea	das Wichtigste verstehen
	main ['meɪn]	= most important	Haupt-
	heading ['hedɪŋ]		Überschrift
	paragraph ['pærəgrɑ:f]	Your grammar pages have got ~s. A new ~ starts on a new line.	Abschnitt
	to **welcome s.b.** ['welkəm ˌsʌmbədɪ]	Thousands of Romans *welcomed* Hadrian.	jdn. willkommen heißen
	°**border** ['bɔ:də]	The ~ shows where one country ends and another begins.	Grenze
	field [fi:ld]	A farmer has to work **in** the ~s.	Feld, Wiese, Weide
	false [fɔ:ls]	The thieves gave ~ names to the police.	falsch, künstlich
	tooth, teeth (*pl*) [tu:θ, ti:θ]	tooth – teeth, foot – feet, goose – geese	Zahn, Zähne
	°**rebellion** [rɪ'beljən]	Die Betonung ist anders als im Deutschen.	Rebellion, Aufstand
	to **lead, led, led** [li:d, led, led]	In the past, the king often *led* his army into battle.	führen
	to **burn** [bɜ:n]	Don't ~ that newspaper! I haven't read it yet.	(ver-/nieder-)brennen
	°**fort** [fɔ:t]	A strong building which helps to defend a place.	Fort, Heerlager
2	to **get s.th. right** [ˌget sʌmθɪŋ 'raɪt]	= to understand what s.th. really means	etwas richtig verstehen
	to **translate** [træns'leɪt]	Can you ~ this letter for me, Mario? It's in Italian.	übersetzen

3	to **pick out** [ˌpɪk‿ˈaʊt]	Can you ~ my face **in** the photo?	heraussuchen
	°to **function** [ˈfʌŋkʃn]	How does this machine ~?	funktionieren
	personal [ˈpɜːsnl]	Can I ask you a ~ question?	persönlich
4	°**remains** (*pl*) [rɪˈmeɪnz]	In the south of Germany you can find a lot of Roman ~.	Überreste

Part 3: **Reacting to a text**

	to **react to s.th.** [rɪˈækt tə ˌsʌmθɪŋ]	How did your parents ~ to our plans for the weekend?	auf etwas reagieren
1	**author** [ˈɔːθə]	= writer	Autor
	next door [ˌnekst ˈdɔː]	Your neighbour lives ~ to you.	nebenan
	thin [θɪn]	*thin* ⟷ fat	dünn
	⟨pointed face⟩ [ˌpɔɪntɪd ˈfeɪs]		spitzes Gesicht
	though (= although) [ðəʊ = ɔːlˈðəʊ]	~ she had to hurry, she stopped and talked to a friend.	obwohl
	everyday life [ˌevrɪdeɪ ˈlaɪf]	the life you lead every day	der Alltag
	room [ruːm]	We haven't got enough ~ for a big dog.	Platz
	to **wish** [wɪʃ]	I ~ you a happy birthday.	wünschen
	to **pretend** [prɪˈtend]	He ~ed to be ill although he wasn't.	etwas vorgeben, so tun als ob
	outside [ˌaʊtˈsaɪd]	*outside* ⟷ inside	außerhalb von
	tongue [tʌŋ]	here: another word for 'language'	Zunge, Sprache
	change [tʃeɪndʒ]	*change* → to change, changeable	Veränderung, Wechsel
3	to **feel sorry for s.o.** [fiːl ˈsɒrɪ fə ˌsʌmwʌn]	We all *felt sorry for her* when we heard the bad news.	Mitleid mit jdm. haben
4	to **remind s.o. of s.th.** [rɪˈmaɪnd ˌsʌmwʌn ɒv ˈsʌmθɪŋ]	I can't remember that photo. ABER: That photo *reminds me of your birthday.*	jdn. an etwas erinnern

Englisch – so oft wie möglich

- **Sprich Englisch so oft wie möglich.**
  Vielleicht ist in deiner Nachbarschaft jemand, mit dem du dich nur auf Englisch unterhalten kannst. Oder hast du vielleicht im Urlaub Gelegenheit, Englisch zu sprechen? Nimm an einem Schüleraustausch teil, wenn du kannst. Und hab keine Angst vor Fehlern. Wer dich nicht versteht, wird nachfragen. Versuche es dann mit anderen Wörtern und Wendungen.
- **Höre Englisch so oft wie möglich.**
  Englische Musik, englisches Radio und Fernsehen bieten dazu gute Möglichkeiten. Versuche einzelne Wörter herauszuhören und ihre Bedeutung zu erschließen oder ungefähr zu erraten. Wenn möglich, sieh dir Filme, die du schon kennst, noch einmal auf Englisch an. Manchmal haben z.B. auch Bibliotheken englische Videos. Du wirst staunen, was du alles verstehst.
- **Lies Englisch so oft wie möglich.**
  Bibliotheken haben auch oft englische Bücher, Zeitungen und Zeitschriften. Vielleicht findest du auch etwas über deine Hobbys. Beginne aber mit kürzeren Texten – Comics sind z.B. gut geeignet – und gib nicht bei den ersten unbekannten Wörtern auf. *Workshop C* gibt dir Tipps dazu.
- **Schreibe Englisch so oft wie möglich.**
  Wie wäre es mit einer Brieffreundschaft? Frage doch mal deinen Lehrer oder deine Lehrerin in der Schule. Oft haben auch deutsche Vereine englischsprachige Partnervereine, die dir dabei weiterhelfen könnten. Auch über das Internet kannst du Kontakte auf Englisch knüpfen. Vielleicht kannst du deinen Brieffreund oder deine Brieffreundin auch einmal besuchen. Vergiss nicht, dass du dich oft mit Jugendlichen aus der ganzen Welt auf Englisch verständigen kannst.

Unit 4 The Environment

ORANGE GREEN

to break, broke, broken [breɪk, brəʊk, 'brəʊkn]	brechen, zerbrechen	**role play** ['rəʊl ˌpleɪ]	Rollenspiel
earth [ɜ:θ]	Erde	**soap** [səʊp]	Seife

Step A **A trip to a theme park**

environment [ɪn'vaɪərənmənt]	The world around us is our ~.	Umwelt
°**theme park** ['θi:m ˌpɑ:k]		Erlebnispark, Vergnügungspark
Alton Towers [ˌɔ:ltən 'taʊəz]		*großer Erlebnispark in England*
mile [maɪl]	A ~ is about 1,600 metres.	Meile
traffic ['træfɪk]	= buses, lorries, bikes, vans, cars, taxis on the roads	Verkehr
motorway ['məʊtəweɪ]	Cars are allowed to drive fast on a ~.	Autobahn
°**roadworks** ['rəʊdwɜ:ks]		Baustelle, Straßenarbeiten
°**traffic jam** ['træfɪk ˌdʒæm]	All the traffic stops in a ~.	Verkehrsstau
service station ['sɜ:vɪs ˌsteɪʃn]	At a ~ there's food and drink for you and petrol for the car.	Raststätte
petrol ['petrəl]	You can't drive a car without ~.	Benzin
roundabout ['raʊndəbaʊt]	There are ~s on the roads and at the fair.	Kreisverkehr
traffic lights *(pl)* ['træfɪk ˌlaɪts]	~ tell you when to stop and when to go.	Verkehrsampel

Some towns in the heart of England

1

Derby ['dɑ:bɪ]	**Ellastone** ['eləstəʊn]	**Sudbury** ['sʌdbərɪ]
Mayfield ['meɪfi:ld]	**Uttoxeter** [ju:'tɒksɪtə]	**Ashbourne** ['æʃbɔ:n]

2a)	**light** [laɪt]	*light* ⟷ heavy	leicht, gering

Step A **In the car**

copy ['kɒpɪ]	Can you lend me your ~ of the newspaper?	Ausgabe, Kopie, Exemplar
It says … [ˌɪt 'sez]		Es heißt hier …, Hier steht …
to **pollute** [pə'lu:t]	We mustn't use things that ~ the environment.	verschmutzen
to **cause** [kɔ:z]		verursachen
pollution [pə'lu:ʃn]	Traffic on the roads causes ~.	Verschmutzung
air [eə]	Factories and cars pollute the ~.	Luft

	to **switch off** [ˌswɪtʃ ˈɒf]	And what does 'switch **on**' mean then?	ausschalten
3	**energy** [ˈenədʒɪ]	You need a lot of ~ to run a mile.	Energie
	to **waste** [weɪst]	Don't ~ time. Hurry up!	verschwenden
	to **recycle** [ˌriːˈsaɪkl]	Don't waste paper. ~ it!	recyceln, wiederverwerten
	to **destroy** [dɪˈstrɔɪ]	Pollution is slowly ~ing our environment.	zerstören
	to **give s.th. up** [ˌgɪv sʌmθɪŋ ˈʌp]	He should *give up smoking*. It's not healthy.	etw. aufgeben, aufhören mit etw.
	light [ˈlaɪt]	You need a ~ to read at night.	Licht
	plastic [ˈplæstɪk]	a ~ bag, a ~ cup, a ~ duck, ...	Plastik

Step B **An article in Our Earth magazine**

	to **cut down** [ˌkʌt ˈdaʊn]	They ~ a lot of trees for the new motorway.	absägen, fällen
	wide [waɪd]	The table is 0.75m high, 2m long and 1m ~.	breit, weit
	to **damage** [ˈdæmɪdʒ]	In the accident a van ~d a car.	beschädigen
	Greendale [ˈgriːndeɪl]		*Ortsname*
	°**bulldozer** [ˈbʊldəʊzə]	You can sometimes see a ~ where there are roadworks.	Bulldozer, Planierraupe
	to **pull down** [ˌpʊl ˈdaʊn]	They ~ed ~ a lot of old houses.	abreißen
	not ... **any more** [ˈnɒt ˌenɪ ˈmɔː]	I *won't* climb mountains *any more*. I hurt my leg last time.	nicht/kein ... mehr
1	°**passive** [ˈpæsɪv]		Passiv

Step B **Saving the environment**

	°**the Stone Age** [ðə ˈstəʊn eɪdʒ]		die Steinzeit
	Rugby [ˈrʌgbɪ]		*Ort in Mittelengland*
	instead of [ɪnˈsted‿ɒv]	Let's have fish ~ meat today.	statt, anstatt
	to **injure** [ˈɪndʒə]	Three people were ~d in the accident.	verletzen
	public transport [ˌpʌblɪk ˈtrænspɔːt]	He hasn't got a car so he goes by ~.	öffentliche Verkehrsmittel
	public [ˈpʌblɪk]	a ~ library, ~ toilets, a ~ path, ...	öffentlich
	transport [ˈtrænspɔːt]		Transport
	to **improve** [ˌɪmˈpruːv]	Going to England for a holiday can help to ~ your English.	(sich) verbessern
	law [lɔː]	We need more ~s against pollution.	Gesetz
	Birmingham [ˈbɜːmɪŋəm]		*Industriestadt in Mittelengland*
	°**bottle bank** [ˈbɒtl ˌbæŋk]	If you put your old bottles in a ~, they will be recycled.	Glascontainer
	to **pass** [pɑːs]	Laws are ~ed in parliament.	(Gesetze) verabschieden; vorbeigehen an
	Bournemouth [ˈbɔːnməθ]		*Stadt an der Südküste Englands*
5	**It's up to you.** [ɪts‿ʌp tə ˈjuː]	Would you like to go to the cinema or to the disco? – I don't mind. ~.	Es kommt auf dich an., Du entscheidest.
8	**owner** [ˈəʊnə]	This bike is mine. I'm the ~.	Besitzer/in, Eigentümer/in
⟨9⟩	driving licence [ˈdraɪvɪŋ ˌlaɪsəns]		Führerschein

Step C **Tomorrow**

Vocabulary

	to **enter** ['entə]	= to go in(to)	betreten, hineingehen (in)
	model [mɒdl]	My parents want to buy a new car but I don't like the new ~s.	Modell
	°**assembly line** [ə'semblɪ ˌlaɪn]	On an ~ many people work together to make the same thing.	Fließband
	°**air stream travel** ['eə stri:m ˌtrævl]		Luftstromtransport
	God [gɒd]		Gott
	°**Japanese** [dʒæpə'ni:z]	Our neighbours' new car is ~.	japanisch, Japanisch, Japaner/in
	technology [tek'nɒlədʒɪ]	Achte auf die Betonung.	Technologie, Technik
	reason ['ri:sən]	Why are you so angry? What's the ~?	Grund
	freedom ['fri:dəm]	free → *freedom*	Freiheit
	biology [baɪ'ɒlədʒɪ]	~ is about things that are alive, like animals or trees.	Biologie
	section ['sekʃn]		Abteilung
	to **touch** [tʌtʃ]	A sign in a museum: "Please do not ~."	berühren, anfassen
	to **have a baby** [ˌhæv ə 'beɪbɪ]		ein Baby bekommen
3	**human** ['hju:mən]	Beachte die Aussprache.	Mensch
4a)	**phrase** [freɪz]	= a sentence, a clause	(Teil-)Satz, Wendung
b)	**expression** [ɪk'spreʃn]	Do you know another ~ for "I can't stand"?	Ausdruck
⟨7⟩	truck [trʌk]		Lastwagen
	midway [ˌmɪd'weɪ]		auf halbem Weg
	Fairlane cruiser [ˌfeəleɪn 'kru:zə]		*Name eines Fahrzeugs*
	headlights (*pl*) ['hedlaɪts]		Scheinwerfer
	driving rain [ˌdraɪvɪŋ 'reɪn]		starker Regen
	window frame ['wɪndəʊ ˌfreɪm]		Fensterrahmen
	star [stɑ:]		Stern, Star
	to hitch a ride [ˌhɪtʃ ə 'raɪd]		per Anhalter fahren
	chorus ['kɔ:rəs]		Refrain
	whizzkid ['wɪzˌkɪd]		Draufgänger
	two-wheel stallion [ˌtʊ: wi:l 'stæljən]		*Motorrad*
	ten-ton lorry [ˌten tʌn 'lɒrɪ]		Zehntonner-Lastwagen
	Got a bead on you. [ˌgɒtə 'bi:d‿ɒn jʊ:]		*etwa:* Hat dich im Visier.
	Ain't no use setting up with a bad companion.		*etwa:* Es hat keinen Zweck, dich mit mir anzulegen.
	Ain't nobody get the better of you-know-who.		*etwa:* Niemand kommt gegen mich an.
	Ain't no route. ['eint ˌnəʊ 'rʊ:t]		*etwa:* Es gibt keine Straße.
	Ain't nobody know ... [eint 'nəʊbədɪ nəʊ]		*etwa:* Keiner weiß ...
	roadway ['rəʊdweɪ]		Straße
	Gonna keep on driving. [gɒnə ˌki:p‿ɒn 'draɪvɪŋ]		*etwa:* Ich werde weiterfahren.
	to truck on [ˌtrʌk 'ɒn]		weiter mit dem Lastwagen fahren
8	**cartoon** [kɑ:'tu:n]	You can find ~s in comics and newspapers.	Bilderwitz, Karikatur
	°**multi-storey car park** [ˌmʌlti stɔ:rɪ 'kɑ: pɑ:k]	Usually there are a lot of floors in a ~.	Parkhochhaus
	system ['sɪstəm]	Achte auf die Betonung.	System

Let's play with words

1 Opposite pairs

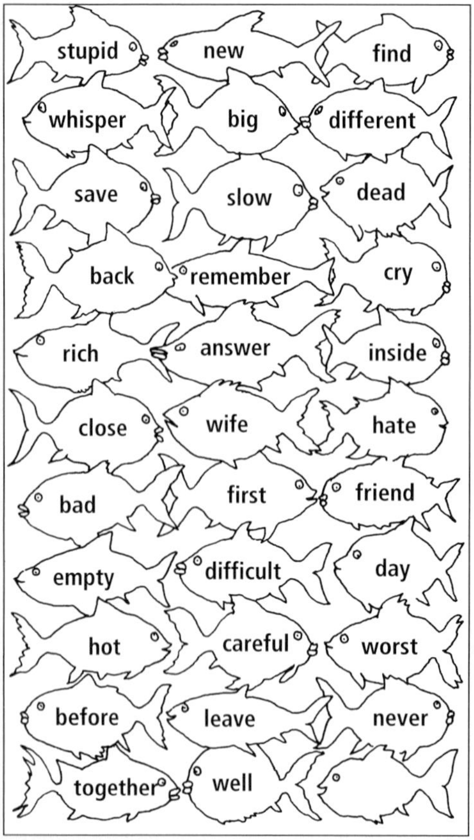

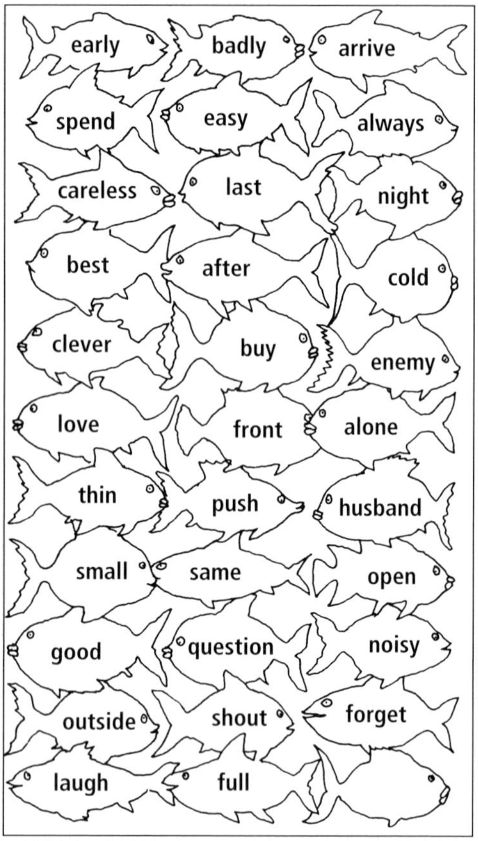

Make a list of 27 opposite pairs, but be careful – there are five fish in each tank without a partner fish in the other tank!

2 Let's play with opposites

Now you know a lot of opposite pairs. How many of them do you and your friends remember together? Collect them and make a game out of your lists.
Write the first word of the opposite pair on the one side of the card, and the opposite of it on the other side. Then you can start the game. The first player gets all the cards, looks at one side of the first card and says the opposite word. Every player has got 30 seconds to call out as many pairs as possible.

Workshop D Let's write

ORANGE GREEN

action ['ækʃn]	Handlung, Geschehen	**healthy** ['helθɪ]	gesund
adverb ['ædvɜːb]	Adverb	**puzzle** ['pʌzl]	Rätsel

Part 1: **Getting ideas together**

	review [rɪ'vjuː]	a piece of writing in a magazine or newspaper about a film, book, game etc.	Besprechung, Rezension eines Buches, Films, etc.
	°**graphics** *(pl)* ['græfɪks]		Grafik, Bild
1	**not only** … **but also** [nɒt 'əʊnlɪ, bʌt 'ɔːlsəʊ]	Mrs Croft *not only* works for radio *but* she *also* writes in her free time.	nicht nur …, sondern auch
	°**dragon** ['drægən]	 a *dragon* a kite 	Drache
	°**level** [levl]		Niveau, Stufe
	colourful ['kʌləfʊl]	*colourful* ⟷ colourless → colour, to colour in	bunt, farbig, farbenfroh
	especially [ɪ'speʃəlɪ]	Robert likes fruit, ~ apples.	besonders
	on the whole [ˌɒn ðə 'həʊl]	= all in all	im Großen und Ganzen
	introduction [ˌɪntrə'dʌkʃn]	the first part of a piece of writing	Einleitung
	opinion [ə'pɪnjən]	What's your ~ about computer games?	Meinung
2	°**lipstick** ['lɪpstɪk]	All these are sticks: lipstick, hockeystick, walking stick 	Lippenstift
	in my opinion [ɪn 'maɪ əˌpɪnjən]		meiner Meinung nach
	It's **worth buying.** [ɪts ˌwɜːθ 'baɪɪŋ]	Beachte die unterschiedliche Satzkonstruktion: This book is *worth buying.* Es lohnt sich, dieses Buch zu kaufen.	Es lohnt sich, … zu kaufen.
	°**boyfriend** ['bɔɪfrend]	*boyfriend* → girlfriend, penfriend	(fester) Freund
	°to **click on s.th.** ['klɪk ɒn ˌsʌmθɪŋ]		etwas anklicken (*mit der Computer-Maus*)
	motorbike ['məʊtəbaɪk]	motor ⊕ → way / → bike / → boat	Motorrad
	violence ['vaɪələns]	fighting and shooting = ~.	Gewalt
	screen [skriːn]	Do you know other computer words?	Bildschirm, Leinwand
5	**brainstorming** ['breɪnstɔːmɪŋ]	to collect ideas	Ideen sammeln
	°**etc** [ɪt'setərə]		usw.

Vocabulary

Part 2: **Writing the text**

⟨5⟩	Frankly, … ['fræŋklɪ]		Ehrlich gesagt, …

Part 3: **Checking the text**

1	**style** [staɪl]	way of doing, making, speaking, writing s.th.	Stil
	negative ['negətɪv]		negativ
	°**punctuation** [ˌpʌŋktʃʊ'eɪʃn]	Beachte Schreibung und Aussprache.	Zeichensetzung
	capital letter [ˌkæpɪtl 'letə]	In a letter you put a *comma* after 'Dear Peter' but you go on with a *capital letter.*	Großbuchstabe
	comma ['kɒmə]		Komma
2b)	**clear** ['klɪə]	*clear* ⟷ unclear	klar, deutlich
3	**skill** [skɪl]	Reading and writing are the first ~s you learn at school.	Fähigkeit, Fertigkeit
	about [ə'baʊt]	'about' hat verschiedene Bedeutungen: a book about history Our school is *about* five miles away.	etwa, circa
⟨4⟩	Congratulations! [kənˌgrætʃʊ'leɪʃnz]		Herzlichen Glückwunsch!
	to reach [riːtʃ]		erreichen

Speaking and talking

to agree – zustimmen
to answer – antworten
to ask – fragen
to call – rufen
to cry – schreien
to describe – beschreiben
to explain – erklären
to give a talk – eine Rede/ein Referat halten
to give information/a tip – informieren/einen Tipp geben
to invite – einladen
to leave/take a message – eine Nachricht hinterlassen/entgegennehmen
to make a call – jdn. anrufen
to make a request – einen Wunsch/eine Bitte äußern
to phone s.o. – jdn. anrufen
to promise – versprechen
to remind s.o. of s.th. – jdn. an etw. erinnern
to say – sagen
to scream – schreien, kreischen
to shout – rufen, schreien
to sound (annoyed) – (verärgert) klingen
to speak – sprechen
to spell – buchstabieren
to talk (about) – sprechen (über)
to tell – erzählen
to tell lies – lügen
to translate – übersetzen
to welcome s.o. – jdn. willkommen heißen
to whisper – flüstern

Unit 5 Great Britain and the sea

ORANGE GREEN

ghost [gəʊst]	Geist, Gespenst	**mechanic** [mɪˈkænɪk]	Mechaniker/in
to hold [həʊld]	halten	**to rescue** [ˈreskjuː]	retten, bergen

Step A **An island country**

	lonely [ˈləʊnlɪ]	*lonely* → alone	einsam
	⟨fever⟩ [ˈfiːvə]		Fieber
	⟨John Masefield⟩ [ˌdʒɒn ˈmeɪzfiːld]		*brit. Autor*
	the North Sea [ðə ˌnɔːθ ˈsiː]		Nordsee
	oil [ɔɪl]		Öl
	flat [flæt]	*flat* ⟷ steep	flach
	cliff [klɪf]		Klippe
	close to [ˈkləʊs tə]	= near	nahe bei
	°**unpredictable** [ˌʌnprɪˈdɪktəbl]	The weather in the mountains changes quickly. It can be very ~.	unberechenbar
	calm [kɑːm]	Beachte die Aussprache. Das ‘l’ wird nicht gesprochen.	ruhig
	wave [weɪv]		Welle
	rough [rʌf]	*rough* sea ⟷ calm sea	rau, stürmisch
	°**tides** [taɪdz]		die Gezeiten
	°**tide** [taɪd]	 low *tide* = Ebbe high *tide* = Flut 	Flut, Ebbe
	coastguard [ˈkəʊstgɑːd]	*coastguard* → coast	Küstenwacht
	°**lifeboat** [ˈlaɪfbəʊt]		Rettungsboot
2	to **be into s.th.** [bɪ ˈɪntʊ ˌsʌmθɪŋ]	to like doing s.th. very much	etwas sehr gern machen
c)	**blood** [blʌd]	Beachte die Aussprache.	Blut
3b)	**description** [dɪˈskrɪpʃn]	*description* → to describe	Beschreibung
⟨5⟩	stormy [ˈstɔːmɪ]		stürmisch
	lifeboatman [ˈlaɪfbəʊtmən]		Seenotrettungsmann
	extra-ordinary [ekˈstrɔːdnrɪ]		ungewöhnlich, speziell; besonders mittelmäßig
	Thing about the sea is … [ˈθɪŋ‿əˌbaʊt ðə ˈsiː ɪz]		*etwa:* Mit dem Meer ist das so …
	Splash! [splæʃ]		Platsch!

Vocabulary

Step B **Out in the North Sea**

	°**oil rig** ['ɔːl rɪg]		Ölbohrplattform
	helicopter ['helɪkɒptə]		Hubschrauber
2a)	**fisherman** ['fɪʃəmən]	*fisherman* → fish	Fischer
3a)	°**conditional** [kən'dɪʃənl]	would + infinitive = *conditional*	das Konditional

Step B **The lifeboat service**

	°**crew** [kruː]	group of people who work together on a ship or plane	Mannschaft, Besatzung
	to **inform s.o. about s.th** [ɪn'fɔːm ˌsʌmwʌn ə'baʊt ˌsʌmθɪŋ]	*to inform* → information	jdn. über etw. informieren
	safety ['seɪftɪ]	*safety* → safe	Sicherheit
6a)	**instructions** (*pl*) [ɪn'strʌkʃnz]	The *crew* on a plane gives you *safety instructions* before the flight.	Gebrauchsanweisung, Anweisungen
	radio ['reɪdɪəʊ]		Radio, Funkgerät
	⟨to slip⟩ [slɪp]		ausrutschen
	⟨darling⟩ ['dɑːlɪŋ]		Liebling

b)	**tide table** ['taɪd ˌteɪbl]	a table, a *tide table*, a timetable	Gezeitentabelle
	°**lifejacket** ['laɪfdʒækɪt]	At sea it is important to wear a ~.	Schwimmweste
8	°**tanker** ['tæŋkə]		Tanker
⟨9⟩	sloop ['sluːp]		*historischer Segelschiffstyp*
	Nassau ['næsɔː]		*Ort auf den Bahamas*
	We did roam ... [wiː dɪd rəʊm]		*etwa:* Wir trieben uns herum ...
	broke-up [ˌbrəʊk‿'ʌp]		kaputt, erledigt
	to hoist up [ˌhɔɪst‿'ʌp]		(Segel) hissen
	sail [seɪl]		Segel
	mainsail ['meɪnseɪl]		Großsegel
	to set [set]		setzen
	ashore [ə'ʃɔː]		an Land
	to get drunk [ˌget 'drʌŋk]		sich betrinken
	to break into s.th. [breɪk 'ɪntə ˌsʌmθɪŋ]		einbrechen in/bei
	captain ['kæptɪn]		Kapitän
	trunk [trʌŋk]		Schrankkoffer
	constable ['kʌnstəbl]		Gendarm, Polizist

Step C **Sea Rescue**

	rescue ['reskju:]	*rescue* → to rescue	Rettung
1a)	**trapped** ['træpt]		eingeschlossen, abgeschnitten
	⟨lifeguard⟩ ['laɪfgɑ:d]		Rettungsschwimmer/in
	⟨to be on patrol⟩ [ˌɒn pə'trəʊl]		auf Kontrollgang sein
	⟨otherwise⟩ ['ʌðəwaɪz]		sonst, ansonsten
	to **dial** ['daɪəl]	She *dialled* 999 and asked for the coastguard.	(Telefonnummer) wählen, eintippen
	⟨maritime⟩ ['mærɪtaɪm]		Meeres-
	emergency [ɪ'mɜ:dʒənsɪ]	Only use that door in an ~.	Notfall
	⟨to co-ordinate⟩ [ˌkəʊ'ɔ:dɪneɪt]		koordinieren
	search [sɜ:tʃ]	 a *search* and rescue helicopter	Suche
	⟨red flare⟩ ['fleə]		Leuchtrakete
2	**kid** [kɪd]	= child	Kind
	engine ['endʒɪn]	There is an ~ in a car, in a plane, in a lot of machines ...	Motor, Maschine
	onto ['ɒntu:]		auf ... hinauf
	serious ['sɪərɪəs]	Pollution is a ~ problem.	ernst
	Broad Haven [ˌbrɔ:d 'heɪvn]		*Küstenort in Wales*
	Nolton Haven [ˌnɒltn 'heɪvn]		*Küstenort in Wales*
	°**nightmare** ['naɪtmeə]	= a bad dream	Alptraum
	Druidston ['dru:ɪdstn]		*Küstenort in Wales*
	Milford Haven [ˌmɪlfəd 'heɪvn]		*Küstenort in Wales*
	one by one [ˌwʌn baɪ 'wʌn]	= one after the other	einer nach dem anderen
	to **turn s.th. over** [ˌtɜ:n sʌmθɪŋ 'əʊvə]	The waves *turned the boat over.*	etw. umdrehen, umwerfen, zum Kentern bringen
	might [maɪt]	it *might* be = it could be	könnte
	Hold on! [ˌhəʊld 'ɒn]		Festhalten!
	brave [breɪv]	Nicht mit dem ähnlichen deutschen Wort verwechseln.	tapfer, mutig
	medal [medl]		Medaille
4c)	to **leave out** [ˌli:v 'aʊt]	*to leave out* ⟷ to add	auslassen, weglassen

Step D **Let's check**

⟨4⟩	diet ['daɪət]		Diät, Ernährung

Alphabetical word list

In dieser alphabetischen Liste ist das gesamte Vokabular von *Green Line New 1, 2* und *3* enthalten. Namen werden in einer gesonderten Liste nach dem Vokabular aufgeführt.

Die mit einem ° gekennzeichneten Wörter zeichnen den rezeptiven Wortschatz aus. In Bundesländern, in denen nicht ausdrücklich rezeptiver Wortschatz verlangt wird, werden diese Wörter genauso behandelt wie der übrige Wortschatz. Die rezeptiv gekennzeichneten Wörter können innerhalb der Unit, in der sie erstmalig vorkommen, eigenständig von den Schülerinnen und Schülern angewandt werden. Falls sie in späteren Units auftauchen, werden sie nur mit Hilfe von Vorgaben verlangt.

Der Wortschatz aus Übungen und Texten, die in Spitzklammern ⟨ ⟩ stehen, ist wahlfrei.
Das Zeichen * nach einem Verb bedeutet: unregelmäßiges Verb.
Die Zahlen verweisen auf das erstmalige Vorkommen der Wörter, z. B.
about [ə'baʊt] über **I** = Green Line New Band 1
above [ə'bʌv] über **II 5**, 42 = Green Line New Band 2, Unit 5, Seite 42

A

a [ə] ein/eine **I**
'A' level ['eɪ ˌlevl] *britische Abiturprüfung* **III 2**, 33
to be **able to** [bɪ‿'eɪbl tə] können **II**
about [ə'baʊt] über **I**
to talk about ['tɔːk‿əˌbaʊt] reden über, sprechen über **I**
to write about ['raɪt‿əˌbaʊt] schreiben über **I**
What about ...? ['wɒt‿əˌbaʊt] Was ist mit ...?, Wie wär's mit ...? **I**
about [ə'baʊt] etwa, circa **III WSD**, 77
above [ə'bʌv] über **II**
accent ['æksent] Akzent **III WSA**, 9
accident ['æksɪdənt] Unfall **I**
across [ə'krɒs] (quer) über **III 1**, 22
to **act** [ækt] sich verhalten **III 1**, 23; spielen, nachspielen **I**
to **act normal** [ˌækt 'nɔːml] sich normal verhalten **III 1**, 23
action ['ækʃn] Handlung, Geschehen **II**
activity [æk'tɪvətɪ] Tätigkeit, Unternehmung **I**
actor ['æktə] Schauspieler **II**
°**AD** [ˌeɪ 'diː] nach Christus **III 3**, 50
to **add** [æd] hinzufügen **II**
address [ə'dres] Adresse, Anschrift **II**
adjective ['ædʒɪktɪv] Adjektiv **II**
adult ['ædʌlt] Erwachsener **II**
adventure [əd'ventʃə] Abenteuer **II**
adverb ['ædvɜːb] Adverb **II**
advice *(no pl)* [əd'vaɪs] Rat(schlag) **III 2**, 40
⟨to affect⟩ [ə'fekt] beeinflussen, sich auswirken auf **III WSC**, 59
°**African** ['æfrɪkən] afrikanisch, Afrikaner/in **III 1**, 16
after ['ɑːftə] nach **I**
after a time [ˌɑːftər‿ə 'taɪm] nach einer Weile **II**
after all ['ɑːftər‿ˌɔːl] trotz allem, doch **III 2**, 40
afternoon [ˌɑːftə'nuːn] Nachmittag **I**
in the afternoon [ɪn ðɪ‿ˌɑːftə'nuːn] am Nachmittag, nachmittags **I**
this afternoon [ðɪs‿ˌɑːftə'nuːn] heute Nachmittag **I**
afterwards ['ɑːftəwədz] nachher, später, danach **III 1**, 22
again [ə'gen] noch einmal, wieder **I**
against [ə'genst] gegen **III 2**, 40
age [eɪdʒ] Alter **II**
the Middle Ages [ðə ˌmɪdl 'eɪdʒɪz] das Mittelalter **II**
travel **agent's** ['trævl‿ˌeɪdʒənts] Reisebüro **II**
ago [ə'gəʊ] vor **II**
a hundred years ago [ə ˌhʌndrəd 'jɪəz‿əˌgəʊ] vor hundert Jahren **II**
a long time ago [ə ˌlɒŋ taɪm‿ə'gəʊ] lange her **II**
to **agree** [ə'griː] zustimmen, der gleichen Meinung sein **III 1**, 20
⟨Ain't no route.⟩ ['eɪnt ˌnəʊ 'ruːt] *etwa:* Es gibt keine Straße. **III 4**, 72
⟨Ain't no use setting up with a bad companion.⟩ *etwa:* Es hat keinen Zweck, dich mit mir anzulegen. **III 4**, 72
⟨Ain't nobody get the better of you-know-who.⟩ *etwa:* Niemand kommt gegen mich an. **III 4**, 72
⟨Ain't nobody know ...⟩ [eɪnt 'nəʊbədɪ nəʊ] *etwa:* Keiner weiß ... **III 4**, 72
⟨I ain't gonna lose.⟩ [aɪ 'eɪnt ˌgɒnə 'luːz] Ich werde nicht verlieren. **III WSB**, 29
air [eə] Luft **III 4**, 64
°air stream travel ['eə striːm ˌtrævl] Luftstromtransport **III 4**, 69
airport ['eəpɔːt] Flughafen **I**
alive [ə'laɪv] lebendig, am Leben **III WSA**, 7
all [ɔːl] ganz, völlig **I**
all over ['ɔːl‿ˌəʊvə] überall (auf) **I**
all right [ˌɔːl 'raɪt] in Ordnung **II**
all [ɔːl] alle/alles **I**
to be **allowed to** [bɪ‿ə'laʊd tə] dürfen **II**
almost ['ɔːlməʊst] fast **II**
alone [ə'ləʊn] allein **II**
Leave me alone! ['liːv mɪ‿ə'ləʊn] Lass mich in Ruhe! **II**
along [ə'lɒŋ] entlang **III 1**, 23
alphabet ['ælfəbet] Alphabet **I**
alphabetical [ælfə'betɪkl] alphabetisch **II**
already [ɔːl'redɪ] schon, bereits **I**
although [ɔːl'ðəʊ] obwohl **II**
always ['ɔːlweɪz] immer **I**
ambulance ['æmbjʊləns] Krankenwagen **I**
American [ə'merɪkən] amerikanisch, Amerikaner/in **II**
an [ən] ein/eine **I**
and [ænd/ənd] und **I**
and so on [ənd 'səʊ ɒn] und so weiter **II**
angry ['æŋgrɪ] böse, verärgert **I**
animal ['ænɪml] Tier **I**
anorak ['ænəræk] Anorak **I**
another [ə'nʌðə] ein anderer/eine andere/ein anderes; noch ein/eine **I**
answer ['ɑːnsə] Antwort **I**
answering machine ['ɑːnsərɪŋ məˌʃiːn] Anrufbeantworter **III WSA**, 10
to **answer** ['ɑːnsə] antworten, beantworten **I**

any ['enɪ] etwas, einige, irgend- **I**
anybody ['enɪbɒdɪ] (irgend)jemand **II**
anyone ['enɪwʌn] (irgend)jemand **II**
anything ['enɪθɪŋ] (irgend)etwas **I**
anyway ['enɪweɪ] jedenfalls, sowieso **II**
anywhere ['enɪweə] irgendwo **II**
to **appear** [ə'pɪə] erscheinen **III 2**, 40
appendix [ə'pendɪks] Blinddarm **II**
apple ['æpl] Apfel **I**
April ['eɪprəl] April **I**
area ['eərɪə] Gegend, Gebiet **III 3**, 46
arm [ɑ:m] Arm **I**
army ['ɑ:mɪ] Armee **III 1**, 19
around [ə'raʊnd] um **II**
° **arrangement** [ə'reɪndʒmənt] Plan **III 2**, 38
to **arrive** [ə'raɪv] ankommen **I**
arrow ['ærəʊ] Pfeil **II**
Art [ɑ:t] Kunst **II**
article ['ɑ:tɪkl] Artikel **III WSB**, 31
as [æz] in der Rolle von, als **II**
as ... **as** [əz ... əz] so ... wie **II**
as [æz] während **II**
as soon as [əz 'su:n_əz] sobald **II**
⟨ashore⟩ [ə'ʃɔ:] an Land **III 5**, 83
to **ask** [ɑ:sk] fragen **I**
  to ask for ['ɑ:sk fə] bitten um **I**
assembly [ə'semblɪ] Versammlung **I**
  Assembly Hall [ə'semblɪ ˌhɔ:l] Versammlungssaal, Aula **II**
° **assembly line** [ə'semblɪ ˌlaɪn] Fließband **III 4**, 69
assistant [ə'sɪstənt] Helfer/in, Assistent/in **I**
  shop assistant ['ʃɒp_əˌsɪstənt] Verkäufer/in **I**
  vet's assistant ['vets_əˌsɪstənt] Tierarzthelfer/in **I**
at [æt/ət] an; um *(bei Zeitangaben)* **I**
  at first [ət 'fɜ:st] zuerst **II**
  at home [ət 'həʊm] zu Hause **I**
  at last [ət 'lɑ:st] schließlich, zuletzt **I**
  at least [ət 'li:st] wenigstens **II**
  at lunchtime [ət 'lʌntʃtaɪm] in der Mittagspause **II**
  at night [ət 'naɪt] nachts **II**
  at once [ət 'wʌns] sofort **II**
  at the bottom of [ət ðə 'bɒtəm_əv] ganz unten, hinten **I**
  at the doctor's [ət ðə 'dɒktəz] beim Arzt **II**
  at the door [ət ðə 'dɔ:] an der Tür **I**
  at the top of ... [ət ðə 'tɒp_əv] ganz oben **I**
athletics [æθ'letɪks] Leichtathletik **III WSB**, 26
° **attraction** [ə'trækʃn] Attraktion **III 1**, 14
August ['ɔ:gəst] August **I**
aunt [ɑ:nt] Tante **I**
  aunty ['ɑ:ntɪ] *Anrede für eine Tante* **I**
author ['ɔ:θə] Autor/in **III WSC**, 60
autograph ['ɔ:təgrɑ:f] Autogramm **II**
autumn ['ɔ:təm] Herbst **I**
away [ə'weɪ] weg, fort **I**
  Go away! [ˌgəʊ_ə'weɪ] Geh weg!, Weg mit dir! **II**
  to give away [ˌgɪv_ə'weɪ] weggeben, verschenken **II**

B

baby ['beɪbɪ] Baby **I**
  to have a baby [ˌhəv ə 'beɪbɪ] ein Baby bekommen **III 4**, 69
babysitting ['beɪbɪˌsɪtɪŋ] Babysitten **II**
back [bæk] hintere/hinterer/hinteres, Hinter- **III 2**, 36
back [bæk] zurück **I**
  back door [ˌbæk 'dɔ:] Hintertür **I**
bad [bæd] schlecht, schlimm **I**
badminton ['bædmɪntən] Federballspiel **I**
bag [bæg] Tasche **I**
bagpipes ['bægpaɪps] Dudelsack **II**
ball [bɔ:l] Ball **I**
banana [bə'nɑ:nə] Banane **I**
band [bænd] (Musik-)Gruppe **II**
  brass band [ˌbrɑ:s 'bænd] Blasorchester **II**
bank [bæŋk] Bank **I**
  bank clerk ['bæŋk ˌklɑ:k] Bankangestellte/r **I**
bar [bɑ:] Tafel, Stück **I**
to **bark** [bɑ:k] bellen **I**
bat [bæt] Schläger *(für Tischtennis)* **III WSB**, 29
bath [bɑ:θ] Bad, Badewanne **I**
  bubble bath ['bʌbl ˌbɑ:θ] Schaumbad **I**
  to have a bath [ˌhæv_ə 'bɑ:θ] baden, ein Bad nehmen **I**
bathroom ['bɑ:θrʊm] Badezimmer **I**
battle ['bætl] Kampf, Schlacht **III 1**, 19
° **BC** [ˌbi: 'si:] vor Christus **III 3**, 50
to **be*** [bɪ] sein **I**
  to be able to [bɪ_'eɪbl tə] können **II**
  to be allowed to [bɪ_ə'laʊd tə] dürfen **II**
  to be annoyed [ˌbɪ ə'nɔɪd] ärgerlich sein **III 2**, 40
  to be called [bɪ 'kɔ:ld] heißen **II**
  to be careful [bɪ 'keəfʊl] vorsichtig sein, Acht geben **I**
  to be excited [bɪ_ɪk'saɪtɪd] aufgeregt sein **I**
  ⟨to be excused⟩ [ˌbɪ ɪk'skju:zd] den Unterricht verlassen **III 2**, 33
  to be finished [bɪ 'fɪnɪʃt] fertig sein **I**
  to be fun [bɪ 'fʌn] Spaß machen **I**
  to be going to [bɪ 'gəʊɪŋ tə] werden **I**
  to be good at ... [bɪ 'gʊd_ət] gut sein in ... **I**
  to be in a hurry [ˌbɪ ɪn_ə 'hʌrɪ] es eilig haben **III 2**, 40
  ⟨to be in use⟩ [ˌbɪ ɪn 'ju:s] benutzt werden **III WSC**, 59
  to be into s.th. [bɪ 'ɪntʊ ˌsʌmθɪŋ] etw. sehr gern machen **III 5**, 78
  to be lucky [bɪ 'lʌkɪ] Glück haben **I**
  to be on [bɪ_'ɒn] eingeschaltet sein **I**
  to be pleased with [ˌbɪ 'pli:zd ˌwɪð] mit etw. zufrieden sein, sich über etw. freuen **III 2**, 34
  to be quiet [bɪ 'kwaɪət] ruhig sein, still sein **I**
  to be right [bɪ 'raɪt] Recht haben **II**
  to be scared of [bɪ 'skeəd_əv] Angst haben vor **II**
  to be sure [bɪ 'ʃɔ:] sicher sein **I**
  to be surprised [bɪ sə'praɪzd] überrascht sein **I**
  to be tired of s.th. [bɪ 'taɪəd_ɒv] genug von etw. haben **III 1**, 21
beach [bi:tʃ] Strand **I**
bean [bi:n] Bohne **II**
bear [beə] Bär **II**
beard [bɪəd] Bart **II**
beautiful ['bju:təfʊl] schön **II**
because [bɪ'kɒz] weil **I**
to **become*** [bɪ'kʌm] werden **III 1**, 19
bed [bed] Bett **I**
  B&B (= bed and breakfast) [ˌbi:_ən_'bi:] Privatpension **III 3**, 45
  bed and breakfast place [ˌbed_ənd 'brekfəst pleɪs] Frühstückspension **II**
  to get out of bed on the wrong side [get_aʊt_əv ˌbed_ɒn ðə rɒŋ 'saɪd] mit dem falschen Fuß aufstehen **II**
bedroom ['bedrʊm] Schlafzimmer **I**
beef [bi:f] Rindfleisch **II**
  roast beef [ˌrəʊst 'bi:f] Rinderbraten **II**
° **Beefeater** ['bi:fˌi:tə] *Wächter im Tower* **III 1**, 19

beetle ['bi:tl] Käfer **I**
before [bɪ'fɔ:] bevor **II;** vor *(zeitlich)* **I**
to **begin*** [bɪ'gɪn] beginnen, anfangen **II**
beginning [bɪ'gɪnɪŋ] Anfang **II**
behind [bɪ'haɪnd] hinter **I**
from behind [ˌfrɒm bɪ'haɪnd] von hinten **II**
Belgian ['beldʒən] belgisch, Belgier/in **III WSA**, 7
to **believe** [bɪ'li:v] glauben **III 3**, 53
°**bell** [bel] Glocke, Klingel **III 2**, 41
bench [bentʃ] Bank *(zum Sitzen)* **III WSB**, 31
to **bend*** [bend] beugen, (ver)biegen **III 1**, 22
to bend down [ˌbend 'daʊn] sich bücken **II**
best [best] beste/bester/bestes **I**
best of all ['best‿əv‿ɔ:l] am allerbesten **I**
better ['betə] besser **I**
⟨Ain't nobody get the better of you-know-who.⟩ *etwa:* Niemand kommt gegen mich an. **III 4**, 72
between [bɪ'twi:n] zwischen **I**
big [bɪg] groß **I**
Big Wheel [ˌbɪg‿'wi:l] Riesenrad **II**
bike [baɪk] Fahrrad **I**
biology [baɪ'ɒlədʒɪ] Biologie **III 4**, 69
bird [bɜ:d] Vogel **II**
bird watcher ['bɜ:d ˌwɒtʃə] Vogelbeobachter/in **II**
biro ['baɪrəʊ] Kugelschreiber, Kuli **I**
birthday ['bɜ:θdeɪ] Geburtstag **I**
biscuit ['bɪskɪt] Keks **I**
dog biscuit ['dɒg ˌbɪskɪt] Hundekuchen **I**
bit [bɪt] Teil, Stück **III 1**, 14
a **bit** [ə‿'bɪt] etwas, ein bisschen **I**
black [blæk] schwarz **I**
blood [blʌd] Blut **III 5**, 78
to **blow*** [bləʊ] blasen **III WSC**, 56
blue [blu:] blau **I**
⟨blues⟩ [blu:z] deprimierte Stimmung **III WSC**, 56
board [bɔ:d] (Schul-)Tafel **III WSB**, 27
notice board ['nəʊtɪs bɔ:d] schwarzes Brett **II**
boarding school ['bɔ:dɪŋ sku:l] Internat **III 2**, 33
boat [bəʊt] Boot **I**
boating lake ['bəʊtɪŋ leɪk] Bootsteich **I**
body ['bɒdɪ] Körper **I**
book [bʊk] Buch **I**
bookshop ['bʊkʃɒp] Buchhandlung **II**
exercise book ['eksəsaɪz ˌbʊk] (Übungs-)Heft **II**
to **book** [bʊk] buchen, reservieren **III WSA**, 11
°**border** ['bɔ:də] Grenze **III WSC**, 58
boring ['bɔ:rɪŋ] langweilig **I**
She was **born** … [ˌʃi: wəz 'bɔ:n] Sie ist … geboren. **III 1**, 16
both [bəʊθ] beide **II**
to **bother s.o.** ['bɒðə] jdn. stören **II**
bottle ['bɒtl] Flasche **I**
°bottle bank ['bɒtl ˌbæŋk] Glascontainer **III 4**, 66
at the **bottom of** [ət ðə 'bɒtəm‿əv] ganz unten, hinten **I**
bow [bəʊ] Bogen **II**
⟨I've taken my bows.⟩ [aɪv 'teɪkən maɪ 'baʊz] *etwa*: Ich habe viel Applaus bekommen. **III WSB**, 29
box [bɒks] Schachtel, Kiste, Dose **I**
lunch box ['lʌntʃ ˌbɒks] *Dose für belegte Brote zum Mittagessen* **I**
boy [bɔɪ] Junge **I**
°**boyfriend** ['bɔɪfrend] (fester) Freund **III WSD**, 75
⟨brain⟩ [breɪn] Gehirn **III 2**, 33
brainstorming ['breɪnstɔ:mɪŋ] Ideen sammeln **III WSD**, 75
brass band [ˌbrɑ:s 'bænd] Blasorchester **II**
brave [breɪv] tapfer **III 5**, 85
bread [bred] Brot **I**
break [breɪk] Pause **II**
to **break*** [breɪk] brechen, kaputtmachen **II**
⟨to break a horse⟩ [ˌbreɪk‿ə 'hɔ:s] ein Pferd zureiten **III WSC**, 60
⟨to break into s.th.⟩ [breɪk 'ɪntə ˌsʌmθɪŋ] einbrechen in/bei **III 5**, 83
breakable ['breɪkəbl] zerbrechlich **III WSB**, 31
breakfast ['brekfəst] Frühstück **I**
to have breakfast [ˌhæv 'brekfəst] frühstücken **II**
⟨brick⟩ [brɪk] Ziegel **III WSC**, 60
bridge [brɪdʒ] Brücke **III 1**, 14
fire **brigade** ['faɪə brɪˌgeɪd] Feuerwehr **I**
bring-and-buy sale [ˌbrɪŋ‿nd 'baɪ seɪl] Flohmarkt **II**
to **bring*** [brɪŋ] bringen **II**
to bring here [brɪŋ 'hɪə] herbringen **I**
British ['brɪtɪʃ] britisch, Britisch **I**
brochure ['brəʊʃə] Broschüre, Prospekt **II**
⟨broke-up⟩ [ˌbrəʊk 'ʌp] kaputt, erledigt **III 5**, 83
broken ['brəʊkn] zerbrochen, kaputt **I**
brother ['brʌðə] Bruder **I**
brown [braʊn] braun **I**
bubble bath ['bʌbl ˌbɑ:θ] Schaumbad **I**
bucket ['bʌkɪt] Eimer **I**
budgie ['bʌdʒɪ] Wellensittich **II**
to **build*** [bɪld] bauen **III 1**, 19
°**bulldozer** ['bʊldəʊzə] Bulldozer **III 4**, 65
bully ['bʊlɪ] Rabauke, Rüpel, Tyrann **II**
to **bully** ['bʊlɪ] schikanieren, tyrannisieren **II**
burglar ['bɜ:glə] Einbrecher/in **I**
to **burn*** [bɜ:n] (ver-/nieder-)brennen **III WSC**, 58
bus [bʌs] Bus **I**
bus shelter ['bʌs ˌʃeltə] überdachte Bushaltestelle **III WSA**, 12
bus stop ['bʌs‿stɒp] Bushaltestelle **I**
busy ['bɪzɪ] beschäftigt **II**
but [bʌt] aber **I**
butter ['bʌtə] Butter **I**
to **buy*** [baɪ] kaufen **I**
by [baɪ] mit **I**
by heart [baɪ 'hɑ:t] auswendig **II**

C

cabbage ['kæbɪdʒ] Kohl **II**
cage [keɪdʒ] Käfig **II**
cake [keɪk] Kuchen, Torte **I**
fruit cake ['fru:t keɪk] *engl. Kuchen* **II**
calf, calves *(pl)* [kɑ:f] Kalb, Kälber **I**
call [kɔ:l] Anruf **III WSA**, 10
to make a call [ˌmeɪk‿ə 'kɔ:l] jdn. anrufen **III WSA**, 10
to **call** [kɔ:l] nennen **III WSA**, 8; rufen, anrufen **I**
to be called [bɪ 'kɔ:ld] heißen **II**
calm [kɑ:m] ruhig **III 5**, 78
camcorder ['kæmˌkɔ:də] Videokamera **II**
camera ['kæmərə] Fotoapparat, Kamera **I**
°**camp** [kæmp] (Heer-)Lager **III 3**, 45
to go **camping** [ˌgəʊ 'kæmpɪŋ] zelten gehen **I**
can [kæn] können **I**
⟨Can't buy me love.⟩ ['kɑ:nt ˌbaɪ mi: 'lʌv] *etwa:* Liebe kann man nicht kaufen. **III 2**, 41
°to **cancel** ['kænsl] absagen, abbestellen, stornieren **III WSA**, 11
candle ['kændl] Kerze **I**
canteen [kæn'ti:n] Kantine, Cafeteria **I**
capital ['kæpɪtl] Hauptstadt **III 3**, 45
capital letter [ˌkæpɪtl 'letə] Großbuchstabe **III WSD**, 77

⟨captain⟩ ['kæptɪn] Kapitän **III 5**, 83
car [kɑ:] Auto **I**
car park ['kɑ: pɑ:k] Parkhaus, Parkplatz **II**
car wash ['kɑ: wɒʃ] Autowaschanlage **II**
° multi-storey car park [ˌmʌltɪ stɔ:rɪ 'kɑ: pɑ:k] Parkhochhaus **III 4**, 72
caravan ['kærəvæn] Wohnwagen **I**
card [kɑ:d] Karte **I**
⟨to care for⟩ ['keə ˌfɔ:] gerne mögen **III 2**, 41
to be **careful** [bɪ 'keəfʊl] vorsichtig sein, Acht geben **I**
carefully ['keəflɪ] vorsichtig, sorgfältig **II**
careless ['keəlɪs] nachlässig **III WSB**, 31
° **carnival** ['kɑ:nɪvl] Karneval, Volksfest **III 1**, 14
carrot ['kærət] Karotte, Möhre **II**
to **carry** ['kærɪ] tragen **II**
cartoon [kɑ:'tu:n] Karikatur, Bilderwitz **III 4**, 72
case [keɪs] Fall **III 2**, 36
pencil case ['pensl keɪs] Federmäppchen **I**
cassette [kə'set] Kassette **II**
castle ['kɑ:sl] Burg **I**
cat [kæt] Katze **I**
to **catch*** [kætʃ] fangen **II**
to catch up with s.o. [ˌkætʃ 'ʌp wɪð ˌsʌmwʌn] jdn. einholen **III 1**, 23
cathedral [kə'θi:drəl] Kathedrale, Dom **III 1**, 14
to **cause** [kɔ:z] verursachen **III 4**, 64
⟨'cause (= because)⟩ [kɒz = bɪ'kɒz] weil **III WSB**, 29
cave [keɪv] Höhle **II**
CD [si:'di:] CD **I**
CD player [si:'di: pleɪə] CD-Spieler **I**
° **Celtic** ['keltɪk] keltisch **III 3**, 50
centre ['sentə] Zentrum, Mitte **I**
city centre [ˌsɪtɪ 'sentə] Stadtzentrum **I**
shopping centre ['ʃɒpɪŋ ˌsentə] Einkaufszentrum **II**
sports centre ['spɔ:ts ˌsentə] Sportzentrum **II**
° **century** ['sentʃʊrɪ] Jahrhundert **III 3**, 45
° **certificate** [sə'tɪfɪkət] Zeugnis, Urkunde **III 2**, 33
chair [tʃeə] Stuhl **I**
⟨challenge⟩ ['tʃælɪndʒ] Herausforderung **III WSB**, 29
champion ['tʃæmpjən] Champion-, Meister- **II**
chance [tʃɑ:ns] Chance **III 2**, 36
change [tʃeɪndʒ] Veränderung, Wechsel **III WSC**, 60
to **change** [tʃeɪndʒ] (sich) ändern, verändern, wechseln **II**; umsteigen, wechseln **III 1**, 18
changeable ['tʃeɪndʒəbl] wechselhaft **III WSB**, 31
changing room ['tʃeɪndʒɪŋ ˌru:m] Umkleideraum **III WSB**, 29
character ['kærəktə] Person, Charakter **I**
charity ['tʃærətɪ] Wohltätigkeitsverein **II**
cheap [tʃi:p] billig **II**
to **check** [tʃek] überprüfen, kontrollieren **I**
to check in [ˌtʃek_'ɪn] sich anmelden, einchecken **III WSA**, 11
checklist ['tʃeklɪst] Kontrollliste **III 1**, 24
cheer ['tʃɪə] Jubelruf **III 3**, 53
Cheer up! [ˌtʃɪər_'ʌp] Kopf hoch! **III 1**, 22
cheese [tʃi:z] Käse **I**
chemist's ['kemɪsts] Apotheke **II**
chicken ['tʃɪkn] Huhn **I**
child, children *(pl)* [tʃaɪld] Kind, Kinder **I**
Chinese [ˌtʃaɪ'ni:z] chinesisch, Chinesisch, Chinese/Chinesin **II**
chips [tʃɪps] Pommes frites **I**
chocolate ['tʃɒklət] Schokolade **I**
choice [tʃɔɪs] Wahl **III 3**, 49
° **choir** ['kwaɪə] Chor **III 3**, 45
to **choose*** [tʃu:z] wählen, aussuchen **II**
⟨chorus⟩ ['kɔ:rəs] Refrain **III 4**, 72

Christmas ['krɪsməs] Weihnachten **II**
Christmas Day [ˌkrɪsməs 'deɪ] erster Weihnachtsfeiertag **III 1**, 19
church [tʃɜ:tʃ] Kirche **I**
cinema ['sɪnəmə] Kino **I**
circus ['sɜ:kəs] Zirkus, Ring **III 1**, 14
city ['sɪtɪ] Stadt **I**
city centre [ˌsɪtɪ 'sentə] Stadtzentrum **I**
City Information Centre [ˌsɪtɪ_ɪnfə'meɪʃn ˌsentə] Touristeninformation **I**
to **clap** [klæp] klatschen, Beifall geben **II**
class [klɑ:s] Klasse *(in einer deutschen Schule)* **I**
classroom ['klɑ:srʊm] Klassenzimmer **I**
° **clause** [klɔ:z] (Teil-)Satz **III 2**, 37
to **clean** [kli:n] putzen, sauber machen **II**
clean [kli:n] sauber **II**
clear ['klɪə] klar **III WSD**, 77
clerk [klɑ:k] Büroangestellte/r **I**
bank clerk ['bæŋk ˌklɑ:k] Bankangestellte/r **I**
clever ['klevə] intelligent, klug **I**
° to **click on s.th.** ['klɪk ɒn ˌsʌmθɪŋ] etw. anklicken *(mit der Computer-Maus)* **III WSD**, 75
cliff [klɪf] Klippe **III 5**, 78
to **climb up** [ˌklaɪm_'ʌp] heraufklettern **I**
climbing ['klaɪmɪŋ] Bergsteigen, Klettern **II**
clock [klɒk] Uhr **II**
to **close** [kləʊz] (sich) schließen **I**
close to ['kləʊs tə] nahe bei **III 5**, 78
closed [kləʊzd] zu, geschlossen **II**
clothes [kləʊðz] Kleidung **I**
cloud [klaʊd] Wolke **II**
° **clown** [klaʊn] Clown **III 1**, 21
club [klʌb] Klub, Verein **II**
clue [klu:] Anhaltspunkt, Spur **III 2**, 40
⟨to co-ordinate⟩ [ˌkəʊ'ɔ:dɪneɪt] koordinieren **III 5**, 84
coach [kəʊtʃ] Reisebus **II**
coal [kəʊl] Kohle **III 3**, 45
coast [kəʊst] Küste **III 1**, 19
coastguard ['kəʊstgɑ:d] Küstenwacht **III 5**, 78
coat [kəʊt] Mantel **II**
coconut ['kəʊkənʌt] Kokosnuss **II**
coconut shy ['kəʊkənʌt ˌʃaɪ] Wurfbude **II**
coffee ['kɒfɪ] Kaffee **II**
coffee shop ['kɒfɪ ˌʃɒp] Café **II**
to have a **cold** [ˌhæv ə 'kəʊld] erkältet sein **III WSC**, 56
cold [kəʊld] kalt **I**
to **collect** [kə'lekt] abholen; sammeln, einsammeln **I**
colour ['kʌlə] Farbe **I**
to **colour in** [ˌkʌlər_'ɪn] anmalen **I**
colourful ['kʌləfʊl] bunt **III WSD**, 74
to **come*** [kʌm] kommen **I**
Come on. [kʌm_'ɒn] Komm/t schon. **I**
to come in [kʌm_'ɪn] hereinkommen **I**
to come off [kʌm_'ɒf] runterfallen **II**
comic ['kɒmɪk] Comic **I**
comma ['kɒmə] Komma **III WSD**, 77
comment ['kɒment] Kommentar **III 2**, 34
⟨to commit a crime⟩ [kəˌmɪt_ə 'kraɪm] ein Verbrechen begehen **III WSB**, 29
to **compare** [kəm'peə] vergleichen **II**
to **compete in s.th.** [kəm'pi:t] an einem Wettbewerb teilnehmen **III WSB**, 26
competition [ˌkɒmpə'tɪʃn] Wettbewerb, Preisausschreiben **I**
to **complete** [kəm'pli:t] fertig stellen, beenden **II**
complete [kəm'pli:t] komplett, vollständig **III WSC**, 56
compound ['kɒmpaʊnd] zusammengesetztes Wort **II**

°**comprehensive school** [ˌkɒmprɪˈhensɪv ˌskuːl] *Gesamtschule in GB* **III 2**, 33
computer [kəmˈpjuːtə] Computer **I**
to **concentrate** [ˈkɒnsəntreɪt] sich konzentrieren **III WSB**, 30
concert [ˈkɒnsət] Konzert **II**
°**conditional** [kənˈdɪʃənl] das Konditional **III 5**, 81
conference [ˈkɒnfərəns] Konferenz **III 2**, 32
⟨Congratulations!⟩ [kənˌgrætʃʊˈleɪʃnz] Herzlichen Glückwunsch! **III WSD**, 77
conjunction [kənˈdʒʌŋkʃn] Konjunktion, Bindewort **II**
to **conquer** [ˈkɒŋkə] erobern **III 3**, 45
⟨to consider⟩ [kənˈsɪdə] betrachten als **III WSB**, 29
⟨constable⟩ [ˈkʌnstəbl] Gendarm, Polizist **III 5**, 83
context [ˈkɒntekst] Zusammenhang **III WSB**, 26
to **cook** [kʊk] kochen **II**
copy [ˈkɒpɪ] Ausgabe, Kopie, Version **III 4**, 64
to **copy** [ˈkɒpɪ] kopieren, abschreiben **III 1**, 23
corner [ˈkɔːnə] Ecke **II**
cornflakes [ˈkɔːnfleɪks] Cornflakes **I**
to **correct** [kəˈrekt] berichtigen, verbessern **I**
correct [kəˈrekt] richtig, korrekt **II**
corridor [ˈkɒrɪdɔː] Korridor, Gang **II**
to **cost*** [kɒst] kosten **I**
costume [ˈkɒstjuːm] Verkleidung, Kostüm **II**
cottage [ˈkɒtɪdʒ] Häuschen **I**
could [kʊd] konnten, könnten **II**
to **count** [kaʊnt] zählen **I**
counter [ˈkaʊntə] Schalter, Theke **I**
country [ˈkʌntrɪ] Land **II**
countryside [ˈkʌntrɪsaɪd] Landschaft **III 3**, 45
course [kɔːs] Kurs(us) **III 2**, 32
of course [əv‿ˈkɔːs] natürlich, selbstverständlich **I**
°**court** [kɔːt] (Tennis-)Platz **III WSB**, 26
cousin [ˈkʌzn] Cousin/e **I**
⟨to cover⟩ [ˈkʌvə] bedecken **III 3**, 50
cow [kaʊ] Kuh **I**
crab [kræb] Krebs **I**
Crash! [kræʃ] Krach! **II**
crayon [ˈkreɪən] Buntstift **I**
crazy [ˈkreɪzɪ] verrückt **I**
cream [kriːm] Sahne **II**
⟨creature⟩ [ˈkriːtʃə] Kreatur, Wesen **III 2**, 37
°**crew** [kruː] Mannschaft **III 5**, 82
cricket [ˈkrɪkɪt] Kricket (*englischer Rasensport*) **I**
crisps (*pl*) [krɪsps] Kartoffelchips **I**
⟨critic⟩ [ˈkrɪtɪk] Kritiker/in **III WSC**, 58
Croak! [krəʊk] Quak! **I**
to **cross** [krɒs] überqueren **III 1**, 22
crossing [ˈkrɒsɪŋ] Überfahrt mit der Fähre **III WSA**, 7
crowd [kraʊd] Menschenmenge **II**
°**crown** [kraʊn] Krone **III 1**, 21
Crown Jewels [ˌkraʊn ˈdʒuːəlz] Kronjuwelen **III 1**, 21
°They are crowned. [ˌðeɪ ɑː ˈkraʊnd] Sie werden gekrönt. **III 1**, 17
to **cry** [kraɪ, kraɪd, kraɪd] schreien, weinen **III 2**, 40
cup [kʌp] Pokal, Becher **III WSB**, 28; Tasse **II**
cupboard [ˈkʌbəd] Schrank **II**
curry [ˈkʌrɪ] Curry (*indisches Gericht*) **II**
⟨curtain⟩ [ˈkɜːtn] Vorhang, Gardine **III WSB**, 29
⟨I've taken my curtain calls.⟩ [aɪv ˈteɪkən maɪ ˈkɜːtn ˌkɔːlz] *etwa:* Ich habe viele Zugaben gegeben. **III WSB**, 29
customer [ˈkʌstəmə] Kunde/Kundin **II**
to **cut*** [kʌt] schneiden **II**
to cut down [ˌkʌt ˈdaʊn] absägen, fällen **III 4**, 65
to cut out [ˌkʌt‿ˈaʊt] ausschneiden **II**

to **cycle** [ˈsaɪkl] Rad fahren **III WSA**, 12
cyclist [ˈsaɪklɪst] Radfahrer/in **III 1**, 22

D

dad [dæd] Vati, Papi **I**
to **damage** [ˈdæmɪdʒ] beschädigen, zerstören **III 4**, 65
to **dance** [dɑːns] tanzen **III 1**, 20
dancer [ˈdɑːnsə] Tänzer/in **III WSB**, 31
danger [ˈdeɪndʒə] Gefahr **III 3**, 53
dangerous [ˈdeɪndʒərəs] gefährlich **II**
Danish [ˈdeɪnɪʃ] dänisch, Dänisch **III WSA**, 7
⟨darling⟩ [ˈdɑːlɪŋ] Liebling **III 5**, 82
date [deɪt] Datum, Termin **II**
daughter [ˈdɔːtə] Tochter **II**
day [deɪ] Tag **I**
in those days [ɪn ˈðəʊz ˌdeɪz] damals **II**
⟨one day⟩ [ˈwʌn ˌdeɪ] eines Tages, an einem Tag **III WSA**, 13
the day after tomorrow [ðə ˈdeɪ‿ˌɑːftə təˈmɒrəʊ] übermorgen **II**
the day before yesterday [ðə ˈdeɪ bɪˌfɔː ˈjestədeɪ] vorgestern **II**
Day Rider Ticket [ˈdeɪ‿raɪdə ˌtɪkɪt] Tagesticket **I**
dead [ded] tot **I**
dear [dɪə] liebe/lieber/liebes **I**
Oh dear! [əʊ ˈdɪə] Oje!, Meine Güte! **I**
December [dɪˈsembə] Dezember **I**
to **decide** [dɪˈsaɪd] (sich) entscheiden **III WSC**, 56
deck [dek] (Schiffs-)Deck **III WSA**, 8
on deck [ˌɒn ˈdek] an Deck **III WSA**, 8
deep [diːp] tief **II**
to **defend s.th./s.o.** [dɪˈfend ˌsʌmθɪŋ/ˌsʌmwʌn] etw./jdn. verteidigen **III WSC**, 56
definition [defɪˈnɪʃn] Definition **III 2**, 42
department store [dɪˈpɑːtmənt stɔː] Kaufhaus **II**
to **describe** [dɪˈskraɪb] beschreiben **II**
description [dɪˈskrɪpʃn] Beschreibung **III 5**, 79
desk [desk] Schreibtisch, Pult **I**
to **destroy** [dɪˈstrɔɪ] zerstören **III 4**, 64
detail [ˈdiːteɪl] Detail, Einzelheit **II**
°**detention** [dɪˈtenʃn] Nachsitzen, Arrest **III 2**, 32
to **dial** [ˈdaɪəl] (Telefonnummer) wählen, eintippen **III 5**, 84
dialogue [ˈdaɪəlɒg] Dialog, Gespräch **I**
⟨diamond⟩ [ˈdaɪmənd] Diamant **III 2**, 41
diary [ˈdaɪərɪ] Tagebuch, Terminkalender **II**
dice [daɪs] Würfel **I**
dictionary [ˈdɪkʃənrɪ] Wörterbuch, Lexikon **II**
to **die** [daɪ] sterben **I**
⟨diet⟩ [ˈdaɪət] Diät, Ernährung **III 5**, 87
difference [ˈdɪfrəns] Unterschied **III WSA**, 9
different [ˈdɪfrənt] anders, verschieden, unterschiedlich **I**
in different ways [ɪn ˌdɪfrənt‿ˈweɪz] auf verschiedene Weise **II**
difficult [ˈdɪfɪkəlt] schwierig **II**
dining-room [ˈdaɪnɪŋrʊm] Esszimmer **I**
dinner [ˈdɪnə] warmes Mittagessen, Abendessen **III 2**, 40
°dinner lady [ˈdɪnə ˌleɪdɪ] *Dame an der Essensausgabe* **III 2**, 40
dirty [ˈdɜːtɪ] schmutzig, dreckig **I**
disappointed [ˌdɪsəˈpɔɪntɪd] enttäuscht **III 1**, 17
disco [ˈdɪskəʊ] Diskothek **II**
to **dive** [daɪv] tauchen; einen Kopfsprung machen **III WSB**, 29

to **divide** [dɪ'vaɪd] teilen, sich aufteilen **III WSA**, 12
to **do*** [du:] tun, machen **I**
to do the washing-up ['du: ðə ˌwɒʃɪŋ‿'ʌp] den Abwasch machen, spülen **I**
to do well [ˌdu: 'wel] Erfolg haben, gut sein **III 2**, 34
doctor ['dɒktə] Arzt/Ärztin **I**
at the doctor's [ət ðə 'dɒktəz] beim Arzt/Ärztin **II**
the **dodgems** ['dɒdʒəmz] Autoskooter **II**
dog [dɒg] Hund **I**
dog biscuit ['dɒg ˌbɪskɪt] Hundekuchen **I**
dog-free ['dɒgfri:] hundefrei **I**
door [dɔ:] Tür **I**
at the door [ət ðə 'dɔ:] an der Tür **I**
back door [ˌbæk 'dɔ:] Hintertür **I**
front door [ˌfrʌnt 'dɔ:] Haustür **I**
double ['dʌbl] zweimal, Doppel- **I**
double decker bus [ˌdʌbl ˌdekə 'bʌs] Doppeldecker (*Bus*) **III 1**, 14
down [daʊn] herunter, hinunter **I**
downstairs [ˌdaʊn'steəz] unten (*in Gebäuden*) **I**
⟨downward⟩ ['daʊnwəd] abwärts **III WSC**, 60
Dr ['dɒktə] *Anrede für Arzt/Ärztin*, Herr/Frau Doktor **II**
° **dragon** ['drægən] Drache **III WSD**, 74
drama ['drɑ:mə] Schauspiel **I**
to **draw*** [drɔ:] zeichnen **I**
dream [dri:m] Traum **II**
dress [dres] Kleid **II**
to **drink*** [drɪŋk] trinken **I**
to **drive*** [draɪv] fahren **I**
driver ['draɪvə] Fahrer/in **I**
⟨driving licence⟩ ['draɪvɪŋ ˌlaɪsəns] Führerschein **III 4**, 68
⟨driving rain⟩ [ˌdraɪvɪŋ 'reɪn] starker Regen **III 4**, 72
drop [drɒp] Tropfen **II**
to **drop** [drɒp] fallen(lassen) **II**
to **drown** [draʊn] ertrinken, ertränken **II**
dry [draɪ] trocken **II**
duck [dʌk] Ente **I**
⟨dues⟩ (*pl*) [dju:z] Lehrgeld **III WSB**, 29
during ['djʊərɪŋ] während **II**
Dutch [dʌtʃ] holländisch, Holländisch **III WSA**, 7

E

° **e-mail** (= **electronic mail**) ['i:meɪl = ɪlek'trɒnɪk 'meɪl] *elektronischer Briefverkehr* **III 2**, 33
each [i:tʃ] jede/jeder/jedes (einzelne) **II**
each other [ˌi:tʃ‿'ʌðə] einander **III WSB**, 30
⟨eagle⟩ ['i:gl] Adler **III WSC**, 60
ear [ɪə] Ohr **II**
early ['ɜ:lɪ] früh **I**
earth [ɜ:θ] Erde **II**
What on earth ...? [ˌwɒt‿ɒn‿'ɜ:θ] Was in aller Welt ...? **II**
east [i:st] Osten, Ost-, östlich **II**
° **eastbound** ['i:stbaʊnd] Richtung Osten **III 1**, 18
Easter ['i:stə] Ostern **II**
easy ['i:zɪ] leicht, einfach **I**
to **eat*** [i:t] essen **I**
egg [eg] Ei **I**
Egyptian [ɪ'dʒɪpʃn] ägyptisch, Ägypter/in **III 1**, 15
elephant ['elɪfənt] Elefant **II**
else [els] sonst (noch) **I**
emergency [ɪ'mɜ:dʒənsɪ] Notfall **III 5**, 84
⟨emperor⟩ ['empərə] Kaiser, Herrscher **III WSC**, 56
⟨empire⟩ ['empaɪə] Kaiserreich **III WSC**, 56
empty ['emptɪ] leer **I**
end [end] Ende, Schluss **I**
in the end [ˌɪn ðɪ‿'end] schließlich, zum Schluss **II**
ending ['endɪŋ] Ende, Schluss (*bei Geschichten*) **I**
enemy ['enəmɪ] Feind/in **II**
energy ['enədʒɪ] Energie **III 4**, 64
engine ['endʒɪn] Motor, Maschine **III 5**, 84
English ['ɪŋglɪʃ] englisch, Englisch **I**
in English [ɪn‿'ɪnglɪʃ] auf Englisch **I**
to **enjoy** [ɪn'dʒɔɪ] genießen, gern tun **II**
enough [ɪ'nʌf] genug **I**
to **enter** ['entə] betreten **III 4**, 69
environment [ɪn'vaɪərənmənt] Umwelt **III 4**, 62
Er ... [ɜ:] Äh ... **I**
escalator ['eskəleɪtə] Rolltreppe **II**
escape [ɪ'skeɪp] Flucht, Ausbruch **II**
to **escape** [ɪ'skeɪp] fliehen, entkommen **II**
especially [ɪ'speʃəlɪ] besonders **III WSD**, 74
° **etc** [ɪt'setərə] usw. **III WSD**, 75
even ['i:vn] sogar **II**
even more [ˌi:vn 'mɔ:] noch mehr **II**
evening ['i:vnɪŋ] Abend **I**
in the evening [ɪn ðɪ‿'i:vnɪŋ] am Abend, abends **I**
° **event** [ɪ'vent] Ereignis, Sportveranstaltung **III WSB**, 27
ever ['evə] je, jemals **II**
every ['evrɪ] jede/jeder/jedes **I**
⟨on every hand⟩ [ɒn 'evrɪ ˌhænd] überall **III 3**, 50
everyday life [ˌevrɪdeɪ 'laɪf] der Alltag **III WSC**, 60
everyone ['evrɪwʌn] jede/jeder, alle **I**
everything ['evrɪθɪŋ] alles **I**
everywhere ['evrɪweə] überall **II**
exam [ɪg'zæm] Prüfung, Examen **III 2**, 33
to **examine** [ɪg'zæmɪn] untersuchen, prüfen **I**
example [ɪg'zɑ:mpl] Beispiel **I**
for example [fər‿ɪg'zɑ:mpl] zum Beispiel **I**
exchange visit [ɪks'tʃeɪndʒ ˌvɪzɪt] (Schüler-)Austausch **III 1**, 16
to be **excited** [bɪ‿ɪk'saɪtɪd] aufgeregt sein **I**
excitedly [ɪk'saɪtɪdlɪ] aufgeregt **II**
exciting [ɪk'saɪtɪŋ] aufregend, spannend **I**
to **excuse** [ɪks'kju:z] (sich) entschuldigen **I**
Excuse me. [ɪks'kju:z mɪ] Entschuldigung., Entschuldigen Sie bitte. **I**
exercise ['eksəsaɪz] Übung, Aufgabe **I**
exercise book ['eksəsaɪz ˌbʊk] (Übungs-)Heft **II**
⟨exile⟩ ['eksaɪl] Exil **III WSC**, 60
to **exist** [ɪg'zɪst] existieren **III 3**, 50
to **expect** [ɪk'spekt] erwarten **III WSC**, 56
expensive [ɪk'spensɪv] teuer **II**
experience [ɪk'spɪərɪəns] Erlebnis, Erfahrung **III WSA**, 12
experiment [ɪk'sperɪmənt] Experiment **III 2**, 34
to **explain** [ɪk'spleɪn] erklären **II**
express [ɪk'spres] Express(zug) **III WSB**, 27
expression [ɪk'spreʃn] Ausdruck **III 4**, 70
extra ['ekstrə] zusätzlich, Zusatz-, Sonder- **I**
⟨extra-ordinary⟩ [ek'strɔ:dnrɪ] ungewöhnlich, speziell; besonders mittelmäßig **III 5**, 79
eye [aɪ] Auge **I**

F

face [feɪs] Gesicht **II**
face to face [ˌfeɪs tə 'feɪs] persönlich, direkt, vis-a-vis **III WSA**, 10
⟨pointed face⟩ [ˌpɔɪntɪd 'feɪs] spitzes Gesicht **III WSC**, 60

fact [fækt] Tatsache **III WSB**, 27
factory ['fæktərɪ] Fabrik **III 3**, 45
fair [feə] Volksfest, Jahrmarkt **II**
to **fall*** [fɔ:l] fallen **I**
to fall off s.th. [ˌfɔ:l 'ɒf ˌsʌmθɪŋ] von etw. herunterfallen **III 1**, 22
to fall over [ˌfɔ:l‿'əʊvə] hinfallen, umfallen **II**
false [fɔ:ls] falsch **III WSC**, 58
⟨fame⟩ [feɪm] Ruhm **III WSB**, 29
family ['fæməlɪ] Familie **I**
famous ['feɪməs] berühmt **II**
fan [fæn] Fan **II**
fantastic [fæn'tæstɪk] fantastisch, toll **II**
fantasy ['fæntəsɪ] Fantasie **III 2**, 38
far [fɑ:] weit **I**
farm [fɑ:m] Bauernhof **I**
farmer ['fɑ:mə] Bauer/Bäuerin **III 3**, 49
fast [fɑ:st] schnell, rasch **II**
fat [fæt] dick, fett **I**
father ['fɑ:ðə] Vater **I**
favourite ['feɪvərɪt] Lieblings- **I**
⟨feature⟩ ['fi:tʃə] Sonderbeitrag **III WSC**, 59
February ['febrʊərɪ] Februar **I**
to **feed*** [fi:d] füttern **I**
to **feel*** [fi:l] fühlen, sich fühlen **I**
to feel sorry for s.o. [ˌfi:l 'sɒrɪ fə ˌsʌmwʌn] Mitleid mit jdm. haben **III WSC**, 61
to feel well [ˌfi:l 'wel] sich wohl fühlen **II**
feeler ['fi:lə] Fühler **I**
feeling ['fi:lɪŋ] Gefühl **III 3**, 54
ferry ['ferɪ] Fähre **I**
°**festival** ['festəvl] Fest(ival) **III 1**, 16
to **fetch** [fetʃ] holen **III 3**, 53
fete [feɪt] Bazar, Fest **II**
⟨fever⟩ ['fi:və] Fieber **III 5**, 78
a **few** [ə 'fju:] ein paar **II**
field [fi:ld] Feld, Wiese, Weide **III WSC**, 58
to **fight*** [faɪt] (be)kämpfen, kämpfen (gegen) **III 1**, 19
to **fill in s.th.** [ˌfɪl‿'ɪn] etw. einsetzen, ausfüllen **III 1**, 21
film [fɪlm] Film **II**
to **film** [fɪlm] filmen **II**
to **find** [faɪnd] finden **I**
to find out [ˌfaɪnd‿'aʊt] entdecken, herausfinden **II**
to be **fine.** [faɪn] gut gehen **II**
finger ['fɪŋgə] Finger **II**
fish finger [ˌfɪʃ 'fɪŋgə] Fischstäbchen **I**
to **finish** ['fɪnɪʃ] beenden, aufhören **I**
to be finished [ˌbɪ 'fɪnɪʃt] fertig sein **I**
fire brigade ['faɪə brɪˌgeɪd] Feuerwehr **I**
fireman ['faɪəmən] Feuerwehrmann **I**
firm [fɜ:m] Firma **I**
first [fɜ:st] erste/erster/erstes; zuerst **I**
fish [fɪʃ] Fisch **I**
fish finger [ˌfɪʃ 'fɪŋgə] Fischstäbchen **I**
fish tank ['fɪʃ ˌtæŋk] Aquarium **II**
to **fish** [fɪʃ] fischen, angeln **III 3**, 49
fisherman ['fɪʃəmən] Fischer **III 5**, 80
⟨flame⟩ [fleɪm] Flamme **III WSC**, 58
⟨red flare⟩ [ˌred 'fleə] Leuchtrakete **III 5**, 84
flat [flæt] Wohnung **I**
flat [flæt] flach **III 5**, 78
⟨flaw⟩ [flɔ:] Fehler, Loch **III 3**, 50
flight [flaɪt] Flug **III 1**, 16
floor [flɔ:] Boden, Fußboden **I**; Stockwerk **II**
flower ['flaʊə] Blume **III 2**, 38
flowerpot ['flaʊəpɒt] Blumentopf **I**
fly [flaɪ] Fliege **III 1**, 21
to **fly*** [flaɪ] fliegen **II**
folder ['fəʊldə] Hefter, Mappe **I**
to **follow** ['fɒləʊ] folgen, befolgen **III 3**, 52
food [fu:d] Essen, Futter **I**
Food Court ['fu:d ˌkɔ:t] *Imbissbereich im Einkaufszentrum* **II**
foot [fʊt] Fuß **I**
to go on foot [ˌgəʊ‿ɒn 'fʊt] zu Fuß gehen **I**
football ['fʊtbɔ:l] Fußball **I**
for [fɔ:/fə] für **I**
for example [fər‿ɪg'zɑ:mpl] zum Beispiel **I**
for sale [fə 'seɪl] zu verkaufen **II**
weather **forecast** ['weðə ˌfɔ:kɑ:st] Wetterbericht **II**
forest ['fɒrɪst] Wald **II**
to **forget*** [fə'get] vergessen **II**
fork [fɔ:k] Gabel **II**
form [fɔ:m] Form **I**
°**formal** ['fɔ:ml] formal, formell **III WSA**, 8
⟨fortune⟩ ['fɔ:tʃu:n] Glück, Schicksal **III WSB**, 29
⟨Frankly, …⟩ ['fræŋklɪ] Ehrlich gesagt, … **III WSD**, 76
free [fri:] frei **I**; gratis **III 2**, 40
free time [ˌfri:‿'taɪm] Freizeit **I**
freedom ['fri:dəm] Freiheit **III 4**, 69
French [frentʃ] französisch, Französisch **I**
Friday ['fraɪdeɪ] Freitag **I**
friend [frend] Freund/in **I**
friendly ['frendlɪ] freundlich, freundschaftlich **II**
frightening ['fraɪtnɪŋ] Furcht erregend, erschreckend **II**
frog [frɒg] Frosch **I**
from [frɒm/frəm] aus, von **I**
from behind [ˌfrɒm bɪ'haɪnd] von hinten **II**
from … to [frəm … tə] von … bis; von … nach **I**
front [frʌnt] Vorder- **III 1**, 22
front door [ˌfrʌnt 'dɔ:] Haustür **I**
front seat [ˌfrʌnt 'si:t] Vordersitz **II**
in front of [ɪn 'frʌnt‿əv] vor **I**
fruit [fru:t] Obst, Frucht, Früchte **II**
fruit cake ['fru:t keɪk] *engl. Kuchen* **II**
⟨frying pan⟩ ['fraɪɪŋ ˌpæn] Pfanne **III 3**, 50
full [fʊl] voll, ausgebucht **III WSA**, 12
full of ['fʊl‿əv] voll (von) **II**
fun [fʌn] Spaß **I**
great fun [ˌgreɪt 'fʌn] viel Spaß **II**
to be fun [bɪ 'fʌn] Spaß machen **I**
to have fun [hæv 'fʌn] Spaß haben **I**
°to **function** ['fʌŋkʃn] funktionieren **III WSC**, 59
funny ['fʌnɪ] lustig, ulkig, komisch **I**
future ['fju:tʃə] Zukunft **II**

G

gallows ['gæləʊz] Galgen **II**
game [geɪm] Spiel **I**
garage ['gærɑ:dʒ] Garage **I**
garden ['gɑ:dn] Garten **I**
°**GCSE** (= **General Certificate of Secondary Education**) [ˌdʒi: si: es 'i: = ˌdʒenərəl sə'tɪfɪkət‿əv 'sekəndərɪ ˌedʒʊ'keɪʃn] *allgemeiner Abschluss der weiterführenden Schulen in GB* **III 2**, 33
°**general** ['dʒenərəl] allgemeine/allgemeiner/allgemeines **III 2**, 33
Geography [dʒɪ'ɒgrəfɪ] Erdkunde, Geografie **II**
German ['dʒɜ:mən] deutsch, Deutsch, Deutsche/r **I**
°**gerund** ['dʒerənd] Gerundium **III 1**, 20
to **get*** [get] bekommen; fangen, auffangen; holen, erwischen **I**
Get out! [get‿'aʊt] Hinaus mit dir/euch! **I**

Get well. [get 'wel] Gute Besserung. **I**
to get better [ˌget 'betə] besser werden, gesund werden **III 2**, 34
⟨to get drunk⟩ [ˌget 'drʌŋk] sich betrinken **III 5**, 83
to get into trouble [ˌget ɪntʊ 'trʌbl] in Schwierigkeiten geraten **III 2**, 36
to get lost [get 'lɒst] sich verirren, verloren gehen **I**
to get off [get‿'ɒf] aussteigen **I**
to get on [get‿'ɒn] einsteigen **I**
to get out of bed on the wrong side [get‿aʊt‿əv ˌbed‿ɒn ðə rɒŋ 'saɪd] mit dem falschen Fuß aufstehen **II**
to get rid of s.th. [ˌget 'rɪd‿ɒf ˌsʌmθɪŋ] etw. loswerden **III 2**, 36
to get s.th. right [ˌget sʌmθɪŋ 'raɪt] etw. richtig verstehen **III WSC**, 59
to get stuck [get 'stʌk] stecken bleiben **I**
°to get the gist [ˌget ðə 'dʒɪst] das Wichtigste verstehen **III WSC**, 58
to get there ['get ðeə] hinkommen **I**
to get up [get‿'ʌp] aufstehen **I**
to get ... ready [get 'redɪ] (sich) vorbereiten, zubereiten **I**
ghost [gəʊst] Geist, Gespenst **II**
ghost train ['gəʊst ˌtreɪn] Geisterbahn **II**
girl [gɜ:l] Mädchen **I**
°to get the **gist** [ˌget ðə 'dʒɪst] das Wichtigste verstehen **III WSC**, 58
to **give*** [gɪv] geben **I**
to give a talk [ˌgɪv‿ə 'tɔ:k] eine Rede/ein Referat halten **III WSA**, 12
to give away [ˌgɪv‿ə'weɪ] weggeben, verschenken **II**
to give s.th. up [ˌgɪv sʌmθɪŋ 'ʌp] etw. aufgeben, aufhören mit etw. **III 4**, 64
glad [glæd] froh **I**
glass [glɑ:s] Glas **II**
go [gəʊ] Fahrt, Versuch **II**
a go [ə 'gəʊ] pro Fahrt, pro Versuch **II**
to have a go [ˌhæv‿ə'gəʊ] etw. versuchen **II**
to **go*** [gəʊ] gehen, fahren **I**
Go away! [ˌgəʊ‿ə'weɪ] Geh weg!, Weg mit dir! **II**
to go camping [ˌgəʊ 'kæmpɪŋ] zelten gehen **I**
to go crazy [ˌgəʊ 'kreɪzɪ] verrückt werden **III WSA**, 8
to go for a walk [ˌgəʊ fər‿ə 'wɔ:k] spazieren gehen **I**
to go home [gəʊ 'həʊm] nach Hause gehen **I**
to go inside [ˌgəʊ ɪn'saɪd] hineingehen **III 1**, 22
to go on [gəʊ 'ɒn] weitermachen **I**
to go on foot [ˌgəʊ‿ɒn 'fʊt] zu Fuß gehen **I**
to go on for [gəʊ‿'ɒn fə] (an)dauern **II**
to go out for a meal [gəʊ ˌaʊt fɒr‿ə 'mi:l] essen gehen **III 1**, 21
to go sightseeing [gəʊ 'saɪt ˌsi:ɪŋ] auf Besichtigungstour gehen **III 1**, 19
to go swimming [gəʊ 'swɪmɪŋ] schwimmen gehen **I**
to go to ['gəʊ tə] gehen nach/zu **I**
to go to the shops [ˌgəʊ tə‿ðə 'ʃɒps] einkaufen gehen **I**
to go with ['gəʊ ˌwɪð] passen zu, gehören zu **III 3**, 45
to go wrong [ˌgəʊ 'rɒŋ] schief gehen **II**; sich verfahren **II**
goal [gəʊl] Tor *(beim Sport)* **I**
°**goalkeeper** ['gəʊlˌki:pə] Torwart **III WSB**, 26
God [gɒd] Gott **III 4**, 69
to be **going to** [bɪ 'gəʊɪŋ tə] werden **I**
gold [gəʊld] Gold **III WSC**, 57
golf [gɒlf] Golf **III 3**, 49
⟨Gonna keep on driving.⟩ [ˌgɒnə ki:p‿ɒn 'draɪvɪŋ] *etwa:* Ich werde weiterfahren. **III 4**, 72
good [gʊd] gut **I**
Good morning. [ˌgʊd 'mɔ:nɪŋ] Guten Morgen. **I**
to be good at ... [bɪ 'gʊd‿ət] gut sein in ... **I**
Goodbye. [ˌgʊd'baɪ] Auf Wiedersehen., Tschüs. **I**
goose, geese *(pl)* [gu:s, gi:s] Gans, Gänse **II**
Gosh! [gɒʃ] *Ausruf des Erstaunens* **II**
have **got** [ˌhæv 'gɒt] haben, besitzen **I**
⟨Got a bead on you.⟩ [ˌgɒt ə 'bi:d‿ɒn ju:] *etwa:* Hat dich im Visier. **III 4**, 72
graffiti [grə'fi:tɪ] Graffiti **III 2**, 36
grammar school ['græmə sku:l] *Gymnasium in GB* **III 2**, 33
grandma ['grænmɑ:] Oma **I**
grandpa ['grænpɑ:] Opa **I**
°**graphics** *(pl)* ['græfɪks] Grafik, Bild **III WSD**, 74
great [greɪt] toll, großartig **I**
great big ['greɪt ˌbɪg] riesengroß **II**
great fun [ˌgreɪt 'fʌn] viel Spaß **II**
great uncle [greɪt‿'ʌŋkl] Großonkel **II**
Greek [gri:k] griechisch, Griechisch **I**
green [gri:n] grün **I**
ground [graʊnd] Boden **III WSB**, 31
group [gru:p] Gruppe **I**
youth group ['ju:θ ˌgru:p] Jugendgruppe **II**
to **grow*** [grəʊ] wachsen, (an)pflanzen **II**
grumpy ['grʌmpɪ] mürrisch **II**
guard [gɑ:d] Wächter **III 1**, 19
to **guess** [ges] vermuten, (er)raten **III WSB**, 26
guest [gest] Gast **I**
guest house ['gest‿haʊs] Pension, Gästehaus **I**
guitar [gɪ'tɑ:] Gitarre **I**
gym (= **gymnasium**) [dʒɪm = dʒɪm'neɪzjəm] Turnhalle, Sporthalle **III WSB**, 26

H

hair [heə] Haar, Haare **II**
haircut ['heəkʌt] Haarschnitt, Frisur **II**
half [hɑ:f] die Hälfte **II**
half an hour [ˌhɑ:f‿ən‿'aʊə] eine halbe Stunde **II**
half past (eleven) ['hɑ:f pɑ:st] halb (zwölf) **I**
hall [hɔ:l] Diele, Flur **I**
ham [hæm] gekochter Schinken **I**
⟨hammer⟩ ['hæmə] Hammer **III 3**, 50
hamster ['hæmstə] Hamster **II**
hand [hænd] Hand **I**
handle ['hændl] (Hand-)Griff **III 3**, 52
hangman ['hæŋmən] Henker **II**
to **happen** ['hæpən] passieren, geschehen **II**
happy ['hæpɪ] glücklich, fröhlich **I**
hard [hɑ:d] hart, schwer **II**
hat [hæt] Hut **II**
to **hate** [heɪt] hassen **III 1**, 20
to **have*** [hæv] haben **I**
have got [hæv 'gɒt] haben, besitzen **I**
to have a baby [ˌhæv ə 'beɪbɪ] ein Baby bekommen **III 4**, 69
to have a bath [ˌhæv‿ə 'bɑ:θ] baden, ein Bad nehmen **I**
to have a go [hæv‿ə 'gəʊ] etw. versuchen **II**
to have a look [hæv‿ə 'lʊk] sich etw. ansehen **I**
to have a ride on [ˌhæv‿ə'raɪd‿ɒn] fahren auf **II**
to have breakfast [ˌhæv 'brekfəst] frühstücken **II**
to have fun [hæv 'fʌn] Spaß haben **I**
to have lunch [hæv 'lʌntʃ] zu Mittag essen **I**
to have on [ˌhæv 'ɒn] anhaben *(Kleidung)* **II**
to have to ['hæv ˌtu:] müssen **II**
he [hi:] er **I**
head [hed] Kopf **I**
headache ['hedeɪk] Kopfweh **II**

heading ['hedɪŋ] Überschrift **III WSC**, 58
⟨headlights *(pl)*⟩ ['hedlaɪts] Scheinwerfer **III 4**, 72
headteacher [ˌhed'tiːtʃə] Schuldirektor/in **I**
healthy ['helθɪ] gesund **I**
healthy living [ˌhelθɪ 'lɪvɪŋ] gesunde Lebensweise **I**
to **hear*** [hɪə] hören **I**
heart [hɑːt] Herz **II**
by heart [baɪ 'hɑːt] auswendig **II**
⟨to heat⟩ [hiːt] erhitzen, heiß machen **III 3**, 50
⟨heather⟩ ['heðə] Heidekraut **III WSC**, 56
⟨central heating⟩ [ˌsentrəl 'hiːtɪŋ] Zentralheizung **III WSC**, 58
heavy ['hevɪ] schwer **III 3**, 45
helicopter ['helɪkɒptə] Hubschrauber **III 5**, 80
Hello. [hə'ləʊ] Hallo., Guten Tag. **I**
to say hello to [ˌseɪ hə'ləʊ‿tə] grüßen **I**
helmet ['helmɪt] Helm **II**
help [help] Hilfe **I**
to **help** [help] helfen **I**
helper ['helpə] Helfer/in **II**
helpful ['helpfʊl] hilfsbereit **III WSB**, 31
helpless ['helplɪs] hilflos **III WSB**, 31
her [hɜː] ihr/ihre; ihr/sie **I**
here [hɪə] hier **I**
Here you are. [ˌhɪə juː‿'ɑː] Hier, bitte schön. **I**
hers [hɜːz] ihr/ihre **II**
herself [hɜː'self] (sie/ihr) selbst **III WSB**, 30
Hey! [heɪ] He!, Oh! **I**
Hi! [haɪ] Hallo! **I**
to **hide*** [haɪd] (sich) verstecken **II**
high jump ['haɪ dʒʌmp] Hochsprung **III WSB**, 26
high [haɪ] hoch **II**
hill [hɪl] Hügel **I**
him [hɪm] ihm/ihn **I**
himself [hɪm'self] (ihn/ihm) selbst **III WSB**, 30
°**Hindu** ['hɪnduː] hinduistisch, Hindu **III 1**, 14
to **hire** ['haɪə] mieten **II**
his [hɪz] sein/seine **I**; seine/seiner/seines **II**
History ['hɪstrɪ] Geschichte **II**
to **hit*** [hɪt] schlagen **II**
⟨to hitch a ride⟩ [ˌhɪtʃ ə 'raɪd] per Anhalter fahren **III 4**, 72
hobby ['hɒbɪ] Hobby **II**
hockey ['hɒkɪ] Hockey **I**
hockey stick ['hɒkɪ stɪk] Hockeyschläger **III WSB**, 29
⟨to hoist up⟩ [ˌhɔɪst 'ʌp] (Segel) hissen **III 5**, 83
to **hold*** [həʊld] halten **II**
Hold on! [ˌhəʊld 'ɒn] Festhalten! **III 5**, 85
hole [həʊl] Loch **I**
holidays *(pl)* ['hɒlɪdeɪz] Ferien **I**
on holiday [ɒn 'hɒlɪdeɪ] im Urlaub **I**
home [həʊm] Zuhause, Heim **I**
at home [ət 'həʊm] zu Hause **I**
home [həʊm] nach Hause **I**
to go home [gəʊ 'həʊm] nach Hause gehen **I**
homework *(no pl)* ['həʊmwɜːk] Hausaufgabe/Hausaufgaben **I**
hood [hʊd] Kapuze **II**
to **hope** [həʊp] hoffen **I**
horse [hɔːs] Pferd **II**
⟨horse-breeder⟩ ['hɔːs ˌbriːdə] Pferdezüchter **III WSC**, 60
hospital ['hɒspɪtl] Krankenhaus **I**
hot [hɒt] heiß **I**; scharf (gewürzt) **III 1**, 21
hot dog [ˌhɒt 'dɒg] Hotdog **II**
hotel [həʊ'tel] Hotel **I**
hour ['aʊə] Stunde **II**
half an hour [ˌhɑːf‿ən‿'aʊə] eine halbe Stunde **II**
house [haʊs] Haus **I**
housekeeper ['haʊsˌkiːpə] Haushälter/in **II**
housework ['haʊswɜːk] Hausarbeit **I**
hovercraft ['hɒvəkrɑːft] Luftkissenboot **I**
how [haʊ] wie **I**
How are you? [ˌhaʊ‿'ɑː juː] Wie geht es dir/euch/Ihnen? **I**
How many? [haʊ 'menɪ] Wie viele? **I**
How much? [haʊ 'mʌtʃ] Wie viel? **I**
however [haʊ'evə] jedoch **III 1**, 19
huge [hjuːdʒ] groß, riesig **III 3**, 46
human ['hjuːmən] Mensch **III 4**, 69
⟨the human race⟩ [ðə ˌhjuːmən 'reɪs] die Menschheit **III WSB**, 29
Humanities *(pl)* [hjuː'mænətɪz] *(in der Schule)* Geschichte und Erdkunde **II**
hungry ['hʌŋgrɪ] hungrig **I**
⟨hunter⟩ ['hʌntə] Jäger/in **III WSC**, 60
to **hurry** ['hʌrɪ] sich beeilen **II**
Hurry up! [ˌhʌrɪ 'ʌp] Beeil dich! **III 1**, 22
to **hurt*** [hɜːt] schmerzen, weh tun **I**; verletzen **II**
husband ['hʌzbənd] Ehemann **III 1**, 23
⟨hut⟩ [hʌt] Hütte **III WSC**, 57

I

I [aɪ] ich **I**
ice cream [ˌaɪs‿'kriːm] Eiskrem **I**
ice rink ['aɪsrɪŋk] Eisstadion **II**
idea [aɪ'dɪə] Idee **I**
idiot ['ɪdɪət] Idiot/in **II**
if [ɪf] wenn **II**
ill [ɪl] krank **II**
to **imagine** [ɪ'mædʒɪn] sich vorstellen **III WSA**, 7
important [ɪm'pɔːtnt] wichtig **II**
to **improve** [ɪm'pruːv] (sich) verbessern **III 4**, 66
in [ɪn] in **I**
in different ways [ɪn ˌdɪfrənt‿'weɪz] auf verschiedene Weise **II**
in front of [ɪn 'frʌnt‿əv] vor **I**
in my opinion [ɪn 'maɪ əˌpɪnjən] meiner Meinung nach **III WSD**, 75
in the end [ˌɪn ðɪ‿'end] schließlich, zum Schluss **II**
in the evening [ɪn ðɪ‿'iːvnɪŋ] am Abend, abends **I**
in the middle of [ɪn ðə 'mɪdl‿əv] in der Mitte von, mitten in **II**
in those days [ɪn 'ðəʊz ˌdeɪz] damals **II**
in time [ˌɪn 'taɪm] rechtzeitig **II**
Indian ['ɪndjən] indisch, Inder/in **II**
industry ['ɪndəstrɪ] Industrie **III 3**, 45
infinitive [ɪn'fɪnətɪv] Infinitiv, Grundform **II**
to **inform s.o. about s.th** [ɪn'fɔːm ˌsʌmwʌn ə'baʊt ˌsʌmθɪŋ] jdn. über etw. informieren **III 5**, 82
information [ɪnfə'meɪʃn] Information/en, Auskunft/Auskünfte **II**
to **injure** ['ɪndʒə] verletzen **III 4**, 66
inn [ɪn] Gasthaus **III 3**, 52
inside [ɪn'saɪd] drinnen **I**; hinein, in(nerhalb von) **III 3**, 46
instead of [ɪn'sted‿ˌɒv] statt, anstatt **III 4**, 66
instructions *(pl)* [ɪn'strʌkʃnz] Gebrauchsanweisung, Anweisungen **III 5**, 82
instrument ['ɪnstrʊmənt] Instrument **III 3**, 48
interest in s.th. ['ɪntrəst] Interesse an etw. **III 2**, 34

to be **interested in s.th.** [ˌbɪ ˈɪntrəstɪd‿ɪn] sich für etw. interessieren **III 1**, 21
interesting [ˈɪntrəstɪŋ] interessant **II**
international [ˌɪntəˈnæʃənl] international **III WSA**, 7
to **interview s.o.** [ˈɪntəvjuː ˌsʌmwʌn] jdn. interviewen **III 3**, 48
into [ˈɪntʊ] in, hinein **I**
introduction [ˌɪntrəˈdʌkʃn] Einleitung **III WSD**, 74
to **invade** [ɪnˈveɪd] besetzen, einmarschieren in **III 3**, 50
invitation [ɪnvɪˈteɪʃn] Einladung **I**
to **invite** [ɪnˈvaɪt] einladen **II**
Irish [ˈaɪrɪʃ] irisch, Irisch **III WSA**, 9
⟨iron⟩ [ˈaɪən] Eisen **III 3**, 50
irregular [ɪˈregjʊlə] unregelmäßig **I**
is [ɪz] ist **I**
island [ˈaɪlənd] Insel **II**
it [ɪt] es/er/sie; es/ihn/sie/ihm/ihr **I**
Italian [ɪˈtæljən] italienisch, Italienisch, Italiener/in **I**
its [ɪts] sein/seine, ihr/ihre **I**
itself [ɪtˈself] (es/ihm) selbst **III WSB**, 30

J

jacket [ˈdʒækɪt] Jacke **II**
January [ˈdʒænjʊərɪ] Januar **I**
°**Japanese** [dʒæpəˈniːz] japanisch, Japanisch, Japaner/in **III 4**, 69
jazz dance [ˈdʒæz ˌdɑːns] Jazztanz **III WSB**, 26
jealous of s.th/s.o. [ˈdʒeləs əv ˌsʌmθɪŋ/ˌsʌmwʌn] eifersüchtig auf etw./jdn. **III 2**, 41
jeans [dʒiːnz] Jeans **I**
job [dʒɒb] Beruf, Arbeit, Arbeitsplatz **I**
°to **jog** [dʒɒg] joggen **III WSB**, 26
to **join** [dʒɔɪn] beitreten, Mitglied werden **II**
joke [dʒəʊk] Witz, Scherz **I**
July [dʒuːˈlaɪ] Juli **I**
jump [dʒʌmp] Sprung **II**
to **jump** [dʒʌmp] springen **II**
June [dʒuːn] Juni **I**
junior [ˈdʒuːnjə] Unterstufen- **II**
just [dʒʌst] gerade, eben, nur, genau **I**
just the thing [ˌdʒʌst ðə ˈθɪŋ] genau das Richtige **II**
just then [ˌdʒʌst ˈðen] in diesem Moment **II**

K

to **keep*** [kiːp] (be)halten **II**
⟨to keep on doing s.th.⟩ [ˈkiːp‿ˌɒn ˈduːɪŋ ˌsʌmθɪŋ] etw. weitermachen **III WSB**, 29
key [kiː] Schlüssel **III WSA**, 12
to **kick** [kɪk] treten, mit dem Fuß stoßen, kicken **I**
kid [kɪd] Kind **III 5**, 84
to **kill** [kɪl] töten **II**
kilo [ˈkiːləʊ] Kilo **III WSB**, 27
kilt [kɪlt] Schottenrock **II**
kind [kaɪnd] Art **II**
king [kɪŋ] König **III 1**, 17
kingdom [ˈkɪŋdəm] Königreich **III 3**, 52
kitchen [ˈkɪtʃən] Küche **I**
kite [kaɪt] Drachen **I**
knee [niː] Knie **II**
knife, knives (*pl*) [naɪf, naɪvz] Messer **I**
°**knight** [naɪt] Ritter **III 3**, 51
to **know*** [nəʊ] wissen, kennen **I**
⟨Ain't nobody know …⟩ [eɪnt ˈnəʊbədɪ nəʊ] *etwa: Keiner weiß …* **III 4**, 72

knuckle [ˈnʌkl] Fingerknöchel **II**
white knuckle ride [ˌwaɪt nʌkl ˈraɪd] *wilde Fahrt auf Achterbahn und Ähnlichem* **II**

L

lace [leɪs] Spitze (*Gewebeart*) **II**
⟨lad⟩ [læd] Junge, junger Mann **III 3**, 50
ladder [ˈlædə] Leiter **I**
lady [ˈleɪdɪ] Dame **II**
lake [leɪk] See, Teich **I**
lamb [læm] Lamm **I**
land [lænd] Land **III 3**, 50
to **land** [lænd] landen, an Land gehen **III 1**, 16
language [ˈlæŋgwɪdʒ] Sprache **III WSA**, 7
last [lɑːst] letzte/letzter/letztes **I**
at last [ət ˈlɑːst] schließlich, zuletzt **I**
late [leɪt] spät, zu spät **I**
to work late [ˌwɜːk ˈleɪt] länger arbeiten **I**
⟨Latin⟩ [ˈlætɪn] lateinisch, Latein **III WSC**, 58
laugh [lɑːf] Lachen **II**
to **laugh** [lɑːf] lachen **I**
to laugh at [ˈlɑːf‿æt] sich lustig machen über **II**
law [lɔː] Gesetz **III 4**, 66
to **lay*** [leɪ] legen **I**
lazy [ˈleɪzɪ] faul **III 2**, 34
to **lead*** [liːd] führen **III WSC**, 58
leaflet [ˈliːflɪt] Prospekt, Informationsblatt **II**
to **learn*** [lɜːn] lernen **I**
learner [ˈlɜːnə] Lernende/r **III WSB**, 31
to **leave*** [liːv] abfahren, verlassen, zurücklassen **I**
Leave me alone! [ˈliːv mɪ‿əˈləʊn] Lass mich in Ruhe! **II**
to leave free [ˌliːv ˈfriː] frei lassen, offen lassen **III 2**, 38
to leave out [ˌliːv ˈaʊt] auslassen, weglassen **III 5**, 86
left [left] links **I**
on the left [ɒn ðə ˈleft] auf der linken Seite **I**
leg [leg] Bein **I**
⟨legion⟩ [ˈliːdʒn] Legion, Regiment **III WSC**, 60
lemonade [ˌleməˈneɪd] Limonade **I**
to **lend*** [lend] leihen, verleihen **I**
lesson [ˈlesn] Unterrichtsstunde **I**
to **let*** [let] lassen **II**
let's [lets] lass uns/lasst uns **I**
letter [ˈletə] Brief; Buchstabe **I**
letterbox [ˈletəbɒks] Briefkasten **I**
°**level** [levl] Niveau, Höhe **III WSD**, 74
library [ˈlaɪbrərɪ] Bibliothek, Bücherei **III 2**, 32
⟨lice⟩ (*pl*) [laɪs] Läuse **III WSC**, 56
lie [laɪ] Lüge **III 2**, 41
to **lie*** [laɪ] liegen **I**
to lie down [ˌlaɪ ˈdaʊn] sich hinlegen **II**
life [laɪf] Leben **II**
°**lifeboat** [ˈlaɪfbəʊt] Rettungsboot **III 5**, 78
⟨lifeboatman⟩ [ˈlaɪfbəʊtmən] Seenotrettungsmann **III 5**, 79
⟨lifeguard⟩ [ˈlaɪfgɑːd] Rettungsschwimmer/in **III 5**, 84
°**lifejacket** [ˈlaɪfdʒækɪt] Schwimmweste **III 5**, 82
lift [lɪft] Aufzug, Fahrstuhl **II**
light [laɪt] Licht **III 4**, 64
light [laɪt] leicht, gering **III 4**, 63
lightning [ˈlaɪtnɪŋ] Blitz **II**
to **like** [laɪk] mögen, gern haben **I**
I'd like … [aɪd ˈlaɪk] Ich möchte …, Ich hätte gern … **II**
like [laɪk] (so) wie **I**
like this [ˌlaɪk ˈðɪs] so **I**

⟨limerick⟩ [ˈlɪmərɪk] *gereimter brit. Witz mit 5 Zeilen* **III 2**, 37
line [laɪn] Linie, Zeile **II**
lion [ˈlaɪən] Löwe **II**
°**lipstick** [ˈlɪpstɪk] Lippenstift **III WSD**, 75
list [lɪst] Liste **I**
shopping list [ˈʃɒpɪŋ ˌlɪst] Einkaufsliste **II**
to **listen** [ˈlɪsn] zuhören **I**
listening practice [ˈlɪsnɪŋ ˌpræktɪs] Hörverstehensübung **I**
little [ˈlɪtl] klein **I**
a **little** [ə ˈlɪtl] ein bisschen **II**
to **live** [lɪv] leben, wohnen **I**
live [laɪv] live, direkt **II**
living-room [ˈlɪvɪŋrʊm] Wohnzimmer **I**
⟨local⟩ [ˈləʊkl] einheimisch **III WSC**, 59
loch [lɒk] (schottischer) See **II**
to **lock** [lɒk] abschließen **III WSA**, 12
locked [lɒkt] abgeschlossen **I**
Londoner [ˈlʌndənə] Londoner/in **III 1**, 16
lonely [ˈləʊnlɪ] einsam **III 5**, 78
long [lɒŋ] lang **I**
a long time ago [ə ˌlɒŋ taɪm‿əˈgəʊ] lange her **II**
a long way [ə ˌlɒŋ‿ˈweɪ] eine weite Entfernung **II**
look [lʊk] Blick **III 3**, 53
to have a look [hæv‿ə ˈlʊk] sich etw. ansehen **I**
to **look** [lʊk] aussehen; sehen, ansehen **I**
to look after [ˌlʊk‿ˈɑːftə] aufpassen, hüten **II**
to look at [ˈlʊk‿ət] anschauen **I**
to look down [ˌlʊk ˈdaʊn] nach unten sehen **II**
to look for [ˈlʊk fə] suchen **I**
to look round [ˌlʊk ˈraʊnd] sich umsehen **II**
to **lose*** [luːz] verlieren **III WSA**, 12
⟨I ain't gonna lose.⟩ [aɪ ˈeɪnt ˌgɒnə ˈluːz] Ich werde nicht verlieren. **III WSB**, 29
⟨loser⟩ [ˈluːzə] Verlierer/in **III WSB**, 29
to get **lost** [get ˈlɒst] sich verirren, verloren gehen **I**
a **lot of** [ə ˈlɒt‿əv] viel, viele **I**
lots of [ˈlɒts‿əv] viele **III WSA**, 7
loud [laʊd] laut **II**
love [lʌv] alles Liebe, herzliche Grüße *(als Briefschluss)*; Liebe **I**
to **love** [lʌv] lieben **I**
lovely [ˈlʌvlɪ] schön, herrlich **II**
lower [ˈləʊə] untere/unterer/unteres **II**
luck [lʌk] Glück **III 3**, 52
What a piece of luck! [ˈwɒt‿ə ˌpiːs‿ɒv ˈlʌk] Was für ein Glück! **III 3**, 52
lucky [ˈlʌkɪ] glücklich, Glücks- **I**
to be lucky [bɪ ˈlʌkɪ] Glück haben **I**
lunch [lʌntʃ] Mittagessen **I**
lunch box [ˈlʌntʃ ˌbɒks] *Dose für belegte Brote zum Mittagessen* **I**
to have lunch [hæv ˈlʌntʃ] zu Mittag essen **I**

M

machine [məˈʃiːn] Maschine, Gerät **III WSA**, 10
answering machine [ˈɑːnsərɪŋ məˌʃiːn] Anrufbeantworter **III WSA**, 10
magazine [ˌmægəˈziːn] Zeitschrift **I**
⟨maiden⟩ [ˈmeɪdn] junges, unverheiratetes Mädchen **III WSC**, 60
main [ˈmeɪn] Haupt- **III WSC**, 58
⟨mainsail⟩ [ˈmeɪnseɪl] Großsegel **III 5**, 83
to **make*** [meɪk] machen **I**
to make a request [ˌmeɪk‿ə rɪˈkwest] eine Bitte äußern, einen Wunsch äußern **I**
to make money [ˌmeɪk ˈmʌnɪ] Geld verdienen **II**
⟨to make s.o. do s.th.⟩ [ˈmeɪk ˌsʌmwʌn ˈduː ˌsʌmθɪŋ] jdn. dazu bringen, etw. zu tun **III WSC**, 60
man, men *(pl)* [mæn, men] Mann, Männer **I**
⟨to man⟩ [mæn] besetzen **III WSC**, 59
many [ˈmenɪ] viele **I**
How many? [haʊ ˈmenɪ] Wie viele? **I**
map [mæp] Landkarte **I**
March [mɑːtʃ] März **I**
⟨to march⟩ [mɑːtʃ] marschieren **III WSC**, 57
⟨maritime⟩ [ˈmærɪtaɪm] Meeres- **III 5**, 84
mark [mɑːk] Note *(in der Schule)* **III 2**, 33
market square [ˌmɑːkɪt ˈskweə] Marktplatz **I**
mascot [ˈmæskət] Maskottchen **I**
match [mætʃ] (Fußball-)Spiel **III WSB**, 26
to **match** [mætʃ] das Dazupassende finden **II**
Maths [mæθs] Mathematikunterricht, Mathe **II**
It doesn't **matter.** [ɪt ˈdʌznt ˈmætə] Es macht nichts. **II**
May [meɪ] Mai **I**
may [meɪ] darf/dürfen, könnte/könnten **I**
maybe [ˈmeɪbiː] vielleicht **I**
me [miː] mir/mich **I**
meal [miːl] Mahlzeit, Essen **II**
to **mean*** [miːn] bedeuten **II**
meaning [ˈmiːnɪŋ] Bedeutung **II**
meat [miːt] Fleisch **II**
mechanic [mɪˈkænɪk] Mechaniker/in **I**
medal [medl] Medaille **III 5**, 85
medicine [ˈmedsɪn] Medizin **II**
to **meet*** [miːt] (sich) kennen lernen **III WSA**, 7; (sich) treffen **I**
meeting [ˈmiːtɪŋ] Treffen, Besprechung **II**
member [ˈmembə] Mitglied **II**
memory [ˈmemərɪ] Gedächtnis, Erinnerung **II**
to **mend** [mend] reparieren **III WSB**, 26
mess [mes] Unordnung **I**
message [ˈmesɪdʒ] Nachricht, Mitteilung **III WSA**, 10
metre [ˈmiːtə] Meter **III WSB**, 26
middle [ˈmɪdl] Mitte **II**
in the middle of [ɪn ðə ˈmɪdl‿əv] in der Mitte von, mitten in **II**
the Middle Ages [ðə ˌmɪdl ˈeɪdʒɪz] das Mittelalter **II**
⟨midway⟩ [ˌmɪdˈweɪ] auf halbem Weg **III 4**, 72
might [maɪt] könnte **III 5**, 85
mile [maɪl] Meile **III 4**, 62
⟨military⟩ [ˈmɪlɪtərɪ] militärisch **III WSC**, 59
milk [mɪlk] Milch **I**
to **milk** [mɪlk] melken **III 3**, 49
milkman [ˈmɪlkmən] Milchmann **II**
million [ˈmɪljən] Million **III 3**, 45
mince [mɪns] Hackfleisch **II**
mind [maɪnd] Verstand, Gedanken **III 3**, 46
°mind map [ˈmaɪnd ˌmæp] *Wörternetz zur Gedächtnisstütze* **III 3**, 46
to **mind** [maɪnd] jdm. etw. ausmachen **II**
Never mind. [ˈnevə ˈmaɪnd] Mach dir nichts daraus., Macht nichts. **I**
mine [maɪn] Bergwerk, Mine **III 3**, 45
mine [maɪn] meine/meiner/meines **II**
minute [ˈmɪnɪt] Minute **I**
°**miracle** [ˈmɪrəkl] Wunder **III 3**, 52
mirror [ˈmɪrə] Spiegel **II**
miserable [ˈmɪzrəbl] unglücklich, elend **II**
to **miss** [mɪs] ⟨vermissen⟩ **III 3**, 50; verpassen **III 3**, 53
missing [ˈmɪsɪŋ] fehlend, nicht da **III 1**, 24

mistake [mɪ'steɪk] Fehler **II**
model [mɒdl] Modell **III 4**, 69
moment ['məʊmənt] Moment, Augenblick **I**
Monday ['mʌndeɪ] Montag **I**
money ['mʌnɪ] Geld **I**
pocket money ['pɒkɪt ˌmʌnɪ] Taschengeld **I**
to make money [ˌmeɪk 'mʌnɪ] Geld verdienen **II**
monkey ['mʌŋkɪ] Affe **II**
monster ['mɒnstə] Monster, Ungeheuer **I**
month [mʌnθ] Monat **I**
⟨monument⟩ ['mɒnjʊmənt] Monument, Bauwerk **III WSC**, 59
more [mɔː] mehr **I**
one more [ˌwʌn 'mɔː] noch ein/eine **I**
morning ['mɔːnɪŋ] Morgen **I**
Good morning. [ˌgʊd 'mɔːnɪŋ] Guten Morgen. **I**
most [məʊst] die meiste/meisten **II**
most of them ['məʊst‿ɒv ˌðəm] die meisten von ihnen **III 1**, 16
mother ['mʌðə] Mutter **I**
motorbike ['məʊtəbaɪk] Motorrad **III WSD**, 75
motorway ['məʊtəweɪ] Autobahn **III 4**, 63
mountain ['maʊntɪn] Berg **I**
mountain rescue ['maʊntɪn 'reskjuː] Bergwacht **II**
mouse, mice *(pl)* [maʊs, maɪs] Maus, Mäuse **II**
mouth [maʊθ] Mund **I**
to **move** [muːv] sich bewegen **III WSB**, 27; umziehen **III 3**, 47
Mr ['mɪstə] Herr (*Anrede für Männer*) **I**
Mrs ['mɪsɪz] Frau (*Anrede für verheiratete Frauen*) **I**
°**Ms** [mɪz] Frau (*Anrede für Frauen, ob verheiratet oder nicht)* **III WSB**, 31
much [mʌtʃ] viel **I**
How much? [haʊ 'mʌtʃ] Wie viel? **I**
very much [ˌverɪ 'mʌtʃ] sehr **I**
muddle ['mʌdl] Durcheinander **I**
°**multi-storey car park** [ˌmʌltɪ stɔːrɪ 'kɑː pɑːk] Parkhochhaus **III 4**, 72
mum [mʌm] Mama, Mutti **I**
°**mummy** ['mʌmɪ] Mumie **III 1**, 22
murgh ['mɜːg] *indisches Currygericht* **III 1**, 21
museum [mjuː'zɪəm] Museum **II**
music ['mjuːzɪk] Musik **I**
pop music ['pɒp‿mjuːzɪk] Popmusik **I**
Muslim ['mʊslɪm] islamisch, Moslem/Moslime **III 1**, 16
must [mʌst] müssen **I**
my [maɪ] mein/meine **I**
myself [maɪ'self] (mich/mir) selbst **III WSB**, 30

N

name [neɪm] Name **I**
nasty ['nɑːstɪ] schrecklich, scheußlich **II**
national ['næʃənl] national, National- **III WSB**, 27
nationality [ˌnæʃə'nælɪtɪ] Nationalität **I**
near ['nɪə] nahe, in der Nähe von **I**
nearly ['nɪəlɪ] fast, beinahe **II**
⟨'neath (= beneath)⟩ ['niːθ = bɪ'niːθ] unter **III 3**, 50
to **need** [niːd] brauchen, benötigen **I**
negative ['negətɪv] negativ **III WSD**, 77
neighbour ['neɪbə] Nachbar/in **I**
neighbourhood ['neɪbəhʊd] Nachbarschaft, Wohnviertel **I**
nervous about ['nɜːvəs‿əˌbaʊt] nervös, aufgeregt wegen **II**
never ['nevə] niemals, nie **I**
°Never mind. ['nevə 'maɪnd] Mach dir nichts daraus., Macht nichts. **I**
New Year's Day [ˌnjuː jɪəz 'deɪ] Neujahrstag **III 3**, 52
new [njuː] neu **I**
news [njuːz] Nachricht/en, Neuigkeit/en **II**
newsagent's ['njuːzˌeɪdʒnts] *Laden für Zeitungen, Zeitschriften, Tabakwaren, Süßigkeiten usw.* **II**
newspaper ['njuːsˌpeɪpə] Zeitung **III WSB**, 31
next [nekst] nächste/nächster/nächstes **I**
next time ['nekst‿ˌtaɪm] nächstes Mal **I**
next door [ˌnekst 'dɔː] nebenan **III WSC**, 60
next to ['neks tə] neben **II**
nice [naɪs] nett, schön **I**
night [naɪt] Nacht **I**
at night [ət 'naɪt] nachts **II**
°**nightmare** ['naɪtmeə] Albtraum **III 5**, 84
no [nəʊ] kein/keine; nein **I**
No, thank you. [nəʊ 'θæŋk‿juː] Nein, danke. **I**
no-one ['nəʊˌwʌn] niemand **III WSC**, 57
nobody ['nəʊbədɪ] niemand, keiner **I**
⟨to nod⟩ [nɒd] nicken **III WSC**, 60
noise [nɔɪz] Lärm, Krach, Geräusch **I**
noisy ['nɔɪzɪ] laut **III 2**, 39
non-swimmer [ˌnɒn 'swɪmə] Nichtschwimmer/in **II**
⟨none⟩ [nʌn] niemand **III 3**, 50
normal ['nɔːml] normal **III 1**, 23
Norman ['nɔːmən] normannisch, Normanne **III 1**, 19
north [nɔːθ] Norden, Nord-, nördlich **II**
northbound ['nɔːθbaʊnd] Richtung Norden **III 1**, 18
nose [nəʊz] Nase **II**
not [nɒt] nicht **I**
not ... any more ['nɒt ˌenɪ 'mɔː] nicht/kein ... mehr **III 4**, 65
not only ... but also [nɒt 'əʊnlɪ, bʌt 'ɔːlsəʊ] nicht nur ..., sondern auch **III WSD**, 74
not ... yet [nɒt 'jet] noch nicht **I**
note [nəʊt] Notiz **I**
nothing ['nʌθɪŋ] nichts **I**
notice ['nəʊtɪs] Aushang, Schild **II**
notice board ['nəʊtɪs bɔːd] schwarzes Brett **II**
to **notice** ['nəʊtɪs] bemerken **III 1**, 23
noun [naʊn] Substantiv **II**
November [nəʊ'vembə] November **I**
now [naʊ] jetzt, nun **I**
number ['nʌmbə] Zahl, Nummer **I**
nurse [nɜːs] Krankenschwester, Krankenpfleger **II**
nursery school ['nɜːsrɪ ˌskuːl] Kindergarten **I**

O

oak [əʊk] Eiche **II**
object ['ɒbdʒɪkt] Objekt, Gegenstand **III WSA**, 8
⟨occupation⟩ [ˌɒkjʊ'peɪʃn] Besetzung **III WSC**, 59
at ... **o'clock** [ə'klɒk] um ... Uhr **I**
October [ɒk'təʊbə] Oktober **I**
of [ɒv/əv] von **I**
of course [əv‿'kɔːs] natürlich, selbstverständlich **I**
off [ɒf] ab, weg **II**
Off you go! ['ɒf jʊ ˌgəʊ] Fort mit dir/euch! **II**
office ['ɒfɪs] Büro, Amt **I**
police **officer** [pə'liːs‿ˌɒfɪsə] Polizist/in **I**
official [ə'fɪʃl] offiziell **III 3**, 50
often ['ɒfn] oft **I**
Oh ... [əʊ] Oh ... **I**
oil [ɔɪl] Öl **III 5**, 78
°oil rig ['ɔːl rɪg] Ölbohrplattform **III 5**, 80

OK [ˌəʊˈkeɪ] OK, in Ordnung **I**
old [əʊld] alt **I**
on [ɒn] an **I**
on (Radio Nottingham) [ɒn (ˌreɪdɪəʊ ˈnɒtɪŋəm)] im (Radio Nottingham) **I**
on holiday [ɒn ˈhɒlɪdeɪ] im Urlaub **I**
on the left [ɒn ðə ˈleft] auf der linken Seite **I**
on the right [ɒn ðə ˈraɪt] auf der rechten Seite **I**
on the seventh of … [ɒn ðə ˈsevnθ‿əv] am siebten … **I**
on the telephone [ɒn ðə ˈtelɪfəʊn] am Telefon **I**
to be on [bɪ‿ˈɒn] eingeschaltet sein **I**
to go on [gəʊ ˈɒn] weitermachen **I**
to have on [ˌhæv ˈɒn] anhaben (*Kleidung*) **II**
on the whole [ˌɒn ðə ˈhəʊl] im Großen und Ganzen **III WSD**, 74
one [wʌn] eins **I**
one by one [ˌwʌn baɪ ˈwʌn] einer nach dem anderen **III 5**, 85
one in five [ˌwʌn‿ˌɪn ˈfaɪv] jeder Fünfte **III 3**, 45
one more [ˌwʌn ˈmɔː] noch ein/eine **I**
only [ˈəʊnlɪ] einzige/einziger/einziges **II**; nur, erst **I**
onto [ˈɒntuː] auf … hinauf **III 5**, 84
open [ˈəʊpn] offen, geöffnet **I**
to **open** [ˈəʊpn] öffnen, aufmachen **I**
operation [ˌɒpəˈreɪʃn] Operation **II**
opinion [əˈpɪnjən] Meinung **III WSD**, 74
in my opinion [ˌɪn ˈmaɪ əˈpɪnjən] meiner Meinung nach **III WSD**, 75
°**opponent** [əˈpəʊnənt] Gegner/in **III WSB**, 27
opposite [ˈɒpəzɪt] Gegenteil **I**
opposite [ˈɒpəzɪt] gegenüber **II**
or [ɔː] oder **I**
or so [ˌɔː ˈsəʊ] ungefähr **II**
order [ˈɔːdə] Reihenfolge, Ordnung **I**
to **organize** [ˈɔːgənaɪz] organisieren **II**
other [ˈʌðə] andere/anderer/anderes **I**
⟨otherwise⟩ [ˈʌðəwaɪz] sonst, ansonsten **III 5**, 84
Ouch! [aʊtʃ] Aua! **II**
our [ˈaʊə] unser/unsere **I**
ours [ˈaʊəz] unsere/unserer/unseres **II**
ourselves [ˌaʊəˈselvz] (uns) selbst **III WSB**, 30
out [aʊt] heraus, draußen **I**
out of [ˈaʊt‿əv] aus **II**
out of the way [ˌaʊt‿əv ðə ˈweɪ] aus dem Weg **II**
out of work [ˌaʊt‿əv ˈwɜːk] arbeitslos **III 3**, 47
outlaw [ˈaʊtlɔː] Gesetzlose/r, Vogelfreie/r, Bandit/in **II**
outside [ˌaʊtˈsaɪd] außerhalb von **III WSC**, 60; (draußen) vor **II**; draußen **I**
over [ˈəʊvə] vorbei, zu Ende **II**
over [ˈəʊvə] über **I**
over there [ˌəʊvə ˈðeə] da drüben, dort **I**
own [əʊn] eigen **III WSA**, 12
⟨children of her **own**⟩ [ˈtʃɪldrən ɒv hər‿ˈəʊn] ihre eigenen Kinder **III WSC**, 60
owner [ˈəʊnə] Besitzer/in, Eigentümer/in **III 4**, 68

P

packed lunch [ˌpækt ˈlʌntʃ] Pausenbrot, Lunchpaket **III 2**, 32
packet [ˈpækɪt] Päckchen **I**
page [peɪdʒ] Seite **I**
to **paint** [peɪnt] malen, anstreichen **III 1**, 21
pair [peə] Paar **I**
palace [ˈpælɪs] Palast **III 1**, 14
paper [ˈpeɪpə] Papier **II**
paragraph [ˈpærəgrɑːf] Abschnitt **III WSC**, 58
Pardon? [ˈpɑːdn] Wie bitte? **III 1**, 22
parents (*pl*) [ˈpeərənts] Eltern **I**
park [pɑːk] Park **I**
car park [ˈkɑː pɑːk] Parkhaus, Parkplatz **II**
to **park** [pɑːk] parken **III 3**, 49
part [pɑːt] Rolle, Teil **II**
past **participle** [ˌpɑːst ˈpɑːtɪsɪpl] Partizip Perfekt **II**
partner [ˈpɑːtnə] Partner/in **I**
party [ˈpɑːtɪ] Party, Feier **I**
to **pass** [pɑːs] (Gesetze) verabschieden; vorbeigehen an **III 4**, 66; reichen, weitergeben **I**
°**passive** [ˈpæsɪv] passiv **III 4**, 65
past [pɑːst] die Vergangenheit **III 1**, 20
past participle [ˌpɑːst ˈpɑːtɪsɪpl] Partizip Perfekt **II**
past progressive [ˌpɑːst prəʊˈgresɪv] *Verlaufsform der Vergangenheit* **II**
simple past [ˌsɪmpl ˈpɑːst] Vergangenheitsform **II**
past [pɑːst] an … vorbei **III WSB**, 27; nach (*bei Uhrzeiten*) **I**
path [pɑːθ] Pfad, Weg **II**
patient [ˈpeɪʃnt] Patient/in, Kranke/r **II**
⟨to be on patrol⟩ [ˌɒn pəˈtrəʊl] auf Kontrollgang sein **III 5**, 84
⟨to patter down⟩ [ˌpætə ˈdaʊn] herunterprasseln **III WSC**, 56
to **pay*** [peɪ] (be)zahlen **II**
to pay s.o. back [ˌpeɪ sʌmwʌn ˈbæk] jdm. etw. zurückzahlen **III 2**, 40
PE (= **Physical Education**) [ˌpiː ˈiː =ˌfɪzɪkl edjuːˈkeɪʃn] Sportunterricht **II**
pen [pen] Füller **I**
pence (= **p**) [pens] *britische Geldeinheit* **I**
pencil [ˈpensl] Bleistift **I**
pencil case [ˈpensl keɪs] Federmäppchen **I**
penfriend [ˈpenfrend] Brieffreund/in **III 3**, 47
people (*pl*) [ˈpiːpl] Leute **I**
present **perfect** [ˌpreznt ˈpɜːfɪkt] *englische Vergangenheitsform* **II**
perfect [ˈpɜːfɪkt] perfekt **III WSA**, 7
person [ˈpɜːsn] Person **II**
personal [ˈpɜːsnl] persönlich **III WSC**, 59
pet [pet] Haustier **I**
pet shop [ˈpet ʃɒp] Tierhandlung **II**
petrol [ˈpetrəl] Benzin **III 4**, 63
Phew! [fjuː] *Ausruf* **III WSA**, 7
to **phone** [fəʊn] anrufen **I**
photo [ˈfəʊtəʊ] Foto **I**
to take a photo of [ˌteɪk‿ə ˈfəʊtəʊ‿əv] ein Foto machen von **I**
phrase [freɪz] (Teil-)Satz, Wendung **III 4**, 70
piano [pɪˈænəʊ] Klavier **II**
to **pick out** [ˌpɪk‿ˈaʊt] heraussuchen **III WSC**, 59
to **pick up** [pɪk‿ˈʌp] aufheben, abholen **II**
°**picnic** [ˈpɪknɪk] Picknick **III WSA**, 12
picture [ˈpɪktʃə] Bild **I**
in the picture [ɪn ðə ˈpɪktʃə] auf dem Bild **I**
piece [piːs] Stück **II**
What a piece of luck! [ˈwɒt‿ə ˌpiːs‿ɒv ˈlʌk] Was für ein Glück! **III 3**, 52
pig [pɪg] Schwein **I**
pigeon [ˈpɪdʒɪn] Taube **III 1**, 14
pillow [ˈpɪləʊ] Kopfkissen **II**
pink [pɪŋk] rosa, pink **II**
pint [paɪnt] *britische Mengenangabe* (*etwa 1/2 Liter*) **I**

⟨pipe⟩ [paɪp] Pfeife **III 3**, 50
° **pitch** [pɪtʃ] (Rugby-)Spielfeld **III WSB**, 27
⟨pitcher⟩ ['pɪtʃə] Krug **III 3**, 50
pizza ['pi:tsə] Pizza **II**
place [pleɪs] Ort, Platz **I**
plan [plæn] Plan **I**
to **plan** [plæn] planen **II**
plane [pleɪn] Flugzeug **I**
plastic ['plæstɪk] Plastik **III 4**, 64
plate [pleɪt] Teller **II**
play [pleɪ] Schauspiel, Theaterstück **II**
role play ['rəʊl pleɪ] Rollenspiel **I**
to **play** [pleɪ] spielen **I**
player ['pleɪə] Spieler/in **II**
playground ['pleɪgraʊnd] Schulhof, Spielplatz **I**
in the playground [ɪn ðə 'pleɪgraʊnd] auf dem Schulhof, auf dem Spielplatz **I**
please [pli:z] bitte **I**
to be **pleased with** [ˌbɪ 'pli:zd ˌwɪð] mit etw. zufrieden sein, sich über etw. freuen **III 2**, 34
⟨pleasure cruise⟩ ['pleʒə ˌkru:z] Vergnügungsfahrt **III WSB**, 29
pocket ['pɒkɪt] Tasche *(bei Kleidung)* **I**
pocket money ['pɒkɪt ˌmʌnɪ] Taschengeld **I**
⟨pointed face⟩ [ˌpɔɪntɪd 'feɪs] spitzes Gesicht **III WSC**, 60
⟨poison⟩ ['pɔɪzn] Gift **III WSC**, 58
police [pə'li:s] Polizei **I**
° police officer [pə'li:s‿ˌɒfɪsə] Polizist/in **I**
Polish ['pəʊlɪʃ] polnisch, Polnisch **III WSA**, 7
polite [pə'laɪt] höflich **II**
to **pollute** [pə'lu:t] verschmutzen **III 4**, 64
pollution [pə'lu:ʃn] Verschmutzung **III 4**, 64
pond [pɒnd] Teich **I**
pony ['pəʊnɪ] Pony **II**
pool [pu:l] Schwimmbad **II**
poor [pɔ:] arm **I**
pop music ['pɒp‿mju:zɪk] Popmusik **I**
popcorn ['pɒpkɔ:n] Popcorn **II**
popular ['pɒpjʊlə] beliebt **II**
porridge ['pɒrɪdʒ] Haferbrei **II**
possible ['pɒsəbl] möglich **III 2**, 41
post office ['pəʊst‿ˌɒfɪs] Post, Postamt **I**
postcard ['pəʊstkɑ:d] Postkarte **I**
poster ['pəʊstə] Poster, Plakat **I**
⟨pot⟩ [pɒt] Topf **III 3**, 50
potato, potatoes *(pl)* [pə'teɪtəʊ] Kartoffel, Kartoffeln **II**
° roast potatoes [ˌrəʊst pə'teɪtəʊz] im Ofen gebratene Kartoffeln **II**
pound (= £) [paʊnd] Pfund *(britische Währung)* **I**
pound (=**lb**) [paʊnd] *britische Gewichtseinheit (etwa ein Pfund)* **I**
word **power** ['wɜ:d ˌpaʊə] die Kraft der Wörter **I**
practice ['præktɪs] Übung, Training **I**
listening practice ['lɪsnɪŋ ˌpræktɪs] Hörverstehensübung **I**
sound practice ['saʊnd ˌpræktɪs] Ausspracheübung **I**
to **practise** ['præktɪs] üben **II**
preposition [ˌprepə'zɪʃn] Präposition, Verhältniswort **II**
prescription [prɪ'skrɪpʃn] (Arzt-)Rezept **II**
present ['preznt] Geschenk **I**
present perfect [ˌpreznt 'pɜ:fɪkt] *englische Vergangenheitsform* **II**
° **present perfect progressive** [ˌpreznt ˌpɜ:fɪkt prəʊ'gresɪv] *Verlaufsform des Perfekt* **III 3**, 47
simple **present** [ˌsɪmpl 'preznt] Präsens **II**
to **pretend** [prɪ'tend] etw. vorgeben, so tun als ob **III WSC**, 60
pretty ['prɪtɪ] hübsch **II**
primary school ['praɪmərɪ ˌsku:l] Grundschule **III 2**, 33
prince [prɪns] Prinz **III 3**, 45
prison ['prɪzən] Gefängnis **III 1**, 17
prisoner ['prɪznə] Gefangene/r **II**
to take prisoner [ˌteɪk 'prɪznə] gefangen nehmen **II**
prize [praɪz] Preis, Gewinn **I**
probably ['prɒbəblɪ] wahrscheinlich **II**
problem ['prɒbləm] Problem **I**
professional [prə'feʃənl] professionell **II**
programme ['prəʊgræm] Programm **II**
progress *(no pl)* ['prəʊgres] Fortschritt **III 2**, 34
progressive (form) [prəʊ'gresɪv] Verlaufsform **II**
past progressive [ˌpɑ:st prəʊ'gresɪv] *Verlaufsform der Vergangenheit* **II**
project ['prɒdʒekt] Projekt **III 2**, 34
promenade [ˌprɒmə'nɑ:d] Promenade **I**
to **promise** ['prɒmɪs] versprechen **III 2**, 40
prompter ['prɒmptə] Souffleur/Souffleuse **II**
to **protect** [prə'tekt] (be)schützen **III WSC**, 57
to be **proud of** ['praʊd‿ˌəv] stolz sein auf **II**
public ['pʌblɪk] öffentlich **III 4**, 66
public transport [ˌpʌblɪk 'trænspɔ:t] öffentliche Verkehrsmittel **III 4**, 66
to **pull** [pʊl] ziehen **II**
to pull down [ˌpʊl 'daʊn] abreißen **III 4**, 65
pullover ['pʊlˌəʊvə] Pullover **I**
pump [pʌmp] Luftpumpe **I**
° **punctuation** [ˌpʌŋktʃʊ'eɪʃn] Zeichensetzung **III WSD**, 77
pupil ['pju:pl] Schüler/in **I**
puppet ['pʌpɪt] Marionette **II**
purse [pɜ:s] Portmonee, Geldbeutel **II**
to **push** [pʊʃ] drücken, schubsen, schieben **III 2**, 40
to **put*** [pʊt] setzen, stellen, legen **I**
to put down [ˌpʊt 'daʊn] abstellen, weglegen **II**
to put in [ˌpʊt‿'ɪn] einsetzen, hineintun **I**
to put the telephone down [pʊt ðə 'telɪfəʊn ˌdaʊn] den Hörer auflegen **II**
to put work into s.th. [ˌpʊt 'wɜ:k ɪntʊ ˌsʌmθɪŋ] Arbeit in etw. hineinstecken **III 2**, 34
puzzle ['pʌzl] Rätsel **I**

Q

quarter ['kwɔ:tə] Viertel **I**
quarter past (eleven) ['kwɔ:tə pɑ:st] Viertel nach (elf) **I**
quarter to (twelve) ['kwɔ:tə tə] Viertel vor (zwölf) **I**
queen [kwi:n] Königin **III 1**, 14
question ['kwestʃn] Frage **I**
° question tag ['kwestʃən ˌtæg] *nachgestellte Fragepartikel* **III 3**, 51
questionnaire [ˌkwestʃə'neə] Fragebogen **I**
queue [kju:] (Warte-)Schlange **III 1**, 14
quick [kwɪk] schnell **II**
quiet ['kwaɪət] ruhig, still **I**
quite [kwaɪt] ziemlich **III 1**, 22
quiz [kwɪz] Ratespiel, Quiz **I**

R

rabbit ['ræbɪt] Kaninchen **II**
race [reɪs] Wettlauf, Rennen **I**

Vocabulary

racket ['rækɪt] Schläger *(für Tennis, Squash u. Ä.)* **III WSB**, 29
radio ['reɪdɪəʊ] Radio **I**; Funkgerät **III 5**, 82
railway ['reɪlweɪ] Eisenbahn **III 3**, 45
rain [reɪn] Regen **II**
to **rain** [reɪn] regnen **I**
rainstorm ['reɪnstɔ:m] Unwetter, Regenguss **III WSA**, 12
rainy ['reɪnɪ] regnerisch **III WSA**, 12
°**RE** (= **Religious Education**) [ˌɑ:r‿'i: = rɪ'lɪdʒəs edju:ˌkeɪʃn] Religionsunterricht **II**
⟨to reach⟩ [ri:tʃ] erreichen **III WSD**, 77
to **react to s.th.** [rɪ'ækt tə ˌsʌmθɪŋ] auf etw. reagieren **III WSC**, 60
to **read*** [ri:d] lesen **I**
readable ['ri:dəbl] lesbar **III WSB**, 31
reader ['ri:də] Leser/in **III WSB**, 31
ready ['redɪ] fertig, bereit **I**
real [rɪəl] wirklich, echt **III 3**, 54
really ['rɪəlɪ] wirklich **I**
reason ['ri:sən] Grund **III 4**, 69
rebellion [rɪ'beljən] Rebellion, Aufstand **III WSC**, 58
recipe ['resɪpɪ] (Koch-)Rezept **II**
recording [rɪ'kɔ:dɪŋ] Aufnahme **III WSA**, 9
to **recycle** [ˌri:'saɪkl] wieder verwenden **III 4**, 64
red [red] rot **I**
reduced in size [rɪˌdju:st‿ɪn 'saɪz] verkleinert **I**
°**referee** [ˌrefə'ri:] Schiedsrichter/in **III WSB**, 29
°**reflexive verb** [rɪˌfleksɪv 'vɜ:b] reflexives (rückbezügliches) Verb **III WSB**, 30
⟨refrain⟩ [rɪ'freɪn] Refrain **III WSB**, 29
relative clause [ˌrelətɪv 'klɔ:z] Relativsatz **III 2**, 37
°relative pronoun [ˌrelətɪv 'prəʊnaʊn] Relativpronomen **III 2**, 36
religion [rɪ'lɪdʒən] Religion **III 1**, 19
°**remains** *(pl)* [rɪ'meɪnz] Überreste **III WSC**, 59
to **remember** [rɪ'membə] behalten, sich merken, sich erinnern **I**
to **remind s.o. of s.th.** [rɪ'maɪnd ˌsʌmwʌn ɒv 'sʌmθɪŋ] jdn. an etw. erinnern **III WSC**, 61
to **repair** [rɪ'peə] reparieren **I**
to **repeat** [rɪ'pi:t] wiederholen **III 2**, 33
to repeat a year [rɪ'pi:t‿ə jɪə] eine Klasse wiederholen **III 2**, 33
report [rɪ'pɔ:t] (Zeitungs-)Reportage **II**
request [rɪ'kwest] Bitte, Wunsch **I**
to make a request [ˌmeɪk‿ə rɪ'kwest] eine Bitte äußern, einen Wunsch äußern **I**
rescue ['reskju:] Rettung **III 5**, 84
mountain rescue ['maʊntɪn 'reskju:] Bergwacht **II**
to **rescue** ['reskju:] retten, bergen **II**
to **rest** [rest] sich ausruhen **II**
restaurant ['restərɔ:ŋ] Restaurant **II**
review [rɪ'vju:] Besprechung, Rezension eines Buches, Films, etc. **III WSD**, 74
to **revise** [rɪ'vaɪz] überarbeiten, korrigieren, den Stoff wiederholen **III WSA**, 7
rhyme [raɪm] Reim **I**
rhythm ['rɪðəm] Rhythmus **II**
rich [rɪtʃ] reich **II**
⟨That rids me of Rome.⟩ [ˌðæt 'rɪdz mɪ ɒv rəʊm] *etwa:* Das befreit mich von Rom. **III WSC**, 60
ride [raɪd] Fahrt **II**
to have a ride on [ˌhæv‿ə'raɪd‿ɒn] fahren auf **II**
white knuckle ride [ˌwaɪt nʌkl 'raɪd] *wilde Fahrt auf Achterbahn und Ähnlichem* **II**
to **ride*** [raɪd] reiten, fahren (Fahrrad, Motorrad) **II**
rider ['raɪdə] Reiter/in **III WSB**, 31
riding school ['raɪdɪŋ ˌsku:l] Reitschule **II**
right [raɪt] richtig **I**
Right? [raɪt] Nicht wahr?, Richtig? **I**
to be right [bɪ 'raɪt] Recht haben **II**
right [raɪt] rechts **I**
on the right [ɒn ðə 'raɪt] auf der rechten Seite **I**
right away [raɪt‿ə'weɪ] sofort **I**
ring [rɪŋ] Ring **I**
to **ring*** [rɪŋ] klingeln **II**; läuten **III 2**, 41
river ['rɪvə] Fluss **II**
road (= **Rd.**) [rəʊd] Straße **I**
roadside ['rəʊdsaɪd] Straßenrand **III 3**, 49
⟨roadway⟩ ['rəʊdweɪ] Straße **III 4**, 72
°**roadworks** ['rəʊdwɜ:ks] Straßenarbeiten **III 4**, 63
⟨We did roam ...⟩ [wi: dɪd 'rəʊm] Wir trieben uns herum ... **III 5**, 83
roast beef [ˌrəʊst ' bi:f] Rinderbraten **II**
roast potatoes [ˌrəʊst pə'teɪtəʊz] im Ofen gebratene Kartoffeln **II**
rock [rɒk] Fels **I**
role play ['rəʊl pleɪ] Rollenspiel **I**
°**Roman** ['rəʊmən] römisch, Römer/in **III 1**, 15
room [ru:m] Platz **III WSC**, 60; Raum, Zimmer **I**
rope [rəʊp] Seil, Strick **II**
⟨rose⟩ [rəʊz] Rose **III WSB**, 29
rough [rʌf] rau, grob **III 5**, 78
round [raʊnd] rund, durch ganz ... **III WSA**, 8; um ... herum **I**
roundabout ['raʊndəbaʊt] °Karussell **II**; Kreisverkehr **III 4**, 63
route [ru:t] Weg, Straße **III 3**, 49
⟨Ain't no route.⟩ ['eɪnt ˌnəʊ 'ru:t] *etwa:* Es gibt keine Straße. **III 4**, 72
row [rəʊ] Reihe **II**
to **row** [rəʊ] rudern **II**
°**royal** ['rɔɪəl] königlich **III 1**, 17
rubbish ['rʌbɪʃ] Abfall, Müll **I**
rugby ['rʌgbɪ] *englischer Rasensport* **III WSB**, 26
rule [ru:l] Regel **II**
to **run*** [rʌn] laufen, rennen **I**
to run off [ˌrʌn‿'ɒf] weglaufen **II**
runner ['rʌnə] Läufer/in **III WSB**, 31
Russian ['rʌʃən] russisch, Russisch, Russe/Russin **III WSA**, 7

S

saddlebag ['sædlbæg] Satteltasche **I**
safe [seɪf] sicher **III 2**, 41
safety ['seɪftɪ] Sicherheit **III 5**, 82
⟨sail⟩ [seɪl] Segel **III 5**, 83
salad ['sæləd] gemischter Salat **I**
for **sale** [fə 'seɪl] zu verkaufen **II**
bring-and-buy **sale** [ˌbrɪŋ‿n 'baɪ seɪl] Flohmarkt **II**
the **same** [ðə 'seɪm] derselbe/dieselbe/dasselbe **I**
sand [sænd] Sand **I**
⟨sandal⟩ [sændl] Sandale **III WSC**, 58
sandcastle ['sændkɑ:sl] Sandburg **I**
sandwich ['sænwɪdʒ] Butterbrot **I**
⟨satisfied⟩ ['sætɪsfaɪd] zufrieden **III 2**, 41
Saturday ['sætədeɪ] Samstag, Sonnabend **I**
sauerkraut ['saʊəkraʊt] Sauerkraut **II**
sausage ['sɒsɪdʒ] Würstchen, Wurst **I**
to **save** [seɪv] retten; sparen **I**
to **say*** [seɪ] sagen **I**
It says ... [ˌɪt 'sez] Es heißt hier ..., Hier steht ... **III 4**, 64
to say hello to [ˌseɪ hə'ləʊ‿tə] grüßen **I**

scared ['skeəd] verängstigt **I**
to be scared of ['skeəd‿əv] Angst haben vor **II**
scarf, scarves *(pl)* [skɑːf, skɑːvz] Schal, Schals **III 1**, 23
scene [siːn] Szene **II**
behind the scenes [bɪˌhaɪnd ðə 'siːnz] hinter den Kulissen **II**
school [skuːl] Schule **I**
nursery school ['nɜːsrɪ ˌskuːl] Kindergarten **I**
school report ['skuːl rɪˌpɔːt] Schulzeugnis **III 2**, 34
Science ['saɪəns] Naturwissenschaft/en **II**
Scottish ['skɒtɪʃ] schottisch, Schottisch **III WSA**, 9
to **scream** [skriːm] schreien, kreischen **III WSB**, 30
screen [skriːn] Bildschirm, Leinwand **III WSD**, 75
sea [siː] das Meer, die See **I**
seal [siːl] Robbe **II**
search [sɜːtʃ] Suche **III 5**, 84
at the **seaside** [ət ðə 'siːsaɪd] am Meer, an der See **I**
season ['siːzn] Jahreszeit **I**
seat [siːt] Sitz, Sitzplatz **I**
front seat [ˌfrʌnt 'siːt] Vordersitz **II**
second ['sekənd] Sekunde **III WSB**, 27
secondary school ['sekəndərɪ ˌskuːl] *weiterführende Schule in GB* **III 2**, 33
section ['sekʃn] Abteilung **III 4**, 69
to **see*** [siː] sehen **I**
⟨You see …⟩ [ˌjʊ 'siː] Weißt du, … **III WSC**, 60
See you tomorrow! [ˌsiː juː tə'mɒrəʊ] Bis morgen! **III WSA**, 8
⟨to seek*⟩ [siːk] suchen **III 3**, 50
to **seem** [siːm] scheinen **II**
to **sell*** [sel] verkaufen **I**
to **send*** [send] schicken **II**
sentence ['sentəns] Satz **I**
September [sep'tembə] September **I**
serious ['sɪərɪəs] ernst **III 5**, 84
service ['sɜːvɪs] Dienst, Bedienung **III 3**, 49
service station ['sɜːvɪs ˌsteɪʃn] Tankstelle **III 4**, 63
⟨to set⟩ [set] setzen **III 5**, 83
⟨The sun was setting.⟩ [ðə 'sʌn wɒz 'setɪŋ] Die Sonne ging unter. **III WSC**, 57
to **settle** ['setl] siedeln **III 3**, 50
to settle s.th. ['setl ˌsʌmθɪŋ] etw. erledigen, in Ordnung bringen **III 2**, 36
shall [ʃəl] soll **III 2**, 39
⟨share⟩ [ʃeə] Anteil **III WSB**, 29
she [ʃiː] sie **I**
sheep [ʃiːp] Schaf, Schafe **I**
sheepdog ['ʃiːpˌdɒg] Hirtenhund **I**
shelf, shelves *(pl)* [ʃelf] Regalbrett, Regalbretter; Regal, Regale **I**
sheriff ['ʃerɪf] Sheriff **II**
to **shine*** [ʃaɪn] scheinen, leuchten **III WSC**, 57
shirt [ʃɜːt] Hemd **II**
shock [ʃɒk] Schock **II**
shoe [ʃuː] Schuh **I**
to **shoot*** [ʃuːt] schießen **II**
shop [ʃɒp] Laden, Geschäft **I**
shop assistant ['ʃɒp‿əˌsɪstənt] Verkäufer/in **I**
to go to the shops [ˌgəʊ tə‿ðə 'ʃɒps] einkaufen gehen **I**
shopping centre ['ʃɒpɪŋ ˌsentə] Einkaufszentrum **II**
shopping list ['ʃɒpɪŋ ˌlɪst] Einkaufsliste **II**
short [ʃɔːt] kurz **II**
for short [ˌfə 'ʃɔːt] abgekürzt **III 3**, 45
short cut [ˌʃɔːt 'kʌt] Abkürzung **II**
should [ʃʊd] sollte/n **II**
shoulder ['ʃəʊldə] Schulter **II**
to **shout** [ʃaʊt] rufen, schreien **I**
°**show-off** ['ʃəʊ ɒf] Angeber/in **III 2**, 35
to **show*** [ʃəʊ] zeigen **I**
to **shut*** [ʃʌt] schließen **III 2**, 36
Shut up! [ˌʃʌt 'ʌp] Halt den Mund! **III 2**, 36
side [saɪd] Seite **II**
sight [saɪt] Sehenswürdigkeit, Anblick **III 1**, 14
sign [saɪn] Schild **II**
signal ['sɪgnl] Signal, Hinweis **II**
silly ['sɪlɪ] dumm, albern **I**
simple ['sɪmpl] einfach **II**
simple past [ˌsɪmpl 'pɑːst] Vergangenheitsform **II**
simple present [ˌsɪmpl 'preznt] Präsens **II**
since [sɪns] seit **III 3**, 47
to **sing*** [sɪŋ] singen **I**
singer ['sɪŋə] Sänger/in **II**
sir [sɜː] (mein) Herr **III 3**, 48
sister ['sɪstə] Schwester **I**
to **sit*** [sɪt] sitzen **I**
to sit down [ˌsɪt 'daʊn] sich hinsetzen **I**
to sit up [ˌsɪt‿'ʌp] sich aufsetzen **II**
situation [ˌsɪtjʊ'eɪʃn] Lage, Situation **II**
size [saɪz] Größe **III WSB**, 27
skate [skeɪt] Schlittschuh, Rollschuh **II**
skateboard ['skeɪtbɔːd] Skateboard **I**
skater ['skeɪtə] Skateboardfahrer/in, Rollschuhläufer/in, Schlittschuhläufer/in **II**
to **ski** [skiː] Ski fahren **III 1**, 20
skill [skɪl] Fähigkeit, Fertigkeit **III WSD**, 77
skin [skɪn] Haut **I**
skirt [skɜːt] Rock **II**
sky [skaɪ] Himmel **III WSC**, 56
to **sleep*** [sliːp] schlafen **I**
sleepless ['sliːplɪs] schlaflos **III WSB**, 31
⟨to slip⟩ [slɪp] ausrutschen **III 5**, 82
slippery ['slɪpərɪ] rutschig, glatt **II**
⟨sloop⟩ [sluːp] *historischer Segelschiffstyp* **III 5**, 83
slow [sləʊ] langsam **II**
⟨slung⟩ [slʌŋ] geschlungen **III 3**, 50
small [smɔːl] klein **I**
to **smell*** [smel] riechen, duften **III 1**, 21
smile [smaɪl] Lächeln **II**
to **smile** [smaɪl] lächeln **II**
to **smoke** [sməʊk] rauchen **II**
snack bar ['snækbɑː] Imbissstube **I**
snake [sneɪk] Schlange **I**
snow [snəʊ] Schnee **I**
to **snow** [snəʊ] schneien **III WSA**, 12
so [səʊ] so, also, deshalb **I**
So do you! ['səʊ ˌduː 'juː] Du auch! **III 2**, 39
soap [səʊp] Seife **I**
sock [sɒk] Socke **II**
⟨solder⟩ ['sɒldə] Lötzinn **III 3**, 50
soldier ['səʊldʒə] Soldat/in **III WSC**, 56
some [sʌm] etwas, ein bisschen, ein paar **I**
somebody ['sʌmbədɪ] (irgend)jemand **II**
someone ['sʌmwʌn] jemand **II**
something ['sʌmθɪŋ] etwas **II**
sometimes ['sʌmtaɪmz] manchmal **I**
somewhere ['sʌmweə] irgendwo **II**
son [sʌn] Sohn **II**
song [sɒŋ] Lied **I**
soon [suːn] bald **I**
sore throat [ˌsɔː 'θrəʊt] Halsweh **II**
Sorry. ['sɒrɪ] Entschuldigung., Tut mir Leid. **I**
Sorry about … ['sɒrɪ ˌəbaʊt] Tut mir Leid wegen … **II**
sound [saʊnd] Klang, Geräusch **I**
sound effects ['saʊnd‿ɪˌfekts] Toneffekte **II**
sound practice ['saʊnd ˌpræktɪs] Ausspracheübung **I**
to **sound** [saʊnd] klingen, sich anhören **II**

soup [su:p] Suppe **III 1**, 21
south [saʊθ] Süden, Süd-, südlich **II**
souvenir [ˌsu:vəˈnɪə] Mitbringsel, Souvenir, Andenken **I**
spade [speɪd] Spaten **I**
Spanish [ˈspænɪʃ] spanisch, Spanisch **I**
to **speak*** [spi:k] sprechen **I**
to speak to [ˈspi:k tə] sprechen mit **I**
special help [ˌspeʃl ˈhelp] Förderunterricht **III 2**, 33
special [ˈspeʃl] besondere/besonderer/besonderes **I**
to **spell*** [spel] buchstabieren **I**
to **spend*** [spend] ausgeben; verbringen **I**
⟨Splash!⟩ [splæʃ] Platsch! **III 5**, 79
spoon [spu:n] Löffel **I**
sport [spɔ:t] Sport **I**
Sports Day [ˈspɔ:ts deɪ] Sportfest **III WSB**, 26
sports centre [ˈspɔ:ts ˌsentə] Sportzentrum **II**
sportsfield [ˈspɔ:tsfi:ld] Sportplatz **III WSB**, 26
spot [spɒt] Fleck **I**
spray [spreɪ] Spray **III 2**, 36
to **spray** [spreɪ] sprühen **III 2**, 36
spring [sprɪŋ] Frühling **I**
° **spy** [spaɪ] Spion/in **III 1**, 19
to **spy** [spaɪ] sehen, erspähen **II**
I spy (with my little eye ...) [ˌaɪ ˈspaɪ] Ich sehe was, was du nicht siehst ... (*Spiel*) **II**
square [skweə] Platz, Quadrat **III 1**, 14
stage [steɪdʒ] Bühne **II**
stairs (*pl*) [steəz] Treppe, Treppenhaus **III 2**, 37
stall [stɔ:l] Stand **II**
stamp [stæmp] Briefmarke **I**
to **stand*** [stænd] stehen **I**
I can't stand ... [aɪ ˈkɑ:nt‿ˈstænd] Ich kann ... nicht leiden/ausstehen. **II**
° to stand up [ˌstænd‿ˈʌp] aufstehen **I**
star [stɑ:] Stern, Star, Idol **III WSB**, 27
to **start** [stɑ:t] beginnen, anfangen **I**
to start off [ˌstɑ:t ˈɒf] beginnen, anfangen **III WSC**, 56
statement [ˈsteɪtmənt] Aussage **III 3**, 54
station [ˈsteɪʃn] Bahnhof **I**
statue [ˈstætʃu:] Statue, Denkmal **I**
status [ˈsteɪtəs] Status, Anerkennung **III 3**, 50
stay [steɪ] Aufenthalt **II**
to **stay** [steɪ] bleiben, (zu Besuch) wohnen **I**
to **steal*** [sti:l] stehlen **III 2**, 37
steep [sti:p] steil **II**
° **step** [step] Schritt, Stufe **I**
still [stɪl] ruhig **I**
still [stɪl] noch **I**
stomach-ache [ˈstʌməkeɪk] Bauchweh, Magenschmerzen **II**
stone [stəʊn] Stein **I**
° the Stone Age [ðə ˈstəʊn eɪdʒ] die Steinzeit **III 4**, 66
stop [stɒp] Haltestelle **III 1**, 18
to **stop** [stɒp] aufhören **II**; halten, anhalten **I**; verhindern, stoppen **II**
Stop it! [ˈstɒp‿ɪt] Hör/Hört auf! **II**
department **store** [dɪˈpɑ:tmənt stɔ:] Kaufhaus **II**
⟨stormy⟩ [ˈstɔ:mɪ] stürmisch **III 5**, 79
story [ˈstɔ:rɪ] Geschichte, Erzählung **I**
straight [streɪt] direkt, gerade(wegs) **II**
strange [streɪndʒ] seltsam, merkwürdig **II**
street [stri:t] Straße **I**
⟨to strike s.o.⟩ [ˈstraɪk sʌmwʌn] jdm. auffallen **III WSC**, 60
string [strɪŋ] Saite, Bindfaden **III WSB**, 29
strong [strɒŋ] stark **III 3**, 45
to get **stuck** [get ˈstʌk] stecken bleiben **I**
student [ˈstju:dnt] Student/in **II**
stupid [ˈstju:pɪd] dumm, doof **III 1**, 20
style [staɪl] Stil **III WSD**, 77
subject [ˈsʌbdʒɪkt] Fach **II**; Subjekt **III 1**, 20; Thema **III WSC**, 56
suddenly [ˈsʌdnlɪ] plötzlich **II**
sugar [ˈʃʊgə] Zucker **I**
summary [ˈsʌmərɪ] Zusammenfassung **II**
summer [ˈsʌmə] Sommer **I**
summer fete [ˌsʌmə ˈfeɪt] Sommerbazar, Sommerfest **II**
sun [sʌn] Sonne **III WSC**, 57
Sunday [ˈsʌndeɪ] Sonntag **I**
sunny [ˈsʌnɪ] sonnig **I**
sunroof [ˈsʌnru:f] Schiebedach **II**
super [ˈsu:pə] super, toll **I**
supermarket [ˈsu:pəˌmɑ:kɪt] Supermarkt **I**
⟨I'm (not) supposed to ...⟩ [ˌaɪm nɒt səˈpəʊzd tə] Ich soll (nicht) ... **III WSC**, 60
to be **sure** [bɪ ˈʃɔ:] sicher sein **I**
surprise [səˈpraɪz] Überraschung **I**
to be **surprised** [bɪ səˈpraɪzd] überrascht sein **I**
sweatshirt [ˈswetʃɜ:t] Sweatshirt **I**
sweet [swi:t] Bonbon **I**
sweet [swi:t] süß, niedlich **II**
to **swim*** [swɪm] schwimmen **II**
swimmer [ˈswɪmə] Schwimmer/in **III WSB**, 31
to go **swimming** [gəʊ ˈswɪmɪŋ] schwimmen gehen **I**
swimming pool [ˈswɪmɪŋpu:l] Schwimmbad **II**
swimming things [ˈswɪmɪŋ ˌθɪŋz] Schwimmsachen, Badezeug **I**
Swiss [swɪs] schweizerisch **III WSA**, 7
to **switch off** [ˌswɪtʃ ˈɒf] ausschalten **III 4**, 64
° **sword** [sɔ:d] Schwert **III 3**, 52
system [ˈsɪstəm] System **III 4**, 72

T

T-shirt [ˈti:ʃɜ:t] T-Shirt **I**
table [ˈteɪbl] Tisch **I**
table tennis [ˈteɪbl ˌtenɪs] Tischtennis **II**
° to **tackle** [tækl] angreifen *(beim Sport)* **III WSB**, 27
to **take*** [teɪk] nehmen, mieten **I**
to take a message [ˌteɪk‿ə ˈmesɪdʒ] eine Nachricht entgegennehmen **III WSA**, 10
to take a photo of [ˌteɪk‿ə ˈfəʊtəʊ‿əv] ein Foto machen von **I**
to take an exam [ˌteɪk ən ɪgˈzæm] eine Prüfung machen, ablegen **III 2**, 33
to take for a walk [ˌteɪk fər‿ə ˈwɔ:k] (Hund) ausführen, spazieren führen **II**
to take notes [ˌteɪk ˈnəʊts] Notizen machen **I**
to take off [ˌteɪk‿ˈɒf] ausziehen **II**
to take over [ˌteɪk ˈəʊvə] übernehmen, wegnehmen **III 3**, 52
to take part in s.th. [ˌteɪk ˈpɑ:t‿ɪn] mitmachen bei, teilnehmen an **III 1**, 16
to take place [ˌteɪk ˈpleɪs] stattfinden **III 1**, 16
to take prisoner [ˌteɪk ˈprɪznə] gefangen nehmen **II**
to take s.o. home [teɪk] jdn. nach Hause bringen **I**
takeaway [ˈteɪkəˌweɪ] *Imbissstube, Schnellgaststätte mit Straßenverkauf* **II**
tale [teɪl] Geschichte, Sage **II**
talk [tɔ:k] Referat, Rede, Gespräch **III WSA**, 12
to **talk about** [ˈtɔ:k‿əˌbaʊt] reden über, sprechen über **I**
tall [tɔ:l] groß **III WSB**, 27
fish **tank** [ˈfɪʃ ˌtæŋk] Aquarium **II**

°**tanker** [ˈtæŋkə] Tanker **III 5**, 83
to **taste** [teɪst] schmecken, probieren **II**
taxi [ˈtæksɪ] Taxi **III 1**, 14
tea [tiː] Tee; *Mahlzeit am frühen Abend (Abendbrot)* **I**
tea shop [ˈtiː ˌʃɒp] Café, Teestube **II**
tea-cosy [ˈtiːkəʊzɪ] Teewärmer, Kaffeemütze **II**
to **teach*** [tiːtʃ] unterrichten, lehren **III 3**, 47
teacher [ˈtiːtʃə] Lehrer/in **I**
team [tiːm] Mannschaft **I**
technology [tekˈnɒlədʒɪ] Technologie, Technik **III 4**, 69; Computerunterricht; Technisches Werken **II**
teddy [ˈtedɪ] Teddybär **II**
telephone [ˈtelɪfəʊn] Telefon **I**
on the telephone [ɒn ðə ˈtelɪfəʊn] am Telefon **I**
to **tell*** [tel] erzählen **I**
to tell lies [ˌtel ˈlaɪz] lügen **III 2**, 41
temperature [ˈtemprətʃə] Fieber **II**
°**temple** [ˈtempl] Tempel **III 1**, 14
⟨ten-ton lorry⟩ [ˌten tʌn ˈlɒrɪ] Zehntonner (Lastwagen) **III 4**, 72
tennis [ˈtenɪs] Tennis **I**
table tennis [ˈteɪbl ˌtenɪs] Tischtennis **II**
tense [tens] (grammatische) Zeit **III WSA**, 7
term [tɜːm] Trimester, Schuljahresdrittel **II**
terrible [ˈterəbl] schrecklich, furchtbar **I**
test [test] Test, Probe **II**
to **test s.b. on s.th.** [ˈtest sʌmbədɪ ɒn ˌsʌmθɪŋ] jdn. auf einem Gebiet prüfen **III 2**, 33
text [tekst] Text **I**
than [ðæn, ðən] als **II**
Thank you. [ˈθæŋk‿juː] Danke schön. **I**
No, thank you. [nəʊ ˈθæŋk‿juː] Nein, danke. **I**
Thank you very much [ˈθæŋk‿jʊ verɪ ˈmʌtʃ] Vielen Dank. **I**
Thanks. [θæŋks] Danke. **I**
that [ðæt/ðət] dass **II**
that [ðæt] das (da) **I**
the [ðə/ðiː] der/die/das **I**
theatre [ˈθɪetə] Theater **II**
their [ðeə] ihr/ihre (*Pl*) **I**
theirs [ðeəz] ihr/ihre **II**
them [ðem] sie/ihnen **I**
°**theme park** [ˈθiːm ˌpɑːk] Erlebnispark, Vergnügungspark **III 4**, 62
themselves [ðəmˈselvz] (sich) selbst **III WSB**, 30
then [ðen] dann **I**
just then [ˌdʒʌst ˈðen] in diesem Moment **II**
there [ðeə] da, dort **I**
over there [ˌəʊvə ˈðeə] da drüben, dort **I**
these [ðiːz] diese hier **I**
they [ðeɪ] sie (*Pl*) **I**
thief, thieves (*pl*) [θiːf, θiːvz] Dieb/in, Diebe/Diebinnen **III WSB**, 31
thin [θɪn] dünn **III WSC**, 60
thing [θɪŋ] Ding, Sache **I**
just the thing [ˌdʒʌst ðə ˈθɪŋ] genau das Richtige **II**
⟨Thing about the sea is …⟩ [ˈθɪŋ‿əˌbaʊt ðə ˈsiː ɪz] *etwa:* Mit dem Meer ist das so … **III 5**, 79
to **think*** [θɪŋk] denken, glauben **I**
to think of [ˈθɪŋk‿əv] denken an **II**
to think of s.th. [ˈθɪŋk ɒv ˌsʌmθɪŋ] sich etw. ausdenken, an etw. denken **III 2**, 37
thirsty [ˈθɜːstɪ] durstig **II**
this [ðɪs] dies, diese/dieser/dieses **I**
this afternoon [ðɪs‿ˌɑːftəˈnuːn] heute Nachmittag **I**
those [ðəʊz] die da drüben **I**
though (= **although**) [ðəʊ = ɔːlˈðəʊ] obwohl **III WSC**, 60
thousand [ˈθaʊznd] tausend **I**
throat [θrəʊt] Hals, Rachen **II**
through [θruː] durch **I**
throw [θrəʊ] Wurf **II**
to **throw*** [θrəʊ] werfen **II**
thunder [ˈθʌndə] Donner **II**
thunderstorm [ˈθʌndəstɔːm] Gewitter **II**
Thursday [ˈθɜːzdeɪ] Donnerstag **I**
ticket [ˈtɪkɪt] Fahrkarte, Eintrittskarte **I**
°**tide** [taɪd] Flut **III 5**, 78
tide table [ˈtaɪd ˌteɪbl] Gezeitentabelle **III 5**, 82
to **tidy up** [ˌtaɪdɪ‿ˈʌp] aufräumen **I**
tidy [ˈtaɪdɪ] ordentlich, aufgeräumt **I**
tiger [ˈtaɪgə] Tiger **II**
tights [taɪts] Strumpfhose, Strumpfhosen **II**
till (= **until**) [tɪl = ənˈtɪl] bis **III 3**, 53
time [taɪm] Mal **II;** Zeit, Uhrzeit **I**
a long time ago [ə ˌlɒŋ taɪm‿əˈgəʊ] lange her **II**
after a time [ˌɑːftər‿ə ˈtaɪm] nach einer Weile **II**
free time [ˌfriː‿ˈtaɪm] Freizeit **I**
in time [ˌɪn ˈtaɪm] rechtzeitig **II**
It's time for … [ɪts‿ˈtaɪm fə] Es ist Zeit für … **I**
next time [ˈnekst‿ˌtaɪm] nächstes Mal **I**
⟨time after time⟩ [ˈtaɪm‿ˌɑːftə‿ˈtaɪm] immer wieder **III WSB**, 29
timetable [ˈtaɪmteɪbl] Fahrplan **I**; Stundenplan **II**
⟨tinker⟩ [ˈtɪŋkə] herumziehender Kesselflicker **III 3**, 50
tip [tɪp] Tipp **III WSA**, 7
tired [ˈtaɪəd] müde **I**
title [ˈtaɪtl] Titel **II**
to [tʊ/tə] nach; vor *(bei Uhrzeiten)* **I**
from … to [frəm … tə] von … bis; von … nach **I**
today [təˈdeɪ] heute **I**
⟨toga⟩ [ˈtəʊgə] Toga *(röm. Kleidungsstück)* **III WSC**, 58
together [təˈgeðə] zusammen **I**
toilet [ˈtɔɪlɪt] Toilette **I**
tomato, tomatoes (*pl*) [təˈmɑːtəʊ, təˈmɑːtəʊz] Tomate, Tomaten **III 2**, 40
tomorrow [təˈmɒrəʊ] morgen **I**
the day after tomorrow [ðə ˈdeɪ‿ˌɑːftə təˈmɒrəʊ] übermorgen **II**
°**tone** [təʊn] Ton **III WSA**, 10
tongue [tʌŋ] Zunge, Sprache **III WSC**, 60
tonight [təˈnaɪt] heute Abend/Nacht **III 2**, 38
too [tuː] allzu, zu; auch **I**
tooth, teeth (*pl*) [tuːθ, tiːθ] Zahn, Zähne **III WSC**, 58
top [tɒp] oberste/oberster/oberstes **II**
at the top of … [ət ðə ˈtɒp‿əv] ganz oben **I**
to **touch** [tʌtʃ] berühren, anfassen **III 4**, 69
tourist [ˈtʊərɪst] Tourist **II**
tournament [ˈtɔːnəmənt] Wettkampf, Turnier **III 3**, 52
towards [təˈwɔːdz] auf … zu **II**
tower [ˈtaʊə] Turm **III 1**, 14
town [taʊn] Stadt **I**
°twin town [ˌtwɪn ˈtaʊn] Partnerstadt **I**
in town [ˌɪn ˈtaʊn] in der Stadt **III 2**, 32
toy [tɔɪ] Spielzeug **II**
tractor [ˈtræktə] Traktor, Trecker **I**
traffic [ˈtræfɪk] Verkehr **III 4**, 63
°traffic jam [ˈtræfɪk ˌdʒæm] Verkehrsstau **III 4**, 63
traffic lights (*pl*) [ˈtræfɪk ˌlaɪts] Verkehrsampel, Verkehrsampeln **III 4**, 63
train [treɪn] Zug **I**
ghost train [ˈgəʊst ˌtreɪn] Geisterbahn **II**
to **train** [treɪn] trainieren **III WSB**, 26
trainers (*pl*) [ˈtreɪnəz] Turnschuhe **II**

to **translate** [træns'leɪt] übersetzen **III WSC**, 59
transport ['trænspɔːt] Transport **III 4**, 66
public transport [ˌpʌblɪk 'trænspɔːt] öffentliche Verkehrsmittel **III 4**, 66
trapped [træpt] eingeschlossen, abgeschnitten **III 5**, 84
travel agent's ['trævl‿ˌeɪdʒənts] Reisebüro **II**
to **travel** ['trævl] reisen **II**
tree [triː] Baum **I**
⟨tribe⟩ [traɪb] (Volks-)Stamm **III WSC**, 58
trick [trɪk] Streich, Trick **II**
to **trick** [trɪk] täuschen, austricksen **I**
⟨trifle⟩ ['traɪfl] *etwa:* ein paar Pfennige **III 3**, 50
trip [trɪp] Fahrt, Ausflug, Reise **III 1**, 18
to **trip** [trɪp] stolpern **I**
trouble ['trʌbl] Ärger, Probleme **III 2**, 32
trousers ['traʊzəz] Hose, Hosen **I**
⟨truck⟩ [trʌk] Lastwagen **III 4**, 72
⟨to truck on⟩ [ˌtrʌk 'ɒn] weiter mit dem Lastwagen fahren **III 4**, 72
true [truː] wahr, wirklich **III 3**, 52
trumpet ['trʌmpɪt] Trompete **II**
⟨trunk⟩ [trʌŋk] Schrankkoffer **III 5**, 83
to **try** [traɪ] versuchen, (aus)probieren **II**
to try hard [ˌtraɪ 'hɑːd] (sich) anstrengen **II**
to try harder [ˌtraɪ 'hɑːdə] sich mehr anstrengen **III WSB**, 28
to try on [ˌtraɪ‿'ɒn] ausprobieren, anprobieren **II**
Tuesday ['tjuːzdeɪ] Dienstag **I**
tummy ['tʌmɪ] Bauch, Magen **I**
⟨tunic⟩ ['tjuːnɪk] Tunika *(röm. Kleidungsstück)* **III WSC**, 56
tunnel ['tʌnl] Tunnel **I**
Turkish ['tɜːkɪʃ] türkisch, Türkisch **I**
to **turn** [tɜːn] abbiegen **I**
to turn back [ˌtɜːn 'bæk] zurückgehen **II**
to turn round [ˌtɜːn 'raʊnd] sich umdrehen **II**
to turn s.th. over [ˌtɜːn sʌmθɪŋ 'əʊvə] etw. umdrehen, umwerfen, zum Kentern bringen **III 5**, 85
Your turn. ['jɔː tɜːn] Du bist an der Reihe., Ihr seid an der Reihe., Sie sind an der Reihe. **I**
tutor ['tjuːtə] Klassenlehrer/in **I**
tutor group ['tjuːtə ˌgruːp] Klasse (*in einer englischen Schule*) **I**
TV [ˌtiː'viː] Fernsehen **I**
twice [twaɪs] zweimal **II**
twice a week ['twaɪs‿ə 'wiːk] zweimal die Woche **II**
twin town [ˌtwɪn 'taʊn] Partnerstadt **I**
⟨two-wheel stallion⟩ [ˌtuː wiːl 'stæljən] *Motorrad* **III 4**, 72
typical ['tɪpɪkl] typisch **III WSA**, 7

U

°**Ugh!** [ɜːh] *Ausruf des Ekels* **III 1**, 17
uncle ['ʌŋkl] Onkel **I**
great uncle [greɪt‿'ʌŋkl] Großonkel **II**
under ['ʌndə] unter **I**
underground ['ʌndəgraʊnd] U-Bahn **III 1**, 17
⟨underneath⟩ [ˌʌndə'niːθ] unter **III WSC**, 60
to **understand*** [ˌʌndə'stænd] verstehen **I**
understandable [ˌʌndə'stændəbl] verständlich **III WSB**, 31
uniform ['juːnɪfɔːm] Uniform **I**
unit ['juːnɪt] Lektion, Kapitel, Einheit **I**
°**unpredictable** [ˌʌnprɪ'dɪktəbl] unvorhersagbar **III 5**, 78
untidy [ʌn'taɪdɪ] unordentlich **I**
until [ən'tɪl] bis **II**
up [ʌp] nach oben, herauf **II**
It's up to you. [ɪts‿ʌp tə 'juː] Es kommt auf dich an., Du entscheidest. **III 4**, 67
up here [ˌʌp 'hɪə] hier oben **III 3**, 47
up to ['ʌp tə] auf … zu **II**
upper ['ʌpə] obere/oberer/oberes **II**
to **upset*** **s.b.** [ʌp'set ˌsʌmbədɪ] jdn. ärgern, kränken **III WSA**, 8
upstairs [ˌʌp'steəz] oben (*in Gebäuden*) **I**
us [ʌs] uns **I**
⟨Ain't no use setting out for the bad companion.⟩ *etwa:* Es hat keinen Zweck, dich mit mir anzulegen. **III 4**, 72
to **use** [juːz] benutzen **II**
useful ['juːsfʊl] nützlich **II**
useless ['juːslɪs] nutzlos **III WSB**, 31
usually ['juːʒʊəlɪ] normalerweise, gewöhnlich **I**

V

valley ['vælɪ] Tal **III 3**, 45
van [væn] Kleinlastwagen **II**
⟨to vanish⟩ ['vænɪʃ] verschwinden **III 3**, 50
vegetable ['vedʒtəbl] Gemüse **II**
verb [vɜːb] Verb **I**
very ['verɪ] sehr **I**
very much [ˌverɪ 'mʌtʃ] sehr **I**
vet [vet] Tierarzt/Tierärztin **I**
vet's assistant ['vets‿əˌsɪstənt] Tierarzthelfer/in **I**
video ['vɪdɪəʊ] Video **I**
video recorder ['vɪdɪəʊ rɪˌkɔːdə] Videorekorder **III 3**, 45
village ['vɪlɪdʒ] Dorf **III 3**, 45
violence ['vaɪələns] Gewalt **III WSD**, 75
°**V.I.P.** (= **very important person**) [ˌviː aɪ 'piː] wichtige Persönlichkeit **III 2**, 38
visit ['vɪzɪt] Besuch **II**
to **visit** ['vɪzɪt] besuchen **II**
visitor ['vɪzɪtə] Besucher/in **III 3**, 45
vocabulary [vəʊ'kæbjʊlərɪ] Wortschatz, Vokabular **III WSB**, 27
voice [vɔɪs] Stimme **II**

W

to **wait (for)** ['weɪt fə] warten (auf) **I**
waiter ['weɪtə] Ober, Kellner **III 1**, 21
to **wake up*** [ˌweɪk‿'ʌp] aufwachen, aufwecken **II**
walk [wɔːk] Spaziergang **I**
to go for a walk [ˌgəʊ fər‿ə 'wɔːk] spazieren gehen **I**
to take for a walk [ˌteɪk fər‿ə 'wɔːk] (Hund) ausführen, spazieren führen **II**
to **walk** [wɔːk] zu Fuß gehen **I**
wall [wɔːl] Wand **III 2**, 36
to **want** [wɒnt] wollen **I**
ward [wɔːd] Krankensaal **II**
°**warden** ['wɔːdn] Herbergsvater/-mutter, Leiter/in **III WSA**, 11
warm [wɔːm] warm **I**
to **warn** [wɔːn] warnen **II**
wash [wɒʃ] Wäsche, Waschen **II**
car wash ['kɑː wɒʃ] Autowaschanlage **II**
to **wash** [wɒʃ] (sich) waschen **II**

washable ['wɒʃəbl] waschbar **III WSB**, 31
washing machine ['wɒʃɪŋ_məˌʃiːn] Waschmaschine **III WSB**, 31
washing-up [ˌwɒʃɪŋ_'ʌp] Abwasch **I**
to do the washing-up ['duː ðə ˌwɒʃɪŋ_'ʌp] den Abwasch machen, spülen **I**
to **waste** [weɪst] verschwenden **III 4**, 64
to **watch** [wɒtʃ] gucken, zuschauen **I**
Watch out! ['wɒtʃ_'aʊt] Vorsicht!, Achtung! **I**
water ['wɔːtə] Wasser **I**
wave [weɪv] Welle **III 5**, 78
° **waxwork** ['wækswɜːk] Wachsfigur **III 1**, 17
way [weɪ] Art und Weise **III 2**, 39; Weg **I**
in different ways [ɪn ˌdɪfrənt_'weɪz] auf verschiedene Weise **II**
out of the way [ˌaʊt_əv ðə 'weɪ] aus dem Weg **II**
She's on her way. [ˌɒn hɜː 'weɪ] Sie ist unterwegs. **I**
that way ['ðæt_weɪ] in die Richtung **II**
all the way [ˌɔːl ðə 'weɪ] den ganzen Weg **III 1**, 22
we [wiː] wir **I**
weak [wiːk] schwach **III 2**, 34
to **wear*** [weə] tragen (*Kleidung*) **I**
weather ['weðə] Wetter **I**
weather forecast ['weðə ˌfɔːkɑːst] Wetterbericht **II**
Wednesday ['wenzdeɪ] Mittwoch **I**
week [wiːk] Woche **I**
twice a week [ˌtwaɪs_ə'wiːk] zweimal die Woche **II**
weekend [ˌwiːk'end] Wochenende **II**
to **weigh** [weɪ] wiegen **III WSB**, 27
Welcome to ... ['welkəm tə] Willkommen in ... **I**
to welcome s.b. ['welkəm ˌsʌmbədɪ] jdn. willkommen heißen **III WSC**, 58
⟨to make s.o. welcome⟩ [ˌmeɪk sʌmwʌn 'welkəm] jdn. mit offenen Armen aufnehmen **III WSA**, 13
to feel **well** [ˌfiːl 'wel] sich wohl fühlen **II**
well [wel] gut (*Adverb*) **I**
Well done. [ˌwel 'dʌn] Gut gemacht. **I**
Welsh [welʃ] walisisch, Walisisch **III WSA**, 8
west [west] Westen, West-, westlich **II**
° West Indian [ˌwest_'ɪndjən] westindisch, Westinder/in **III 1**, 16
⟨West of the Sunset⟩ [ˌwest_ˌɒv ðə 'sʌnset] *etwa:* im Totenreich **III WSC**, 60
° **westbound** ['westbaʊnd] Richtung Westen **III 1**, 18
wet [wet] nass **I**
what [wɒt] was **I**
What a ... ['wɒt_ə] Was für ein/eine ... **I**
What about ...? ['wɒt_əˌbaʊt] Was ist mit ...?, Wie wär's mit ...? **I**
What colour is/are ...? [ˌwɒt 'kʌlər_ɪz] Welche Farbe hat/haben ...? **I**
What on earth ...? [ˌwɒt_ɒn 'ɜːθ] Was in aller Welt ...? **II**
What time is it? [wɒt_'taɪm_ɪz_ɪt] Wie spät ist es? **I**
What's ... like? [ˌwɒts ... 'laɪk] Wie ist ...? **I**
wheel [wiːl] Rad **II**
when [wen] wenn **II**; wann **I**; als **I**
where [weə] wo **I**
whether ['weðə] ob **III 3**, 49
which [wɪtʃ] welche/welcher/welches **II**
while [waɪl] Weile **III 2**, 41
while [waɪl] während **II**
⟨whiskers⟩ ['wɪskəz] Schnurrbart **III 3**, 50
to **whisper** ['wɪspə] flüstern **III 1**, 22
white [waɪt] weiß **I**
⟨whizzkid⟩ ['wɪzkɪd] Draufgänger **III 4**, 72
who [huː] wen/wem; wer **I**
whole [həʊl] ganz **III 1**, 17
⟨whom⟩ [huːm] welche, die **III 2**, 37
whose [huːz] wessen **I**
why [waɪ] warum **I**
wide [waɪd] breit, weit **III 4**, 65
wife [waɪf] Ehefrau **III 3**, 53
wig [wɪg] Perücke **II**
wild [waɪld] wild **III 3**, 45
will [wɪl] wird, werden **II**
to **win*** [wɪn] gewinnen **I**
wind [wɪnd] Wind **III WSC**, 56
window ['wɪndəʊ] Fenster **I**
⟨window frame⟩ ['wɪndəʊ ˌfreɪm] Fensterrahmen **III 4**, 72
windy ['wɪndɪ] windig **I**
wine [waɪn] Wein **II**
winner ['wɪnə] Gewinner/in **I**
winter ['wɪntə] Winter **I**
to **wish** [wɪʃ] wünschen **III WSC**, 60
with [wɪð] bei; mit **I**
And with that ... [ˌænd_wɪð 'ðæt] Und damit ... **II**
without [wɪð'aʊt] ohne **I**
° **wizard** ['wɪzəd] Zauberer **III 3**, 52
woman, women (*pl*) ['wʊmən, 'wɪmɪn] Frau, Frauen **I**
to **wonder** ['wʌndə] sich etw. überlegen, sich etw. fragen **III 3**, 49
wonderful ['wʌndəfʊl] wunderbar **II**
word [wɜːd] Wort **I**
° word building ['wɜːd ˌbɪldɪŋ] Wortbildung **III WSB**, 31
word power ['wɜːd ˌpaʊə] die Kraft der Wörter **I**
work [wɜːk] Arbeit **II**
to **work** [wɜːk] arbeiten **I**
to work late [ˌwɜːk 'leɪt] länger arbeiten **I**
worker ['wɜːkə] Arbeiter/in **III WSB**, 31
worksheet ['wɜːkʃiːt] Arbeitsblatt **III 1**, 22
workshop ['wɜːkʃɒp] Werkstatt, Kurs, Schulung **III WSA**, 7
world [wɜːld] Welt **II**
World Cup [ˌwɜːld 'kʌp] Weltmeisterschaft **III WSB**, 27
worried about ['wʌrɪd] besorgt wegen **II**
to **worry** ['wʌrɪ] sich Sorgen machen **I**
worse [wɜːs] schlechter **II**
(the) **worst** [ðə 'wɜːst] am schlechtesten **II**
It's **worth buying.** [ɪts ˌwɜːθ 'baɪɪŋ] Es lohnt sich, ... zu kaufen. **III WSD**, 75
Would you like ...? [ˌwʊd juː 'laɪk] Möchtest du ...?, Möchten Sie ...? **II**
Wow! [waʊ] Super!, Toll! **I**
to **write*** [raɪt] schreiben **I**
to write about ['raɪt_əˌbaʊt] schreiben über **I**
to write down [ˌraɪt 'daʊn] aufschreiben **I**
writer ['raɪtə] Schriftsteller/in, Schreiber/in **III WSB**, 31
writing ['raɪtɪŋ] Schrift **III 2**, 36
wrong [rɒŋ] falsch **I**
to get out of bed on the wrong side [get_aʊt_əv ˌbed_ɒn ðə ˌrɒŋ 'saɪd] mit dem falschen Fuß aufstehen **II**
to go wrong [ˌgəʊ 'rɒŋ] schiefgehen **II**
What's wrong? [ˌwɒts 'rɒŋ] Was ist los? **II**

Y

year [jɪə] Jahr, Jahrgang **I**
yellow ['jeləʊ] gelb **I**
yes [jes] ja **I**
yesterday ['jestədeɪ] gestern **II**
the day before yesterday [ðə 'deɪ bɪˌfɔː 'jestədeɪ] vorgestern **II**
yet [jet] noch **I**; schon **II**
not ... yet [nɒt 'jet] noch nicht **I**
you [juː] du, ihr, Sie; dir/dich/euch/Ihnen **I**
young [jʌŋ] jung **II**
your [jɔː] dein/deine, Ihr/Ihre, euer/eure **I**
Your turn. ['jɔː tɜːn] Du bist an der Reihe., Ihr seid an der Reihe., Sie sind an der Reihe. **I**
yours [jɔːz] deine/r/s, eure/r/s, Ihre/r/s **II**
yourself [jɔː'self] (dich/dir) selbst **III WSB**, 30
yourselves [jɔː'selvz] (euch/Ihnen) selbst **III WSB**, 30
youth group ['juːθ ˌgruːp] Jugendgruppe **II**
youth hostel ['juːθ ˌhɒstl] Jugendherberge **III WSA**, 11

Z

zone [zəʊn] Zone, Bereich **I**
zoo [zuː] Zoo **II**

Boys' names

°**Alan** ['ælən]
°**Arthur** ['ɑ:θə]
Asim [ʌ'si:m]
Barry ['bærɪ]
Charles [tʃɑ:lz]
°**Clive** [klaɪv]
Colin ['kɒlɪn]
⟨Dafydd⟩ ['dævɪθ]
Daniel ['dænjəl]
Darren ['dærən]
David ['deɪvɪd]
°**Eddy** ['edɪ]
Florian ['flɒrɪən]
Gavin ['gævɪn]
Harold ['hærəld]
Harry ['hærɪ]
Hugh [hju:]
°**Jack** [dʒæk]
°**Jeff** [dʒef]
John [dʒɒn]
Jonah ['dʒəʊnə]
Kay [keɪ]
°**Ken** [ken]
°**Kevin** ['kevɪn]
°**Lee** [li:]
°**Lenny** ['lenɪ]
⟨Marcus⟩ ['mɑ:kəs]
Mario ['mærɪəʊ]
Mark [mɑ:k]
°**Michael** ['maɪkl]
Mike [maɪk]
Nigel ['naɪdʒəl]
Owen [əʊɪn]
Pete [pi:t]
°**Peter** ['pi:tə]
Richy ['rɪtʃɪ]
Ricky ['rɪkɪ]
Robert ['rɒbət]
Ryan ['raɪən]
Sam [sæm]
Samuel ['sæmjʊəl]
Simon ['saɪmən]
⟨Stan⟩ [stæn]
Steve [sti:v]
Thomas ['tɒməs]
Tim [tɪm]
Tom [tɒm]
°**Washington** ['wɒʃɪŋtən]
Wayne [weɪn]

Girls' names

Amy ['eɪmɪ]
°**Anna** ['ænə]
°**Annabel** ['ænəbel]
Audrey ['ɔ:drɪ]
Becky ['bekɪ]
⟨Camilla⟩ [kə'mɪlə]
Candy ['kændɪ]
⟨Cottia⟩ ['kɒtɪə]
Ellen ['elɪn]
Emma ['emə]
Fiona [fɪ'əʊnə]
Gwen [gwen]
Helen ['helɪn]
Jackie ['dʒækɪ]
Jane [dʒeɪn]
°**Janet** ['dʒænɪt]
Jenny ['dʒenɪ]
Jill [dʒɪl]
Judy ['dʒu:dɪ]
Julie ['dʒu:lɪ]
Kate [keɪt]
Kim [kɪm]
Lucy ['lu:sɪ]
Maggie ['mægɪ]
°**Mary** ['meərɪ]
Mavis ['meɪvɪs]
Megan ['megən]
Michelle [mi:'ʃel]
°**Nina** ['ni:nə]
Nora ['nɔ:rə]
°**Pat** [pæt]
Paula ['pɔ:lə]
°**Sally** ['sælɪ]
Samira [sə'mɪərə]
Sarah ['seərə]
Shabina [ʃæ'bi:nə]
°**Sue** [su:]
°**Susan** ['su:zn]
Suvina [su:'vi:nə]
Tammy ['tæmɪ]
⟨Valaria⟩ [və'lærɪə]
Victoria [vɪk'tɔ:rɪə]
Virginia [və'dʒɪnjə]
°**Yasmin** [jæz'mi:n]

Surnames

°**Adib** [ə'dɪb]
Anderson ['ændəsn]
°**Barker** ['bɑ:kə]
°**Benson** ['bensn]
°**Blackwell** ['blækwel]
Bloggs [blɒgz]
Brandon ['brændən]
°**Broadwood** ['brɔ:dwʊd]
°**Brown** [braʊn]
Burton ['bɜ:tn]
Cameron ['kæmərən]
°**Campbell** ['kæmbl]
Clark [klɑ:k]
Cooper ['ku:pə]
Croft [krɒft]
Dane [deɪn]
Dart [dɑ:t]
Davis ['deɪvɪs]
Dickens ['dɪkɪnz]
Dixon ['dɪksən]
Duncan ['dʌŋkən]
Grant [grɑ:nt]
°**Greenwood** ['gri:nwʊd]
⟨Gwynn⟩ [gwɪn]
°**Hilton** ['hɪltn]
°**Hunt** [hʌnt]
°**Ismaili** [ˌɪz'meɪlɪ]
Jackson ['dʒæksn]
Jenkins ['dʒeŋkɪnz]
°**Jessop** ['ðʒesəp]
Jones ['dʒəʊnz]
Jonker ['jɒŋkə]
Lee [li:]
Lomu ['ləʊmu:]
MacTavish [mək'tævɪʃ]
°**Martin** ['mɑ:tɪn]
Mason ['meɪsn]
°**Matthew** ['mæθju:]
Mc Carthy [mə'kɑ:θɪ]
°**Miller** ['mɪlə]
°**Muddle** ['mʌdl]
Otis ['əʊtɪs]
Parker ['pɑ:kə]
Patel [pə'tel]
°**Patterson** ['pætəsn]
Penrose ['penrəʊz]
°**Price** [praɪs]
Pritchard ['prɪtʃəd]
°**Richards** ['rɪtʃədz]
°**Ripple** ['rɪpl]
Sheikh [ʃeɪk]
°**Singh** [sɪŋ]
°**Smith** [smɪθ]
Stevenson ['sti:vnsn]
Stuart ['stjʊət]
Taylor ['teɪlə]
Umney ['ʌmni:]
Underwood ['ʌndəwʊd]
Walker ['wɔ:kə]
°**Wall** [wɔ:l]
Warren ['wɒrən]
°**White** [waɪt]
°**Wood** [wʊd]

Geographical names

Aberystwyth [ˌæbəˈrɪstwɪθ]
Africa [ˈæfrɪkə]
the **Alps** (*pl*) [ðə ælps]
Ambleside [ˈæmblsaɪd]
America [əˈmerɪkə]
Antarctica [ænˈtɑːktɪkə]
Arndale Road [ˌɑːndeɪl ˈrəʊd]
Arnot Hill Park [ˌɑːnət hɪl ˈpɑːk]
Ashbourne [ˈæʃbɔːn]
Asia [ˈeɪʃə]
Australia [ɒˈstreɪljə]
Austria [ˈɒstrɪə]
Baker Street [ˈbeɪkə ˌstriːt]
°**Belfast** [ˌbelˈfɑːst]
°**Belgium** [ˈbeldʒəm]
Ben Nevis [ˌben ˈnevɪs]
Berlin [bɜːˈlɪn]
Bethnal Green [ˌbeθnəl ˈgriːn]
Birmingham [ˈbɜːmɪŋəm]
Bournemouth [ˈbɔːnməθ]
Britain [ˈbrɪtn]
⟨Britannia⟩ [brɪˈtænjə]
the **British Isles** [ðə ˌbrɪtɪʃ‿ˈaɪlz]
Broad Haven [ˌbrɔːd ˈheɪvn]
Caerleon [kɑːˈliːən]
Caernarvon [kəˈnɑːvən]
Cardiff [ˈkɑːdɪf]
°**Caribbean** [ˌkærɪˈbiːən]
°the **Channel** [ðə ˈtʃænl]
°**Chicago** [ʃɪˈkɑːgəʊ]
China [ˈtʃaɪnə]
°**Cornwall** [ˈkɔːnwəl]
Coventry [ˈkɒvəntrɪ]
Denmark [ˈdenmɑːk]
Derby [ˈdɑːbɪ]
Druidston [ˈdruːɪdstn]
East Cheam [ˌiːst ˈtʃiːm]
Edinburgh [ˈedɪnbrə]
Edward's Lane [ˌedwədz ˈleɪn]
Elf Row [ˌelf ˈrəʊ]
Ellastone [ˈeləstəʊn]
Embankment [ɪmˈbæŋkmənt]
England [ˈɪŋglənd]
Europe [ˈjʊərəp]
Fishguard [ˈfɪʃgɑːd]
°**Fort William** [ˌfɔːt‿ˈwɪljəm]
°**France** [frɑːns]
Germany [ˈdʒɜːmənɪ]
Glenarm [glenˈɑːm]
Great Britain [ˌgreɪt ˈbrɪtn]
Greece [ˈgriːs]
Green Park [ˌgriːn ˈpɑːk]
Greendale [ˈgriːndeɪl]
Hastings [ˈheɪstɪŋz]
°**Heathrow Airport** [ˌhiːθrəʊ ˈeəpɔːt]
°the **High Street** [ðə ˈhaɪ ˌstriːt]
Holyhead [ˈhɒlɪhed]
Hull [hʌl]
Hyde Park [ˌhaɪd ˈpɑːk]
India [ˈɪndjə]
Ireland [ˈaɪələnd]
the **Isle of Wight** [ðə ˌaɪl‿əvˈwaɪt]
Italy [ˈɪtəlɪ]
Kent [kent]
Knightsbridge [ˈnaɪtsbrɪdʒ]
the **Lake District** [ðə ˈleɪk ˌdɪstrɪkt]
Larwood Grove [ˌlɑːwʊd ˈgrəʊv]
°**Leeds** [liːdz]
Leicester Square [ˌlestə ˈskweə]
Loch Lomond [ˌlɒk ˈləʊmənd]
Loch Ness [ˌlɒk ˈnes]
⟨Londinium⟩ [lʌnˈdɪnjəm]
London [ˈlʌndən]
Luton [ˈluːtn]
°**M6** [ˌem ˈsɪks]
Malham [ˈmæləm]
Mansfield Road [ˌmænsfiːld ˈrəʊd]
Mayfield [ˈmeɪfiːld]
⟨the Mediterranean Sea⟩ [ˌmedɪtəˈreɪnjən ˈsiː]
Milford Haven [ˌmɪlfəd ˈheɪvn]
⟨Nassau⟩ [ˈnæsɔː]
°the **Netherlands** [ðə ˈneðələndz]
New Zealand [ˌnjuː ˈziːlənd]
Nolton Haven [ˌnɒltn ˈheɪvn]
Normandy [ˈnɔːməndɪ]
the **North Sea** [ðə ˈnɔːθ ˌsiː]
North America [ˌnɔːθ‿əˈmerɪkə]
°**Northallerton** [nɔːˈθælətən]
Northern Ireland [ˌnɒːðn‿ˈaɪələnd]
Notting Hill Gate
Nottingham [ˈnɒtɪŋəm]
Paddington [ˈpædɪŋtən]
Pakistan [ˌpɑːkɪˈstɑːn]
°**Paris** [ˈpærɪs]
Piccadilly Circus [ˌpɪkədɪlɪ ˈsɜːkəs]
°**Poland** [ˈpəʊlənd]
Regent's Park [ˌriːdʒənts ˈpɑːk]
the **Republic of Ireland** [ðə rɪˌpʌblɪk‿ɒv‿ˈaɪələnd]
River Thames [ˌrɪvə ˈtemz]
Rome [rəʊm]
Rotterdam [rɒtəˈdæm]
Rugby [ˈrʌgbɪ]
Russia [ˈrʌʃə]
Scarborough [ˈskɑːbrə]
°**Scotland** [ˈskɒtlənd]
Shadwell [ˈʃædwəl]
Sherwood [ˈʃɜːwʊd]
Sherwood Forest [ˌʃɜːwʊd ˈfɒrɪst]
Skegness [skegˈnes]
Snowdon [ˈsnəʊdn]
Snowdonia National Park [snəʊˈdəʊnjə ˌnæʃənl ˈpɑːk]
South Africa [ˌsaʊθ‿ˈæfrɪkə]
South America [ˌsaʊθ‿əˈmerɪkə]
Spain [speɪn]
Sudbury [ˈsʌdbərɪ]
Swansea [ˈswɒnzɪ]
Switzerland [ˈswɪtsələnd]
Tenby [ˈtenbɪ]
Tonga [ˈtɒŋgə]
Trafalgar Square [trəˌfælgə ˈskweə]
°**Truro** [ˈtrʊərəʊ]
Turkey [ˈtɜːkɪ]
Twycross Zoo [ˌtwaɪkrɒs ˈzuː]
the **UK** (= **the United Kingdom**) [ðə ˌjuː ˈkeɪ]
Uttoxeter [juːˈtɒksɪtə]
Wales [weɪlz]
the **West Indies** [ˌwest‿ˈɪndɪz]
York [jɔːk]
°**Yorkshire** [ˈjɔːkʃə]

Other names

All Blacks [ˌɔːl ˈblæks]
Alton Towers [ˌɔːltən ˈtaʊəz]
Angles *(pl)* [ˈæŋglz]
Belle [bel]
Big Ben [ˌbɪg ˈben]
⟨Boudicca⟩ [bəʊˈdɪkə]
the **British Museum** [ðə ˌbrɪtɪʃ mjuːˈzɪəm]
Britons *(pl)* [ˈbrɪtnz]
Buckingham Palace [ˌbʌkɪŋəm ˈpælɪs]
Camelot [ˈkæmɪlɒt]
Canterville Chase [ˌkæntəvɪl ˈtʃeɪs]
° **Celts** *(pl)* [kelts]
Central Line [ˈsentrəl ˌlaɪn]
the **Circle Line** [ðə ˈsɜːkl ˌlaɪn]
City Information Centre [ˌsɪtɪ‿ɪnfəˈmeɪʃn ˌsentə]
⟨Claudius⟩ [ˈklɔːdjəs]
Covent Garden [ˌkɒvənt ˈgɑːdn]
District Line [ˈdɪstrɪkt ˌlaɪn]
Dracula [ˈdrækjʊlə]
Edward the Confessor [ˌedwəd ðə kənˈfesə]
⟨Fairlane cruiser⟩ [ˌfeəleɪn ˈkruːzə]
° **Friar Tuck** [ˌfraɪə ˈtʌk]
° **Goose Fair** [ˌguːs ˈfeə]
° **Greenwood School** [ˌgriːnwʊd ˈskuːl]
⟨Hadrian⟩ [ˈheɪdrɪən]
Harrods [ˈhærədz]
Haywood School [ˌheɪwʊd ˈskuːl]
the **Houses of Parliament** [ðə ˌhaʊzɪz‿əv ˈpɑːləmənt]
⟨Iceni⟩ [aɪˈsiːnɪ]
Jackie [ˈdʒækɪ]
⟨John Masefield⟩ [ˌdʒɒn ˈmeɪsfiːld]
Jubilee Line [ˈdʒuːbɪliː ˌlaɪn]
Just Jeans [ˌdʒʌst ˈdʒiːnz]
King Arthur [ˌkɪŋ ˈɑːθə]
Lace Museum [ˌleɪs mjuːˈzɪəm]
London Bridge [ˌlʌndən ˈbrɪdʒ]
the **London Dungeon** [ðə ˌlʌndən ˈdʌnʒən]
London Zoo [ˌlʌndən ˈzuː]
Madame Tussaud's [ˌmædəm təˈsɔːdz]
the **Major Oak** [ðə ˌmeɪdʒər‿ˈəʊk]
Maxi [ˈmæksɪ]
Merlin [ˈmɜːlɪn]
Michael Jackson [ˌmaɪkl ˈdʒæksn]
Mini [ˈmɪnɪ]
Monny [ˈmɒnɪ]
the **Museum of London** [ðə mjuːˌzɪəm‿əv ˈlʌndən]
the **Museum of the Moving Image** [ðə mjuːˌzɪəm‿əv ðə ˌmuːvɪŋ‿ˈɪmɪdʒ]
Newstead Abbey [ˌnjuːstɪd‿ˈæbɪ]
⟨the ninth⟩ [ˌðə ˈnaɪnθ]
Northern Line [ˈnɔːðn ˌlaɪn]
the **Planetarium** [ðə ˌplænɪˈteərɪəm]
the **Queen** [ðə ˈkwiːn]
Queen Igrayne [ˌkwiːn ɪˈgreɪn]
Ramadan [ˌræməˈdæn]
° **Robin Hood Statue** [ˌrɒbɪn hʊd ˈstætʃuː]
"Romeo and Juliet" [ˌrəʊmɪəʊ ən ˈdʒuːljət]
⟨Rosemary Sutcliff⟩ [ˌrəʊzmərɪ ˈsʌtklɪf]
⟨Rover⟩ [ˈrəʊvə]
Saxons *(pl)* [ˈsæksnz]
the **Science Museum** [ðə ˈsaɪəns mjuːˌzɪəm]
Selby School [ˈselbɪ ˌskuːl]
Sir Ector [ˌsɜːr‿ˈektə]
° **Sneaky Snake** [ˌsniːkɪ ˈsneɪk]
° **Sniffy** [ˈsnɪfɪ]
° **Snowy** [ˈsnəʊɪ]
° **Spot** [spɒt]
° **Springfield Farm** [ˌsprɪŋfiːld ˈfɑːm]
St John's School for Boys [snt ˌdʒɒnz skuːl fə ˈbɔɪz]
St Paul's Cathedral [snt ˌpɔːlz kəˈθiːdrəl]
° **St Peter's Church** [snt ˌpiːtəz ˈtʃɜːtʃ]
Tabby [ˈtæbɪ]
° **Taj Mahal** [ˌtɑːdʒməˈhɑːl]
Teens [tiːnz]
Tower Bridge [ˌtaʊə ˈbrɪdʒ]
the **Tower of London** [ðə ˌtaʊər‿əv ˈlʌndən]
Trocadero Centre [ˌtrɒkəˈdɪərəʊ ˌsentə]
° **Twinning Office** [ˈtwɪnɪŋ‿ˌɒfɪs]
Two'n'Two [ˌtuːnˈtuː]
King **Uther** [kɪŋ juːθə]
° **Victoria Shopping Centre** [vɪkˌtɔːrɪə ˈʃɒpɪŋ ˌsentə]
Waterloo Bridge [ˌwɔːtəluː ˈbrɪdʒ]
Waterloo Station [ˌwɔːtəluː ˈsteɪʃn]
Wembley Stadium [ˌwemblɪ ˈsteɪdjəm]
Westminster Abbey [ˌwestmɪnstər‿ˈæbɪ]
Westminster Bridge [ˌwestmɪnstə ˈbrɪdʒ]
the **White Tower** [ðə ˌwaɪt ˈtaʊə]
Will Scarlet [ˌwɪl ˈskɑːlət]
William the Conqueror [ˌwɪljəm ðə ˈkɒŋkərə]

List of irregular verbs

infinitive	simple past	past participle	German
be [bi:]	was [wɒz]	been [bi:n]	sein
become [bɪ'kʌm]	became [bɪ'keɪm]	become [bɪ'kʌm]	werden
begin [bɪ'gɪn]	began [bɪ'gæn]	begun [bɪ'gʌn]	beginnen
bend [bend]	bent [bent]	bent [bent]	(sich) bücken, biegen
blow [bləʊ]	blew [blu:]	blown [bləʊn]	blasen
break [breɪk]	broke [brəʊk]	broken ['brəʊkn]	brechen
bring [brɪŋ]	brought [brɔ:t]	brought [brɔ:t]	bringen
burn [bɜ:n]	burned [bɜ:nd] burnt [bɜ:nt]	burned [bɜ:nd] burnt [bɜ:nt]	brennen, verbrennen
build [bɪld]	built [bɪlt]	built [bɪlt]	bauen
buy [baɪ]	bought [bɔ:t]	bought [bɔ:t]	kaufen
catch [kætʃ]	caught [kɔ:t]	caught [kɔ:t]	fangen
choose [tʃu:z]	chose [tʃəʊz]	chosen ['tʃəʊzn]	auswählen
come [kʌm]	came [keɪm]	come [kʌm]	kommen
cost [kɒst]	cost [kɒst]	cost [kɒst]	kosten
cut [kʌt]	cut [kʌt]	cut [kʌt]	schneiden
do [du:]	did [dɪd]	done [dʌn]	machen, tun
draw [drɔ:]	drew [dru:]	drawn [drɔ:n]	zeichnen
drink [drɪŋk]	drank [dræŋk]	drunk [drʌŋk]	trinken
drive [draɪv]	drove [drəʊv]	driven ['drɪvn]	fahren
eat [i:t]	ate [eɪt]	eaten ['i:tn]	essen
fall [fɔ:l]	fell [fel]	fallen ['fɔ:ln]	fallen
feed [fi:d]	fed [fed]	fed [fed]	füttern
feel [fi:l]	felt [felt]	felt [felt]	fühlen
fight [faɪt]	fought [fɔ:t]	fought [fɔ:t]	kämpfen
find [faɪnd]	found [faʊnd]	found [faʊnd]	finden
fly [flaɪ]	flew [flu:]	flown [fləʊn]	fliegen
forget [fə'get]	forgot [fə'gɒt]	forgotten [fə'gɒtn]	vergessen
get [get]	got [gɒt]	got [gɒt]	holen, bekommen
give [gɪv]	gave [geɪv]	given ['gɪvn]	geben
go [gəʊ]	went [went]	gone [gɒn]	gehen
grow [grəʊ]	grew [gru:]	grown [grəʊn]	wachsen, (an)bauen
have [hæv]	had [hæd]	had [hæd]	haben
hear [hɪə]	heard [hɜ:d]	heard [hɜ:d]	hören
hide [haɪd]	hid [hɪd]	hidden ['hɪdn]	(sich) verstecken
hit [hɪt]	hit [hɪt]	hit [hɪt]	schlagen
hold [həʊld]	held [held]	held [held]	halten
hurt [hɜ:t]	hurt [hɜ:t]	hurt [hɜ:t]	verletzen, weh tun
keep [ki:p]	kept [kept]	kept [kept]	(be)halten
know [nəʊ]	knew [nju:]	known [nəʊn]	wissen, kennen
lay [leɪ]	laid [leɪd]	laid [leɪd]	legen
lead [li:d]	led [led]	led [led]	führen
learn [lɜ:n]	learned [lɜ:nt], learnt [lɜ:nt]	learned [lɜ:nt], learnt [lɜ:nt]	lernen
leave [li:v]	left [left]	left [left]	(ver)lassen
lend [lend]	lent [lent]	lent [lent]	(ver)leihen

infinitive	simple past	past participle	German
let [let]	let [let]	let [let]	lassen
lie [laɪ]	lay [leɪ]	lain [leɪn]	liegen
lose [lu:z]	lost [lɒst]	lost [lɒst]	verlieren
make [meɪk]	made [meɪd]	made [meɪd]	machen
mean [mi:n]	meant [ment]	meant [ment]	bedeuten
meet [mi:t]	met [met]	met [met]	treffen, begegnen
pay [peɪ]	paid [peɪd]	paid [peɪd]	zahlen, bezahlen
put [pʊt]	put [pʊt]	put [pʊt]	setzen, stellen, legen
read [ri:d]	read [red]	read [red]	lesen
ride [raɪd]	rode [rəʊd]	ridden ['rɪdn]	reiten, fahren
ring [rɪŋ]	rang [ræŋ]	rung [rʌŋ]	klingeln, anrufen
run [rʌn]	ran [ræn]	run [rʌn]	laufen, rennen
say [seɪ]	said [sed]	said [sed]	sagen
see [si:]	saw [sɔ:]	seen [si:n]	sehen
seek [si:k]	sought [sɔ:t]	sought [sɔ:t]	suchen
sell [sel]	sold [səʊld]	sold [səʊld]	verkaufen
send [send]	sent [sent]	sent [sent]	schicken, senden
shine [ʃaɪn]	shone [ʃɒn]	shone [ʃɒn]	scheinen
shoot [ʃu:t]	shot [ʃɒt]	shot [ʃɒt]	schießen
show [ʃəʊ]	showed [ʃəʊd]	shown [ʃəʊn]	zeigen
shut [ʃʌt]	shut [ʃʌt]	shut [ʃʌt]	schließen
sing [sɪŋ]	sang [sæŋ]	sung [sʌŋ]	singen
sit [sɪt]	sat [sæt]	sat [sæt]	sitzen
sleep [sli:p]	slept [slept]	slept [slept]	schlafen
smell [smel]	smelt [smelt]	smelt [smelt]	riechen
speak [spi:k]	spoke [spəʊk]	spoken ['spəʊkn]	sprechen
spell [spel]	spelled [spelt], spelt [spelt]	spelled [spelt], spelt [spelt]	buchstabieren
spend [spend]	spent [spent]	spent [spent]	ausgeben, verbringen
stand [stænd]	stood [stʊd]	stood [stʊd]	stehen
steal [sti:l]	stole [stəʊlə]	stolen [stəʊlən]	stehlen
swim [swɪm]	swam [swæm]	swum [swʌm]	schwimmen
take [teɪk]	took [tʊk]	taken ['teɪkn]	nehmen, bringen
teach [ti:tʃ]	taught [tɔ:t]	taught [tɔ:t]	lehren
tell [tel]	told [təʊld]	told [təʊld]	erzählen, sagen
think [θɪŋk]	thought [θɔ:t]	thought [θɔ:t]	denken
throw [θrəʊ]	threw [θru:]	thrown [θrəʊn]	werfen
understand [ˌʌndə'stænd]	understood [ˌʌndə'stʊd]	understood [ˌʌndə'stʊd]	verstehen
upset [ʌp'set]	upset [ʌp'set]	upset [ʌp'set]	jmd. ärgern, kränken
wake [weɪk]	woke [wəʊk]	woken ['wəʊkn]	wecken, aufwachen
wear [weə]	wore [wɔ:]	worn [wɔ:n]	tragen (Kleidung)
win [wɪn]	won [wʌn]	won [wʌn]	gewinnen
write [raɪt]	wrote [rəʊt]	written ['rɪtn]	schreiben

⟨In the classroom⟩

What you can say to your friends or to the teacher

When you arrive and leave

What are we going to do today?	Was machen wir heute?
I'm sorry I'm late.	Tut mir Leid, dass ich mich verspätet habe.
I'm sorry, I've forgotten my exercise book.	Tut mir Leid, ich habe mein Heft vergessen.
What's for homework?	Was haben wir als Hausaufgabe auf?
See you next time.	Bis zum nächsten Mal.
Have a nice weekend.	Schönes Wochenende!

If there is a problem ...

How are you?	Wie geht es dir?
Are you feeling ill?	Fühlst du dich krank?
What's the matter with you?	Was fehlt dir denn?
I'm fine, thank you.	Gut, danke.
I'm not feeling well.	Ich fühle mich nicht gut.
I've got a headache.	Ich habe Kopfweh.
Can I open the window, please?	Darf ich bitte das Fenster öffnen?
Can I go to the toilet, please?	Darf ich bitte auf die Toilette gehen?

If you want to ask for help ...

Can you help me, please?	Können Sie mir bitte helfen?
I don't understand this.	Ich verstehe das nicht.
What do we have to do?	Was müssen wir denn machen?
What's that in English/German?	Was heißt das auf Englisch/Deutsch?
Can I say: ...?/What does ... mean?	Kann ich sagen: ...?/Was bedeutet ...?
How do you do this exercise?	Wie macht man diese Übung?
Is this right? I'm not sure.	Ist das richtig? Ich bin nicht sicher.
Sorry, I don't know.	Tut mir Leid, das weiß ich nicht.
Can you write it on the board, please?	Können Sie das bitte an die Tafel schreiben?
Can I ask a question, please?	Kann ich bitte eine Frage stellen?
Pardon? Can you repeat the question/sentence, please?	Wie bitte? Können Sie die Frage/den Satz bitte wiederholen?
Can you play the cassette again, please?	Können Sie die Kassette bitte nochmal abspielen?
Can you play the cassette with pauses, please?	Können Sie die Kassette bitte mit Pausen abspielen?
Can we do another example, please?	Können wir noch ein Beispiel machen?
Thanks./Thank you very much.	Danke./Vielen Dank.

If you work together ...

Can I work with ...?	Kann ich mit ... zusammenarbeiten?
Can I have your crayon/ruler ...?	Kann ich mal deinen Buntstift/dein Lineal haben?
Whose turn is it?	Wer ist dran?

What are we going to do first?	Was machen wir als Erstes?
Let's write … on our poster.	Schreiben wir … auf unser Poster.
Let's put this picture here.	Setzen/Kleben wir das Bild hier hin.
You can be … and I'll be …	Du kannst … spielen, und ich werde … spielen.
Has anybody seen my pencil?	Hat jemand meinen Bleistift gesehen?

If you want to talk about stories, poems, songs, …

I like/don't like this story.	Diese Geschichte gefällt mir/gefällt mir nicht.
I think it's good, interesting, brilliant, funny, really exciting.	Ich finde sie gut, interessant, toll, witzig, wirklich spannend.
I think it's sad, terrible, boring.	Ich finde sie traurig, schrecklich, langweilig.
It was OK, but I've read better ones.	Sie ist ganz nett, aber ich habe schon bessere gelesen.

If you have a discussion …

What do you think?	Was meinst du?
In my opinion …	Meiner Meinung nach …
I think you are right/wrong.	Ich denke, du hast Recht/Unrecht.
On the one hand …, on the other hand …	Einerseits …, anderseits …

… and what the teacher says to you

Open your books at page … .	Schlagt Seite … auf.
Turn to page … .	Blättert auf Seite … um.
Read the text on page … .	Lest den Text auf Seite … .
Who would like to write on the transparency?	Wer möchte auf die Folie schreiben?
Come to the board, please.	Komm bitte an die Tafel.
Who would like to play the cassette?	Wer möchte die Kassette abspielen?
You're going to hear the cassette twice.	Ihr werdet die Kassette zweimal hören.
Rewind the cassette to zero, please.	Spul die Kassette bitte auf Null zurück.
Who would like to play the part of …?	Wer möchte die Rolle von … spielen?
Write the answers in your exercise book.	Schreibt die Antworten in eure Übungshefte.
Would you collect the exercise books/ worksheets, please?	Würdest du bitte die Übungshefte/Arbeitsblätter einsammeln?
Do this exercise for homework.	Macht diese Übung als Hausaufgabe.
Be quiet. Sit down, please.	Seid ruhig. Setz dich/Setzt euch, bitte.
Please speak up.	Sprich/Sprecht bitte lauter.
No prompting, please.	Nicht vorsagen, bitte.
Excellent!	Prima!
You can do better. Try again.	Das kannst du besser. Versuch es noch einmal.
That's it. Well done.	So ist es richtig. Gut gemacht.

Bildquellen:

Cover: Lori Adamski Peek/Tony Stone, London
p. 9: Greenhill, London (Megan); J. Allan Cash Ltd., London (Asim; Glenarm; Welsh hills); Grasser/Mauritius, Stuttgart (Ryan); Ridder/Mauritius, Stuttgart (Kate); Topham Picturepoint, Edenbridge (Luton); C. Bowman/Harding, London (Edinburgh);
p. 10: Mirror Syndication International, London (phone booth);
p. 11: J. Allan Cash Ltd., London (Youth hostel);
p. 16: J. Allan Cash Ltd., London (Notting Hill Carnival); Rolf Richardson/Harding, London (Hindu temple);
p. 17: Nigel Francis/Harding, London (Tower of London); J. Allan Cash Ltd., London (Westminster Abbey; C. Bowman, Buckingham Palace); Julien Niemann/Mirror Syndication International, London (Madame Tussaud's);
p. 18: London Regional Transport (London underground map);
p. 19: J. Allan Cash Ltd., London (Beefeater); The Bayeux Tapestry, © Norman Denny & Josephine Filmer-Sankey, "The Bayeux Tapestry, The Norman Conquest 1066", Collins, London, 1966;
p. 26: Barnaby's Picture Library, London (jogging boys, football match); Mauritius, Stuttgart (jazz dance class); J. Allan Cash Ltd., London (cyclists);
p. 27: Topham Picturepoint, Edenbridge (Jonah Lomu); Mauritius, Stuttgart (boy);
p. 33: Gary Larson Cartoon, © 1996 UPS/Distr. Bulls;
p. 35: Topham Picturepoint, Edenbridge (school);
p. 44: Topham Picturepoint, Edenbridge (Caernarvon Castle), Celtic Picture Library (Snowdon, Roman remains, mine museum, B&B sign); Bernhard Nimtsch/Das Fotoarchiv, Hamburg (factory);
p. 45: Celtic Picture Library (rugby match, sheep, Llanfair sign); J. Allan Cash Ltd., London (Welsh/English road signs);
p. 46: Mirror Syndication International, London (Wales);
p. 47: Tony Stone, London (coast, hills);
p. 49: Topham Picturepoint, Edenbridge (Snowdonia National Park);
p. 50: Celtic Picture Library (stone circle);
p. 56: Barnaby's Picture Library, London (Hadrian's wall);
p. 57: Cartoons, © Terry Deary, "The Rotten Romans", (Illustrated by Martin Brown), Scholastic Children's Books – Hippo, London, 1994, p. 8;
p. 59: Topham Picturepoint, Edenbridge (Hadrian's wall);
p. 62: J. Allan Cash Ltd., London (traffic jam); Alton Towers, Staffordshire (brochure); HMSO Publications Centre, London (road sign);
p. 63: Brian Gibbs/Topham Picturepoint, Edenbridge (service station); J. Allan Cash Ltd., London (roundabout);
p. 67: Poster, © Time Magazine, 1.6.1992, p. 62;
p. 72: Chris Minerva/Transglobe Agency, Hamburg (truck); Cartoon, © Editions Piero, Puteaux Cedex, Frankreich;
p. 78: SC 4046 "Lifeboat and Manby apparatus going off to a stranded vessel", 1831 by Joseph Mallord William Turner (1775–1851), Victoria & Albert Museum, London/Bridgeman Art Library, London); Mirror Syndication International (fisherman, girl); Topham Picturepoint, Edenbridge (ferry);
p. 80: Greenpeace (oil rig);
p. 83: Greenpeace (Sea Empress, bird);
p. 84: Brochure, © The Coastguard Agency, March 1995, TCA/PUB/010;
p. 85: Topham Picturepoint, Edenbridge (lifeboat);
p. 91: ELAR (Eid Greetings); © AGC, Inc. (Hannukah Greetings); EMS publications for Oxfam, Oxford (Season's Greetings); Gibson Greetings Inc., Cincinnati, Ohio, USA (Diwali Greetings);
p. 93: © J. Salmon Ltd., Sevenoaks, Kent;
p. 94: The National Geographic Society, Washington, 1995. Rediscovering Hawaii;
p. 95: Archiv für Kunst und Geschichte, Berlin (Cook).

Textquellen:

p. 29: We are the Champions, by Freddy Mercury, © Queen Music Ltd./EMI Music Publishing Germany, Hamburg;
p. 41: Can't buy me love, by John Lennon/ Paul McCartney, © Northern Songs Ltd.;
p. 50: Bachgen bach o dincer, © traditional, arranged by Dr. Thomas Parry; English adaptation by David Bell;
p. 56: Roman Wall Blues, by W. H. Auden, © "Verse for you, 1", Longmans, Green & Co. Ltd., London, 1958, p. 97;
p. 59: Emperor Hadrian, © "Hadrian's Wall – A souvenir guide to the Roman Wall", English Heritage, Ruislip, Middlesex, England;
p. 60: The Eagle of the Ninth, © Rosemary Sutcliff, Oxford University Press, 1954;
p. 72: 2-4-6-8 Motorway, by Tom Robinson, © Konkwest Music Ltd., Transamerika MV KG, P. Kaminsky;
p. 76/77: Cartoons, © Roland Fiddy, "The Fanatics Guide to Computers", Exley Publications Ltd., Watford, England;
p. 79: Storm Force HQ, RLNI, Poole, Dorset (Stormy Stan);
p. 82: RNLI, Poole, Dorset (Coastguard);
p. 83: Sloop John B., traditional;
p. 92: Nathan and Lara, by David Bygott, Oxford;
p. 96: The little drummer boy, © Chappel & Co. GmbH, Hamburg.

ICELAND
NORWAY
SWEDEN
FINLAND
RUSSIA
ESTONIA
LATVIA
LITHUANIA
RUSSIA
DENMARK
THE UNITED KINGDOM
IRELAND
Nottingham
London
THE NETHER-LANDS
BELGIUM
LUXEMBOURG
GERMANY
POLAND
BELARUS
E U R O P E
THE UKRAINE
CZECH REPUBLIC
SLOVAKIA
MOLDAVIA
FRANCE
SWITZER-LAND
AUSTRIA
HUNGARY
ROMANIA
SLOVENIA
CROATIA
BOSNIA-HERZEGOVINA
SERBIA
PORTUGAL
SPAIN
ITALY
MONTENEGRO
BULGARIA
MACEDONIA
ALBANIA
GREECE
TURKEY
MALTA
0
500
1 000 km
A F R I C A